HOMOSEXUAL ACTS, ACTORS, AND IDENTITIES

Homosexual Acts, Actors, and Identities

Lon G. Nungesser

PRAEGER SPECIAL STUDIES • PRAEGER SCIENTIFIC

New York • Philadelphia • Eastbourne, UK
Toronto • Hong Kong • Tokyo • Sydney

Library of Congress Cataloging in Publication Data

Nungesser, Lon G.
  Homosexual acts, actors, and identities.

  Bibliography: p.
  Includes index.
  1. Homosexuality—Public opinion.   2. Sex—Public
opinion.   3. Stereotype (Psychology)   4. Prejudices.
I. Title
HQ76.25.N87   1983   306.7'66   83-13826
ISBN 0-03-069389-6 (alk. paper)
ISBN 0-03-069391-8 (pbk. : alk. paper)

Published in 1983 by Praeger Publishers
CBS Educational and Professional Publishing
a Division of CBS Inc.
521 Fifth Avenue, New York, New York 10175, USA

3456789   052   987654321

Printed in the United States of America
on acid-free paper

To Bill

PREFACE

A fellow graduate student in New York recently commented that he did not understand why I was writing this text. The answer remains clear to me: because so many twentieth-century Americans puzzle over the wrong questions regarding homosexual acts and actors. The burning questions regarding antihomosexual attitudes are: Where did these prejudiced attitudes about sexuality come from, and how do they function to limit personal choice and well-being? I intend for this book to stimulate meaningful questions about prejudice and human sexuality.

A good example of a bad question is: "What is so 'gay' about being a homosexual, anyway?" Actually, this question reveals more about the inquirer than anything else. My reply to this question must transcend its real purpose, which is not to gather information, but to regulate choice. I must agree that prejudice against homosexual acts and actors can be painful and that stereotyping oneself in damaging ways is not carefree. Yet, the gay experience does contain special treasures. Clearly, for one to be gay does not necessarily mean that one is the victim of a congenital disease. Gay and lesbian identities are personal identifications with social and psychological positions. These positions are imbedded in political history. Good questions affirm real history. Bad questions affirm the inquirer's prejudices.

The most positive outcome of homosexual oppression/liberation is the truth that emerges from sheer contradiction. Sickness emerges when we behave in sickening ways and believe in sickening ideas; transformation becomes favorable because it brings one closer to truth and integrity. The truths about human sexuality and the components of sexual identity set free the human spirit to adapt and evolve. Specifically, social perception and action are transformed from being guided by gender-schematic processing to a more complex impression formation. The salience of gender in self-concept organization becomes less than in sex-typed persons' self-concept organizations. The components of sexual identity contribute equally to social perception and to action in the context of a well-defined self-concept. A holistic love for our own fellow beings emerges along with a world view founded on a remarkable appreciation for life in general. The gay experience provides an opportunity to question traditional lifestyles and values and to create an individual lifestyle based on personal knowledge and clarified social values. The sincere and noble benevolence we hold for our beloved is our most precious treasure, and one for which we struggle ardently.

Lesbian-identified women and gay-identified men constitute a diverse group. It is not really correct to say homosexuals constitute a sexual minority, because such a position distorts the truth about sexuality. It is more accurate to say that everyone is homosexual, or at least as accurate as saying everyone is heterosexual. However, at present only a small portion of humans from all ethnic and socioeconomic classes have publicly identified themselves as gay or lesbian. Many more remain invisible, as though their physical self were some figment of the imagination or were psychological and transhistorical. Most people believe they are only heterosexual organisms.

Gay- and lesbian-identified people have gained enormous strength from the conscious experience of sexual regulation. Those pools of personal power are capable of uniting against sexual oppression, sexism, racism, and spiritual oppression. Enlightened people are capable of having considerable social impact. The impetus for cultural alteration is created as sociosexual enlightenment is shared; this is why "coming out" is a "minority" issue. The time has come to alter U.S. culture. Males and females must be freed from the restricting roles they are required to perform according to gender. We must accept the truth about human sexuality and the social system. In doing so, we must alter the national character of this country, so that when one thinks of "an American," one will no longer think only of a white, heterosexual American, but also of a native American, an Asian American, an Afro-American, a Mexican American, and so on, and sexual Americans of both genders and of diverse heritages. We must make this country one vast encounter group, in which every person serves as a clinician to society, dedicated to immediate change: to a transformation of the national character. A recognition that the human sexual capacity is positive and inclusive, rather than negative (except by virtue of its object) and exclusive, is imperative. This transformation is a necessary and essential part of human development.

The citizens of the United States must take control of the socializing institutions of this country and force them to correct the information they disseminate as they socialize our children. Family, church, state, and school operate on a general body of knowledge called the *normal point of view*, which perpetuates many assumptions and generalizations. Stereotypes of groups of people, as well as the concept of what kinds of behaviors and roles are more common or more normal, are destructively applied; conformity and compliance are valued over individuality, establishing the high school as a prison. Religious guilt has become an un-Godly weapon.

It has been my personal and professional goal to expose the origins and functions of antihomosexual attitudes. I feel that such knowledge will lead to the resolution of fear and prejudice toward homosexual acts and actors. This resolution of fear will create a condition for human growth and social development. Antihomosexual attitudes are the crux of many of the social ills experienced in the United States, including sexism, gender role conformity, spiritual oppression, and crime. This continues to be true in part because sex has been legally defined as the private sphere, and not proper for public discussion. Forms of prejudice may be studied comparatively between both genders, and among the various races, classes, and religions, revealing the essential point requiring resolution. The study of comparative prejudice will transcend traditional approaches by equally acknowledging their truths and their contradictions. The greatest splendor of truth is that it need not be aggressive to expose the authoritarian power hierarchies that create and maintain prejudice.

This book contains my personal gift to you. This gift is the opportunity to rigorously examine attitudes toward homosexual acts, actors, and identities, while critically seeking the origins and bases for these attitudes. You don't have to say you are gay to read this book; if you do, be prepared for a compelling analysis of the psychology of the gay experience. I hope you experience my sharing of subjective truth, and go forth to determine your own history.

ACKNOWLEDGMENTS

While this manuscript was in preparation, several able critics gave it a thoughtful and helpful review. I would like to thank Sandra and Daryl Bem, Cornell University, and Philip Zimbardo, Stanford University, for their assistance in formulating research questions and conducting my empirical studies, and A.P. MacDonald, Jr., University of Massachusetts, for his interest and editorial comment. Thanks to Lynn Abramson, University of Wisconsin, for her thoughtful contributions to my writings on social stereotypes, self-perception, and self-esteem. For encouragement in writing the book, I am grateful to John DeCecco, San Francisco State University, John Gonsiorek, University of Minnesota Medical School, and Robert O. Hawkins, State University of New York School of Allied Health Professions at Stony Brook. I am especially grateful to Steven Morin, Don Clark, and Charles Silverstein for their engaging comments on the topics of gay chauvinism, homophobia, and "homosexual." Thanks to the psychology faculty and students at the State University of New York at Stony Brook for assisting in my critical analysis of ideology and consciousness. I am grateful to Robin Winkler, University of Western Australia, to Mike Storms, University of Kansas, and to Jeffrey Weeks, University of Essex, London, for their helpful comments on sexual identity development.

Contents

LIST OF TABLES

INTRODUCTION

Research and theory pertaining to beliefs about and fears of people labeled "homosexual" have become more productive than in any previous time. The progress even within the last decade has been remarkable, and we now see psychologists, sociologists, anthropologists, and historians tackling problems like the development of sexual identity in component parts, the impact of situations on behavioral manifestations of beliefs about and fears of homosexual acts and actors, and the characteristics of societies that have historically shaped taboos against homosexual acts and actors. We have a long way to go, of course, but the beginnings of a coherent framework for studying ideas about homosexual acts and actors are becoming visible, and an increasing number of exceptionally qualified individuals are researching the psychological processes involved in regulating the homosexual capacity.

PURPOSE AND PERSPECTIVE

The purpose of this book is to explore some of the questions being asked by researchers in the rapidly developing area of beliefs about and fears of homosexual acts, actors, and identities. The book will discuss what kinds of questions and phenomena are being studied, why they are important, and how researchers are attempting to explore the phenomena and answer the questions. In general, this book is a study of why individuals have certain ideas and anticipations of homosexual acts and actors, how situations influence these beliefs and fears, and what characteristics of the cultural complex account for the individual's experience of social control and regulation in psychosocial development.

It is important to note something else about this book's discussion of subjective views of homosexual acts and actors. As stated earlier, the goal is to discuss what kinds of questions are being studied, why the questions are important, and how researchers study the questions. This statement needs, however, to be qualified. There are many people working in the areas of beliefs and fears and of homosexual acts and actors; each researcher has a different idea about the kinds of questions that are most important, the kinds of theories and studies that are most useful, and so on. Note, for example, that the topic to be explored is beliefs about and fears of homosexual acts and actors, rather than personal views of homosexuality or of homosexuals. There is an important reason for this choice of terms, one that sets this text apart from other texts on human sexuality and social psychology. This book separates the act from the person; thus, there are no "homosexuals," or "heterosexuals," in any pure biological or genetic sense. Not all of the theories and experiments discussed adopt this perspective. This book's major contribution is that the separation of the act from the actor advances a study in the contents and processes of prejudice and social stigma in the area of human sexuality.

In this book, I try to capture some of the enthusiasm and direction characteristic of researchers in the field and to communicate it in a way that is understandable to undergraduates, graduates, and professionals in psychology. The organization and content of this text reflect a particular perspective on problems of beliefs and fears of homosexual acts and actors. *The perspective advanced considers the essential composition of human sexuality as inclusive of a range of potential responses, and sexual identity as essentially social and political.* Particular experiments were selected because they exemplify particular points in a clear manner, and I tend to discuss a few prototypical experiments in an area, rather than providing an exhaustive review of the research relevant to any domain. I present two of my own exploratory studies where theoretical questions require immediate examination or demonstration.

ORGANIZATION

Part One (chapters One through Three) focuses on sexual identity and belief. Chapter One delineates the components of sexual identity. Biological and psychological components are examined as they interact with social influences. Beliefs and systems of beliefs are described in Chapter Two. Stereotypes are analyzed, and information-processing implications are presented. Religious beliefs and tradition are considered to be influential in shaping individual belief and scientific paradigm. Chapter three explains sexuality and beliefs about sexuality. Self-concept implications are demonstrated in a study of attitudes about homosexual acts and actors among homosexual males.

Part Two (chapters Four through Six) concentrates on pejorative responding to homosexual acts and actors. Chapter Four explains the acquisition and performance of behavior. The social influence of the presence of other people is examined. Some effects of guilt on compliance are clarified. Chapter Five clarifies the study of prejudice and sexuality. The authoritarian personality is characterized. Issues in interpersonal attribution and emotional labeling are presented. The learning processes of socially stigmatized persons are discussed. A correlational study is presented to demonstrate the character of person-situation deviance. Chapter Six considers fears and phobias of homosexual acts and actors in a rigorous analysis of "homophobia." This analysis highlights the most influential psychological and sociological reports within a twofold framework including analysis from both a personal and a cultural perspective. The central issues of definition, measurement, and diagnostic criteria are carefully examined. Chapter Seven draws conclusions relevant to methodology and suggests some new directions for research.

AUDIENCE

This book is recommended as an upper-division college text for social psychology, human sexuality, and gender role classes in psychology, sociology, and anthropology. The book provides a theoretical base and innovative direction for selected topics classes in prejudice. Graduate-level courses in human sexuality and social stigma will also find it useful, since rigorous cognitive, behavioral, and social analyses are essential to this domain.

As a supplementary text or sourcebook, *Homosexual Acts, Actors, and Identities* can help to extend capabilities for nonprejudiced personal interaction in most psychology seminars. Practicing professionals will also find it useful both as a teaching resource and as a primary resource for research ideas. Clinical psychologists and social workers will find it helpful in generating a deeper appreciation of the problems encountered by individuals due to social values and sexual ideology. *Homosexual Acts, Actors, and Identities* will be an important resource for those developing therapeutic methods of clinical intervention. Furthermore, since the book contains a careful analysis of beliefs and social influence, it will be an essential tool for those interested in shaping public opinion.

HOMOSEXUAL ACTS, ACTORS, AND IDENTITIES

PART ONE:

SEXUAL IDENTITY AND BELIEF

CHAPTER ONE

COMPONENTS OF SEXUAL IDENTITY

The struggle for sexual self-definition is a struggle in the end for control over our bodies. To establish this control we must escape from those ideologies and categorizations which imprison us within the existing social order.

Jeffrey Weeks

Freedom for gay people cannot come solely from a greater assertion of gay rights, but must come from far wider social and cultural shifts involving the transformation of all sexual meanings and definitions. In the present conjuncture we can only begin to achieve this by organizing around the historically given sexual categories and meanings. But we should be aware that our ultimate aim is the disintegration of those categories rather than their reinforcement.

Frank Mort

An individual's sexual identity is influenced by biological and psychological components. In addition to biological gender, there are three psychological components of sexual identity. They are: (1) gender identity, that is, a secure sense of one's genital maleness or femaleness; (2) sexual preference; and (3) gender role identity and gender role behaviors, traits, and interests that are socially considered to be gender specific.

BIOLOGICAL GENDER

This discussion of sexual identity and beliefs about homosexual acts and actors begins with a consideration of biological influences. One's

3

biology shapes one's sexual identity by way of physical development. The critical period prenatally is between the eighth and twentieth weeks, when the secretion of hormones is determined by the chromosomes paired at conception.* If the fetus is a male, testosterone is secreted; if a female, estrogen is secreted, tending to promote estrus and stimulate the development of secondary gender characteristics in the female. Some of these secondary gender characteristics relate to body strength, dominance, and aggression. These secondary characteristics may be considered biological predispositions that interact with the impact of social experience and learning to shape one's overall sexual identity. In short, at birth most persons may be classified by biological gender, as determined by the external genitalia. In cases where biological gender is ambiguous, more detailed criteria are used, including chromosomal configurations, gonads, internal reproductive organs, and hormonal secretions.

The obvious differences in anatomy shape one's self-awareness and set the stage for cultural values to be assigned to one's behaviors and characteristics. In terms of self-awareness, an aroused penis is externally and instrumentally more obvious than an aroused clitoris. Men know very early that their penis is the source of sexual pleasure; from puberty the male is more aware than the female of being a genitally oriented person. Kinsey found evidence supporting these observations. In his survey of American adults, he found that by age 20, 92% of males (Kinsey, Pomeroy, & Martin, 1948) and 33% of females (Kinsey et al., 1953) had masturbated. In 1972, *Playboy* sampled U.S. adults and found that 94% of men had masturbated in their life, while only 63% of women had.

Aggression

Male hormones (androgens) function during prenatal development to masculinize the growing individual. In fact, genetic females exposed to abnormally (for females) high levels of androgens prenatally are masculinized both physically and behaviorally, including elevated levels of threat behavior and rough-and-tumble play (Maccoby & Jacklin, 1974).

Male hormones increase aggressive behavior when they are administered even without prenatal sensitization. Aggressive responses were the main focus of a study on social dominance and the establishment of dominance relations (Joslyn, 1973). These researchers selected three male and three female rhesus monkeys that were separated from their mothers at

---

*I will spare the reader a detour into genetics and embryology; but note that evidence of the critical period in chromosomal determination (46XX as female and 46XY as male) has shown that male and female are actually *overlapping* biological ranges; see, e.g., Luria (1979), p. 165.

3 and 4 months of age for subjects. The three females were regularly injected with testosterone from age 6½ months to 14½ months. The males were untreated. For three periods of several months each the animals were placed together for 30 minutes a day in an observation cage and their social behavior recorded. The three periods were ages 5 to 9½ months, ages 13½ to 16 months, and ages 25 to 27½ months. The findings were that initially, before testosterone treatment of the females began, the males were dominant and showed more aggression than the females. After the onset of testosterone treatment, the frequency of aggression by the females increased; it was approximately equal to that of the males by the end of the first observation period (age 9½ months). During the early portion of the second observation period, two of the females attacked and subdued the two most dominant males. These two females continued to be dominant throughout the second observation period (after the hormone treatment had been discontinued) and also maintained their dominance through the third observation period, almost a year after the cessation of hormonal treatment. At this time, aggression was infrequent within the group, and there was an increased frequency of social play, but the amount of rough-and-tumble play among the males was considerably reduced by comparison with that among males in normal situations, as was their sexual behavior.

Attitudes

Eight studies that have investigated gender differences in pejorative attitudes toward homosexual acts and actors report that males are more negative or threatened than are females (Brown & Amoroso, 1975; Gallup, 1977; Millham, San Miguel, & Kellogg, 1976; Nutt & Sedlacek, 1974; Steffensmeier & Steffensmeier, 1974; Morin, Taylor, & Kielman, 1975; Morin & Wallace, 1976). Six other studies found no significant differences in pejorative attitudes toward homosexual acts and actors among men and women (Levitt & Klassen, 1974; MacDonald & Games, 1974; MacDonald et al., 1973; Morin, 1974; Rooney & Gibbons, 1966; Smith, 1971). Those studies that report finding gender differences assess the degree of threat the nonhomosexual anticipated feeling when in close proximity to the homosexual actor. Those studies that do not report finding gender differences focus more on general, cultural beliefs than on personal and situational anticipations. Further research should use multiple indicators in a path analysis.

The interrelationship of biological gender and aggression reveals that there are significant gender differences that may be related to hormones. It is difficult to discern, however, if these differences are attributed more appropriately to other sources, such as socialization. The secondary gender characteristic aggression appears to be closely related to forms of hostile prejudice, which in turn are laden with social values. In order to explore the impact of biological elements on aggression it is necessary to ask the following questions:

1. Is aggression cross-culturally constant?
2. How early in the child's life is it seen?
3. Is it consistent across different species?
4. Can we devise an experiment to test its biological basis?

The evidence for biological differences in aggression is found in all four areas. First, males are more aggresive than females in all societies for which evidence is available. Second, the differences are found early in life, at a time when there is no evidence that differential socialization pressures have been brought to bear by adults to "shape" aggression differently. Third, similar differences are found in humans and subhuman primates. Fourth, aggression is related to levels of hormones and can be changed by experimental administration of these hormones (Maccoby & Jacklin, 1974; Young, Goy, & Phoenix, 1964).

Gender differences in aggression, as in rough-and-tumble play, have a biological foundation. Specifically, some of these differences may be androgen mediated. That is not to say that aggression is never learned, but rather that the learning process calls for a form of reactivity that is not well understood, and with respect to which males and females may have different degrees of preparedness. In respect to aggression towards homosexual acts and actors, the process involves the acquisition of beliefs about them and subsequent hostility expressed towards them. A biological foundation for *acquiring* pejorative beliefs about and fears of homosexual acts and actors is not proposed. *Pejorative homosexual/homogender responding is viewed here as a product of social learning and behavioral acquisition coupled with biological preparedness; that is why males are more negative and fearful in their action toward homosexual acts and actors than women are.* These gender differences are most accurately attributed to the personal threat of any behavior thought to be socially inappropriate for males as U.S. men. This is a feature of gender role rigidity, also referred to as avoidance of cross-sex behavior. *This personal anxiety is not toward the mythical homosexual, but toward social rejection for unmasculine behavior.* In this sense, "homophobia" is a motivational element used to induce conformity to gender roles. Gender role behavior is confused with gender object choice or preference during socialization in part because guilt can be induced more effectively when the oppressed is in a state of conceptual confusion.

The evidence is strong that males are generally the more aggressive gender. The male is, for biological reasons, in a greater state of readiness to learn and display aggressive behavior. This may explain a gender difference in hostility towards homosexual acts and actors, but it does not explain all individual differences in pejorative responding to homosexual acts and actors. Furthermore, female aggression may be expressed *differently* than male aggression. Apparently the different socialization that results in males' fearing the label of effeminate provides different motivational dynamics. Among males, fear of being labeled unmasculine, e.g., "sissy" or "queer," may be the essential motivational mediator between learned prejudice toward homosexual acts and actors and expressed aggression towards them. We turn now to the development of gender identity and gender role identity for further explanations of the gender differences in pejorative responding to homosexual acts and actors.

GENDER IDENTITY

Gender identity is a sense of one's biological maleness or femaleness. Gender identity has been defined as the individual's basic conviction of being male or female, present by the time the child begins to speak, and developed by the age of three (Green, 1974; Money & Tucker, 1975). Healthy gender identity is also defined as being able to look into the mirror and be perfectly comfortable with the body that one sees there (Bem, 1976). The private sense of one's gender, including the label attached to one's gender by oneself and significant others, that develops early in childhood is called *core gender identity*, whereas the gender identity of postpubescence is called *adult gender identity* (Luria, 1979).

Some individuals experience a conflict between biological gender and gender identity. In such cases, the conflict may be "resolved" by undergoing surgery whereby biological gender is modified to be congruent with gender identity. Individuals who have undergone this particular type of surgery are known as *transsexuals*. Transsexuals may be heterosexual, homosexual, or bisexual.

The relationship between gender identity and beliefs about homosexuality is apparent in much of the scientific research and theory of the past century. This relationship has been considered to be a particularly close and possibly a causally linked one. It was widely believed that identification with the opposite-gender parent, and the failure to transfer identification to the same-gender parent, resulted in a preference for a sexual partner of the same gender. At the turn of the century medical writers indicated that homosexuality resulted from the individual's possessing "traces of psychical hemaphrodisia," with male homosexuals having a female mind (Krafft-Ebbing, 1906). An inverted man "feels he is a woman in search of a man," said Freud (1905). In cases where this searching was not apparent, Sigmund believed men who possess relatively few of the characteristics of the opposite gender search for feminine mental traits in their sexual object.

Similar differences in line with normative societal expectations suggest that homosexuality is an incongruity of gender identity. A model in which transsexualism, transvestism, and homosexuality are seen as functions, from strong to less severe, of opposite-gender identification was presented by Money and Ehrhardt (1968). These researchers adopted a sex-only-for-procreation model that ignores human social development and sex as an emotional, interpersonal, and intrasocial form of communication.

The assumption of opposite-parent, and thus opposite-gender, identification may be another facet of the belief that sexual relations can only occur between opposite-gendered individuals. In other words, where normative social pressure is internalized, the homosexual actor may, in an extreme case, believe that sexual relations can only be male-female and may rationalize in line with this pressure that, if he desires another male, he must be like a female. Therefore, he may opt for changing to a female rather than adopting alternative male behaviors. Others have argued that rigidity of definitions of masculinity may well increase the likelihood of men's making self-attributions of homosexuality when they find themselves deviating from narrow role definitions (Luria, 1979).

Sexual variation may be viewed as a facilitator of interpersonal relationships. One group of researchers suggests that masculinity, femininity, and opposite-gender identification are not aspects of homosexuality but indicators of social stereotypes and their internalization. Ross and his collegues conclude, "All that could be said to differentiate homosexuals from heterosexuals, in the final analysis, is the degree and form of social pressure to which they are subjected" (Ross, Rogers, & McCulloch, 1978, p. 328).

John Gagnon (1979) aptly summarizes the relationship between gender roles and sexual conduct:

> The relation between gender roles and sexual conduct is a function of specific historical-cultural conditions, not the acting out of either a developmental or a biological program. Our dilemma is that we have taken the processes of a single set of historical examples (the United States and Western Europe for a century) and have assumed that they have universal validity. In this sense most of sex and gender research is antihistorical and anticultural. It is often insisted that men and women and sexual conduct are not only the same in similar places, but that all combinations of gender and

sexual activity also have transhistorical meanings. The patterns of gender role and erotic development that we observe in Western European societies and their descendants are only a few of the potential designs available for humans (p. 243).

Sandra Bem (1976) has written an eloquent description of the influence of gender identity on behavior and trait choices:

> But beyond being comfortable with one's own body, one's gender need have no other influence on one's behavior or on one's life style.... although I suggest that a man ought to feel perfectly comfortable about the fact that he has a penis which can become erect, this in no way implies that a man ought to take the more active role in sexual intercourse, nor even that his sexual partners ought all to be female (p. 60).

In sum, it is the child's growing understanding of his or her own anatomy that develops gender identity, coupled with a growing understanding of stereotyped roles prescribed by the prevailing culture, that determines the child's behavioral choices. In this view, the development of gender identity is dependent upon certain aspects of cognitive growth. A child's inferences concerning what behavior is appropriate are partly based on the instances of differential reward and punishment.

The developmental process of gender identity formation reveals an inferred relationship between one's commitment to being male or female and one's choice of sexual partners. The socialization process provides different experiences and pressure for boys and girls. A part of the process of gender role socialization is the initial formation of gender identity. Gender role identity stems from the development of gender identity and is closely related to the development of social stereotypes. Thus, the components of sexual identity adhere in socially valued ways and are presented as a cluster during the socialization of the young.

GENDER ROLE IDENTITY AND GENDER ROLE

Gender role identity is a global self-concept of both one's masculinity and one's femininity. The concept of role originated in the theater, where the actor's script was rolled around a wooden rod called in Latin a *rotula*. "Role" was introduced as a sociological concept in the 1920s by George H. Mead and a group of University of Chicago sociologists. Sociologists generally define *role* in terms of an individual's "position" or the location of an actor or class of actors in a system of social relationships. A role is a set of social expectations or norms and is not necessarily descriptive of what a person actually does. This aspect of sexual identity relates to the feeling of identification with a constellation of behaviors and preferences associated with a masculine or feminine role that is ascribed by biological gender. In childhood, a boy usually comes to understand that he is and always will be a boy (gender identity). He comes to feel that he wants to be a boy and is motivated to behave according to what his conception of what boylike behavior is. However, the 2- or 3-year-old doesn't really know of the relationship between anatomy and behavioral gender roles. Therefore, judgments of gender are made from any cue other than anatomical design. Differential socialization with social stereotypes, involving rewards and punishments, guides the child's development.

Gender role identity is more commonly referred to as social sex role identity (see Storms, 1978; Bem, 1981a). This component of sexual identity is conceptualized in terms of masculinity and femininity. These characteristics are commonly referred to as social sex roles and are largely tied to characteristics of behavior, personality, and appearance. Bakan (1966) considered the masculine orientation to be an agentic one, coupled with a concern for the self as an individual. Femininity was considered a communal orientation, coupled with a concern for the self in relation to others. Parsons (1978) characterized instrumentality as a cognitive focus on getting the job done or the problem solved; he presented expressivity as an affective concern for the welfare of others. The term "gender role" is more appropriate than the term "social sex role," and it will be used whenever possible in this text. "Gender role identity" will be used to denote self-concept rather than behavior or activity preference.

An interesting example of research on the psychosocial determinants of gender identity comes from the work of John Money and his colleagues at Johns Hopkins University. In one case, twins were matched biologically, but assigned and reared differently (Money, 1975). Money reported that at age 7 months the twins were circumcised, and an operating error on one of the twins led to necrosis and sloughing off of the penis. When the boys were 17 months of age, the parents agreed to have the injured twin penecotomized and reassigned to the female gender. At 21 months of age, the first feminizing genital surgery was performed.

It was the parents' behavior, however, that changed most dramatically after the reassignment. Luria (1979) describes this change:

> The parents' behavior became different for the two children after the reassignment. The mother found her son's urinating in the yard amusing; similar behavior by the daughter was considered immodest, not what "nice little girls do." By age four, the little girl

preferred dresses to slacks and took pride in her long hair. The mother described the girl at four-and-one-half as neat and concerned about her apearance, while the brother was unconcerned about being dirty.

Before reassignment and surgery, the boy who was later reassigned had been the dominant twin, the "leader." As a girl at age three, this same child was described as "bossy." Her twin brother was already protective toward her in situations of danger or threat.

The children's toys and activities had been encouraged along gender-differentiated lines. And the encouragement "took." The girl's tomboyishness—common in androgenized females and not rare in nonandrogenized females—was discouraged. The girl got dolls and other girl toys; the boy got cars, tools, and other boy toys. The mother's educational aspirations for both twins remain high and egalitarian; but she feels the fulfillment of her aspirations is more important for her son. (p. 169)

Gender Roles

Masculine and feminine roles may be viewed as bipolar personality traits or behaviors, or as two constellations of traits and behaviors. If they are viewed as bipolar, the individual expresses masculinity at the expense of femininity. If they are viewed as independent continua, the individual may be qualitatively seen as masculine and feminine. Quantitatively, masculinity and femininity can range from very much to very little and may be described in ways that depart from the expressive-instrumental dimension. Individuals who are both masculine and feminine have been termed *androgynous* (Bem, 1974; Spence, Helmreich, & Stapp, 1975), whereas those individuals who are not at all masculine or feminine are *undifferentiated*.

In some rare cases, conflicts arise between biological gender and gender role identity. Green (1974), Green and Money (1969), Rekers and Lovaas (1974), and Rekers et al. (1976) have studied boys who developed what they considered very feminine behaviors and traits. Some of these boys are called *transvestites*. A transvestite is a person who dresses in clothing ordinarily worn by a person of the other gender. Transvestites are commonly heterosexual.

Theories of Gender Role Socialization

Identification and social learning theories of gender role socialization offer some explanation of role acquisition. Identification theories

have their origins in Freud's psychoanalytic psychology. Childrens' relationships with their parents, particularly their same-gender parent, affect
their developing personalities through the process of *identification*. This
process involves the child's molding its own "ego-ideal" after that of the
parent model. Psychoanalytic theory assumes that boys form defensive
identifications while girls form anaclitic identifications. This is because
females are not motivated by a fear of castration to identify with either the
mother or the father. Through identification, children acquire complete,
complex patterns of behavior, attitudes, feelings, wishes, and standards of
conduct that constitute a gender role. These integrated patterns of behavior
are stable across situations and over time. Some data support predictions
based on identification theory, but reinforcement principles yield the same
predictions and explain the data equally well (Parsons & Croke, 1978).
Identification theorists also assume that children are stimulated by some
internal drive or unconscious and powerful motive to model the parents'
gender role behaviors. For Sigmund Freud the motivation was Oedipal
conflict—fear of castration and penis envy. Anna Freud suggested that the
motive was fear of loss of love from one's parent; the data are sparse and far
from conclusive. Yet many continue to assume that identification results
from a unique emotional tie to the same-gender parent and that the child
will "turn out" just like the same-gender parent. Data indicate that the
presence of a same-gender parent is not absolutely essential for gender
stereotyping to occur; in fact, the same-gender parent may not be the
primary source for gender role learning among children (Maccoby &
Jacklin, 1974).

Social learning theory explains gender role socialization in terms of
behavioral laws. Identification and emulation encompass the same be-
behavioral phenomenon; the principles of reinforcement and modeling
describe the process in simpler terms. *Any consistency that does occur across
various situations or over time is attributed to the way that society responds to that
behavioral phenomenon.* Growing children are thus described as continuing
to adopt new behaviors and to alter or eliminate old behaviors from their
repertoires, according to societal expectations and reward contingencies.
An emotional bond is not necessary for imitation to occur, but nurturance
on the part of the model may facilitate imitation. Rather than seeing
children as motivated by internal drives, the social learning theorist views
the external social environment as motivating. The mechanisms underlying
gender role acquisition are reinforcement and punishment. The process of
modeling assumes that children learn from attending to and learning
correctly the behavior of the model. Not all behavior learned will be
performed. Evidence indicates that children do attend more to models of

the same gender but that imitation is controlled by the model's power, dominance, and warmth. The acquisition and performance of behavior will be described more fully in Chapter Four.

Neither identification nor social learning theories are sufficient to explain the part socialization plays in gender role acquisition. Children are not viewed as active learners in the social environment (Parsons, 1978).

In contrast to the identification theories, the cognitive-developmental explanations assume the motivational basis for the acquisition of behaviors is a positive, internal desire for mastery. In comparison to the social learning approach, the cognitive-developmental view suggests children are actively gathering information rather than passively modeling behavior. Another important difference between the cognitive-developmental theories and both social learning and identification theories concerns the causal relationships between gender stereotyped identity, cultural stereotypes, and actual attributes. Both social learning theory and identification theory suggest gender stereotyped identity is the product of identification with the stereotypes and actual imitation of gender role attributes. In contrast, Kohlberg (1966) has suggested that gender typed identity and knowledge of gender role stereotypes produce gender role attributes. Cognitive-developmental theories also assume that the emergence of gender as an important social category is the result of the child's cognitive system rather than the result of either psychosexual dynamics or the impact of external models and rewards. Thus, a cognitive-developmental model of gender role acquisition contains these three conclusions: (1) gender emerges as an early classificatory cue; (2) gender forms the basis for stable and persistent stereotypes throughout the preschool and early elementary years; and (3) changes in these stereotypes depend on the exposure of the child to egalitarian models and information and on the child's cognitive maturity. Culture functions in the acquisition of gender roles insofar as the system of categories, the nature of the categories, and the extent and rigidity of children's generalizations reflect the culture's values (Parsons, 1978).

From the basis of Piaget's four stages of cognitive development, Kohlberg (1966) argued that children pass through three major cognitive steps in the process of acquiring gender role behaviors. First, by age 4 gender identity develops out of the awareness that people come in two genders and the child belongs to one of them. Gender becomes an organizer for social information and the categorical foundation for later stereotypes. Second, children develop a system (schema) of values for the attitudes and behaviors associated with the other gender; egocentric thinking and stable gender identity characterize this stage of cognitive development. Third, because of the differential valuing and modeling of same-gender attributes and attitudes, an emotional attachment or identification develops with the parent of the same gender.

Thus, according to Kohlberg, gender role identity is established early in life and thereafter serves to mediate the influence of gender role stereotypes on the individual's development of gender role attributes. Gender role identity guides the individual's attachment to, evaluation of, and desire to emulate gender role prototypes (specific adult role models) and gender role stereotypes (abstract role models). The gender role attributes adopted by the individual are a product of the individual's gender role identity and perception of gender role stereotypes.

In contrast to the cognitive-developmental theory outlined by Kohlberg, Kagan (1964a) views gender role identity as the product of gender role stereotypes and gender role attributes. That is, developing individuals compare their own attributes against gender role stereotypes to arrive at a relativistic self-concept of their gender role identity. Using social learning theory, Kagan (1958) explained the acquisition of this component of sexual identity as governed by the following contingencies:

1.   Children must want approval.

2.   Adult caretakers must give children approval for developing stereotypic behavior.

3.   Males must learn to behave like boys and females must learn to behave like girls.

Kagan describes the relationship of the child to the caretaker model:

1.   The model must be perceived by the child as nurturant.

2.   The model must be perceived by the child as in control of the resources desired by the child.

3.   The child must perceive some objective basis of similarity between itself and the model.

Kagan's and Kohlberg's theories of gender role identity are tested in a study conducted by Storms (1979). Both of these theories predict a relationship between one's gender role identity, gender role attributes, and perception of gender role stereotypes. Kagan asserts that identity is the product of stereotypes and attributes, whereas Kohlberg asserts that identity and stereotypes give rise to one's attributes.

The subjects that Storms selected to participate in the test of these two theories were 104 male and 110 female students in an introductory social psychology class at a state university in the Midwest. The instruments used included the *Sex Role Identity Scale* (SRIS), developed to measure a global self-concept of one's masculinity and femininity. The SRIS contains three masculine and three feminine items and shows good psychometric properties. In addition, Spence and Helmreich's (1978) *Personal Attributes Questionnaire* (PAQ) was administered as a measure of subjects' sex role attributes. Subjects' stereotypes were measured by modified versions of the PAQ; stereotype ratings of the typical male and of the typical female were thus obtained using exactly the same scales as for the self-ratings. The results indicated sex role identity was conceptualized by these subjects as unidimensional. Masculinity items correlated negatively with femininity items better than −.64 for men and −.74 for women. Kagan's and Kohlberg's theories made different predictions relevant to two correlational analyses: Kagan's theory predicts a causal link, and therefore a correlation between sex role stereotypes and sex role identity. Kohlberg's theory does not predict this correlation because it views sex role stereotypes and sex role identity as two independent variables. Kagan's theory was not upheld by the obtained correlation coefficients. Kagan's and Kohlberg's theories also lead to opposing predictions about the relationship between sex role attributes and sex role stereotypes. Kohlberg's theory posits a causal link, and therefore a correlation, between the two, whereas Kagan's theory predicts no such relationship. The obtained correlations reached significance in the direction predicted by Kohlberg's theory.

Socializing Boys Versus Girls

Maccoby and Jacklin (1974) explore the following set of hypotheses concerning processes underlying differential treatment of children:

1. Parents treat children so as to shape them toward the behavior deemed appropriate for their sex.

2. Because of innate differences in characteristics manifested early in life, boys and girls stimulate their parents differently and hence elicit different treatment from them.

3. Parents base their behavior toward a child on their conception of what a child of a given sex is likely to be like.
    a. Parents devote special attention to training children to overcome what they believe to be their natural weaknesses.
    b. Parents accept as inevitable, and do not attempt to change, behavior they believe to be "natural" for a given sex.

c. Parents tend to notice, and react to, whatever behavior is seen as unusual for a child of a given sex.

4. A parent's behavior toward a child will depend, in some degree, upon the sex of the child.
   a. Each parent wants to be a model for the same-sex child.
   b. Parents transfer to their children some of the behavior they are accustomed to display towards adults of the two sexes.
   c. Parents will tend to identify more strongly with the same-sex child (pp. 305–306).

In their comprehensive review, Maccoby and Jacklin (1974) conclude that there is substantial evidence that parents do encourage certain attitudes and behaviors, in part through providing certain toys for their children. Moreover, parents discourage their children—particularly their sons—from engaging in activities they consider appropriate only for the female gender. The authors conclude, "It would appear that feminine behavior in a boy is likely to be interpreted as a sign of possible homosexual tendencies, and as such, it is a danger signal to parents and triggers powerful anxieties in them—perhaps especially in fathers" (p. 339).

Following an analysis of parental sex anxiety in relation to the parents' care-taking interactions with infant sons and daughters, Sears (1965, p. 159) comments, "Sex anxiety is essentially homosexual in males." In other words, both parents are likely to find their own sex anxieties more stimulated by the sexual qualities of a son than by those of a daughter, and hence will avoid too intimate physical contact with him.

Furthermore, boys have been found to have more intense socialization experiences than girls. In an early and frequently cited article, Hartley (1959) reported the findings from interviews with forty-one 8- and 11-year-old boys. She considered the dilemmas that boys face regarding socialization to involve the fact that masculine norms are enforced earlier and more strictly for boys than girls. This creates an anxiety-provoking situation in which unclear demands, based on reasons beyond the child's understanding, are harshly enforced. A second problem, particularly for boys, is the relative absence of the father. Consequently, much of male behavior has to be learned by trial and error; the peer groups' over-simplified and overemphasized physical strength and athletic skills model of masculinity becomes the primary source of information and practice for the child. The greatest source of difficulty for the male child is that he is placed under the jurisdiction of the despised female for most of his waking day. This, it is argued, creates a role conflict, because he is simultaneously taught to be independent and to disdain "sissies."

The boys in Hartley's study saw the demands of the male role as including such things as having to fight if a bully comes along, to be athletic, and to be smart. When asked what was expected of boys, the replies included that they believed grown-ups to expect them to get dirty, to be naughty, to mess up the house, not to be crybabies, and not to be softies. Girls were seen as afraid very often, as needing to know how to cook, and as keeping themselves occupied with dolls, fussing over babies, and talking about dresses. Women were believed to be indecisive, to lack the strength in the head or in the body to do most jobs, and to die more often than men. Four patterns of responses were identified in the data. They were: (1) overstriving with explicit hostility expressed against the other gender and with marked rigidity concerning the differentiation between role activities assigned to men and those assigned to women, (2) overstriving with less hostility but with marked rigidity, (3) a tendency to give up the struggle to live up to the male role accompanied by protest against social expectations, and (4) a successful, well-balanced implementation of the role, marked with clear differentiation of the roles but with flexibility in activities assigned to each.

As a result of the socialization process, men learn that homosexuality represents a failure to live up to accepted masculine norms such as competitiveness with other men, absence of emotional expression (particularly in the presence of other men), and sexual potency with women. According to Lewis (1978), accepting the traditional male expectations reinforces efforts to be competitive, to fear homosexuality, and to avoid personal vulnerability and openness. For men who identify themselves as homosexual, the outcome of internalizing traditional male norms and the normative point of view is accepting that homosexuality is associated with failure to live up to these norms, resulting in feelings of guilt and failure and a negative identity (Altman, 1973; Fasteau, 1976).

Recent research shows that people perceive homosexual men as less masculine than heterosexual men. In a survey of readers of *Psychology Today* (Tavris, 1977), 70% of the heterosexual respondents reported that they believe homosexual men to be "not fully masculine." That study also revealed that homosexual men were much more likely than heterosexual men to rate themselves "less masculine than average" (40% compared with 7%). Furthermore, homosexual men rate themselves "more feminine than average" to a greater degree than heterosexual men (36% compared with 19%).

Lethal Aspects of Masculinity

A male's acceptance of traditional male role expectations strongly reinforces his efforts to be competitive, to fear homosexuality and to avoid personal vulnerability and openness.

Robert Lewis

The major theses of a book by Jourard (1971) include that people are healthiest and most personally developed only insofar as they gain courage to be themselves with others and when they find goals that have meaning to them. Jourard believes that normal personalities are role functional, but not necessarily healthy. His examination of the sociology of illness tabulates disease incidence and suggests that people sicken because they behave in sickening ways. Sickness means the body's protests are being ignored, and thus the sick person is in need of restoring systematic integrity. Nondisclosure, stress, and sickness are related. Jourard discusses some lethal aspects of the male role that cause men to die sooner than women. Men are obliged to hide the ongoing flow of their spontaneous inner experience in order to meet the demands of the male role—to be tough, objective, striving, achieving, and emotionally inexpressive. Jourard stimulated a generation of research with his observation that disclosure begets disclosure. That is, when a man discloses little personal information to others, they disclose little to him. Jourard argued that this is why men lack insight and empathy. The instrumental role training males experience promotes an interpersonal style of I–it relating to people. Manliness and incompetence at loving are discussed in light of the notion that loving oneself or others requires knowledge of the unique characteristics of the beloved. Because men disclose less and receive less disclosure it is harder for them to be loved. According to Jourard, retirement may cause death among men because masculine identity and self-esteem—factors in spiritual health for men—are a narrow base. Jourard's writings suggest research on both the amount, or breadth, of verbal disclosure and the personalness, or depth, of verbal disclosure, as they relate to mental, physical, and spiritual well-being.

Several types of inexpressive male roles have been delineated by researchers. These scientists assume it is more mature and healthy to express positive feelings toward another when that other is present than it is to not express them, and that the reason men often do not express positive feelings toward others is because of the role they believe they are expected to play in society. Working from these assumptions, Balswick (1981) discusses six types of inexpressive male roles: cowboys, good ol' boys, playboys, conboys, locker-room boys, and parlor-room boys.

The concept of role as used by Balswick serves to explain inexpressiveness as what results from the ego's conception of itself, its perceptions of the alter's (potential target person's) role, and its perception of the alter's expectation of it. Interpretation of the social situation is a key variable in understanding inexpressiveness. Three criteria are used to classify male inexpressiveness: (1) whether feelings are present, (2) whether the subject is pretending to express feelings, and (3) whether the potential object of expressiveness is male or female. Thus, feeling, nonverbal roles include playing the role of cowboy toward females and the role of a good ol' boy toward males. The feeling, nonverbal male learns to relate to females by assuming the strong, silent he-man role. Good ol' boys grow up together and stick together through thick and thin. The good ol' boy is feeling but nonverbal. Nonfeeling, verbal roles call for a display of feelings when, in reality, the male has no feelings within. The playboy is "a skilled manipulator of women, knowing when to turn the lights down, what music to play on the stereo, which drinks to serve and which topics of conversation to engage in," says Balswick (p. 365). The playboy reduces sexuality to a packageable consumption item that can be handled without responsibility. The conboy becomes a skilled manipulator of other males through his ability to convince them he really likes and cares for them.

The nonfeeling, nonverbal roles include locker-room boys and parlor-room boys. Males who are nonfeeling and nonverbal toward females but expressive of their feelings toward males will be viewed by females as locker-room boys. Males who are nonfeeling and nonverbal toward males but expressive of their feelings toward females will be viewed by other males as parlor-room boys. Two implications are stated in conclusion by Balswick. They are: (1) inexpressive behavior is immature, and (2) this behavior may be called forth by roles that exist within the social structure of U.S. society.

Within the category of agentic and communal traits, there are a number of "masculine" and "feminine" characteristics that are socially undesirable and have consequences for their possessors or those about them that may be deleterious. That is, a strong sense of agency, unmitigated by a sense of communion, is destructive. One group of researchers set out to explore the negative and positive components of psychological masculinity and femininity and their relationships to neurotic and acting-out behaviors. Spence, Helmreich, and Holahan (1979) set out to explore the possibility that different patterns of positive and negative masculine (M) and feminine (F) scale scores would be related to neurotic and acting-out behavior. They developed the Extended Personal Attributes Questionnaire (EPAQ) to measure positive and negative traits that might be considered masculine and feminine. A sixteen-item self-report measure of self-esteem and social competence was administered along with a thirty-nine-item biographical questionnaire measuring acting out and emotional distress. Their subjects were 220 male and 363 female students in introductory psychology at a large southwestern university. They report finding significant differences between the sexes in the predicted direction on all six scales of the EPAQ. For both males and females, positively valued masculine traits contribute more than any other gender role traits to self-esteem. The strongest relationship found between neuroticism and the gender role attributes was a negative correlation between positively valued masculinity and neuroticism. The most neurotic males were found to have the lowest socially desirable gender specific masculinity scores and the lowest desirable masculine traits for either gender. The only other significant finding was for males, who are less neurotic if they have feminine traits positively valued for both genders but more neurotic if they have more negatively valued feminine traits (sex-specific), e.g., passive-aggressive verbal style, spinelessness, servility, and gullibility.

The reaction that an individual has to stressful events may also be a function of gender role learning. The Type A behavior pattern, character-ized by rapid speaking/walking/eating, impatience, difficulty in relaxing, time urgency, acquisitiveness, preoccupation with work and advancement, and concern about the evaluation of peers and supervisors, has been linked to coronary heart disease (Harrison, 1978; Glass, 1977; Lovallo & Pishkin, 1980). Several studies reveal that Type A people do behave differently than Type B people; for example, As perform at elevated levels either with or without deadlines when solving complex math problems. Their achieve-ment motivation has been shown by superior memory, and their sup-pression of fatigue was demonstrated by continuous walking on a treadmill. That Type As are impatient with delay was shown by a study using differential rates of low reinforcement; Type As get tense and won't wait long enough before responding again after prior reinforcement. The coronary-prone behavior pattern might best be described as a characteristic style of responding to environmental stressors that threaten an individual's sense of control. In fact, Type A people react to uncontrollable events initially hyperresponsively—they are more motivated to control. However, extended exposure to such events results in hyporesponsiveness. Research on control and heart disease has shown that salient and negative events that are perceived as out of one's control lead to helplessness and heart disease (Glass, 1977). Type A individuals are more motivated to succeed in a conflict situation, and this leads the Type As to exaggerate the amount of dispositional information they believe they infer from observing the behavior of future opponents (Smith & Brehm, 1981); and because they are so competitive, Type As grow to avoid working with others so as to not impair their own performance (Gastorf, Suls, & Sanders, 1980).

Androgyny

The concept of adrogyny is predicated on the assumption that it is possible, in principle, for individuals to be both masculine and feminine. One researcher designed a study to look more closely at the specific processes that might be responsible for behavioral restriction (Bem, 1976). On one hand, Bem supposed it is possible that gender stereotyped individuals fail to engage in the cross-gender behavior simply because it does not occur to them or because they do not feel sufficiently skilled at it. In other words, it might be that cross-gender behavior is not motivationally problematic for gender stereotyped individuals and that they would willingly engage in such behavior if the situation were constructed to encourage it.

On the other hand, Bem believed it likely that cross-gender behavior is motivationally problematic for gender stereotyped individuals and that they actively avoid it as a result. This avoidance could emerge because gender stereotyped individuals are motivated to present a public image of masculinity or femininity to those around them. But, in either case, the individuals actively prefer gender-appropriate activities, even in situations where those gender-appropriate behaviors could incur some costs (Bem & Lenney, 1976). Furthermore, they experience discomfort and temporary loss of self-esteem if they are actually required to perform cross-gender behavior, according to Bem's research. However, masculine and feminine behaviors and characteristics that do not directly implicate instrumentality and expressiveness tend to be only weakly related to broadly defined masculine and feminine personality traits (Spence, Helmreich, & Holahan, 1979). Thus, some traits and behaviors are more centrally related to gender role stereotypes and have more impact upon self-esteem.

Through a process of socialization, a child adopts a set of behaviors, traits, interests, and mannerisms that are culturally ascribed according to gender. Even though one's actual attributes are independent of one's sexual preferences, the cooccurrence of these two elements of sexual identity is confused—at least, their covariance is overestimated—by many parents, socialization agents, and scientists. In other words, parents (especially fathers) fear that a boy preferring music to football may be showing "signs" of homosexuality. The result is the pervasive occurrence of emotional and behavioral rigidity or gender role comformity. This conformity includes pejorative beliefs about and fears of homosexual acts and actors.

SEXUAL PREFERENCE

Another psychological component of sexual identity is sexual preference. Like biological gender and gender role, sexual preference is best understood not in absolute but in relative terms. However, sexual behavior may be referred to by the biological gender of the persons involved in sexual acts or relations. In other words, if one is involved with someone of the same biological gender as one's own, the involvement is considered homosexual. If the involvement is with someone of the other gender, it is considered to be heterosexual. Persons are not considered to be homosexual or heterosexual, except when they, through a process of politics and personality, come to refer to themselves as such. Social identity labels based on sexual behavior may be problematic, as behaviors reflecting sexual preference appear to be nonstatic. Preferences in sexual behaviors and partners may change over a person's lifetime. Furthermore, that aspect of human nature called sexual preference is not bipolar, but homosexual and heterosexual relations may be expressed independently. Hence, the specific terms "homosexual acts" and "homosexual actors" and "heterosexual acts" and "heterosexual actors" will be adopted to this text. Generally, the terms "sexual acts" and "sexual actors" may be used. A word of caution: My view of human sexuality does not consider that sexual acts are instinctual, and thus independent of sexual actors, but rather that sexual drive, identity, and lifestyle are matters of human capacity, learning, and forced choice. I believe gender identity should not be confused with sexual preference, nor should sexual preference be thought to stem from inappropriate parental identification, fear of women as sexual beings, or symbolic fixation in the Oedipus complex. I prefer the term sexual *preference* to sexual *orientation* because the latter denotes some organic orientation or tendency. *Thus, I will focus on positive preferences in sensuous and affective relations rather than genetic, hormonal, or environmental determinants.*

A frequently cited attempt was made by Kinsey Pomeroy, and Martin (1948) to categorize people according to sexual acts. They devised a seven-point rating scale (with categories ranging from 0 to 6) that measured the balance of heterosexual and homosexual *behavior leading to orgasm*. At one end of this scale (in Category 0) they placed those whose experiences were exclusively heterosexual, and at the other end (in Category 6) they placed those whose experiences were exclusively homosexual. Between these two extremes were those who had had both heterosexual experiences and homosexual experiences in various degrees (categories 1 to 5). The exact breakdown follows:

0. Exclusively heterosexual behavior.

1. Largely heterosexual, but incidental homosexual behavior.

2. Largely heterosexual, but more than incidental homosexual behavior.

3. Equal amount of heterosexual and homosexual behavior.

4. Largely homosexual, but more than incidental heterosexual behavior.

5. Largely homosexual, but incidental heterosexual behavior.

6. Exclusively homosexual behavior.

Kinsey concluded from data collected from detailed sex histories that the world was not to be divided into heterosexuals and homosexuals. "Only the human mind invents categories and tries to force facts into separated pigeon-holes (p. 639)," he was convinced. In fact, he concluded it was simply wrong-headed to distinguish between two discrete populations, heterosexual and homosexual.

Kinsey et al. (1953) summarize their research on homosexual patterns of sexual preference in the following:

> The inherent physiological capacity of an animal to respond to any sufficient stimulus seems, then, the basic explanation of the fact that some individuals respond to stimuli originating in other individuals of their own sex—and it appears to indicate that every individual could so respond if the opportunity offered and one were not conditioned against making such responses. There is no need of hypothesizing peculiar hormonal factors that make certain individuals especially liable to engage in homosexual activity, and we know of no data which prove the existence of such hormonal factors. There are no sufficient data to show that specific hereditary factors are involved. Theories of childhood attachments to one or the other parent, theories of fixation at some infantile level of sexual development, interpretations of homosexuality as neurotic or psychopathic behavior or moral degeneracy, and other philosophic interpretations are not supported by scientific research, and are contrary to the specific data on ours series of female and male histories. The data indicate that the factors leading to homosexual behavior are: (1) the basic physiologic capacity of every mammal to respond to any sufficient stimulus; (2) the accident which leads an individual into his or her first sexual experience with a person of the same sex, (3) the conditioning effects of such experience; and (4) the indirect but powerful conditioning which the opinions of other persons and the social codes may have on an individual's decision to accept or reject this type of sexual contact (p. 447).

A more palatable conceptualization of human sexual responsiveness has appeared in the contemporary psychological literature that views sexual preference as having *two* independent aspects. One is physical preference, and the other aspect is affectional preference. Physical preference has two independent continua of heterosexuality and homosexuality. In the same fashion, affectional preference is viewed as having one continuum for heterosexual affection and another for homosexual affection (Shively & DeCecco, 1977).

Sexual preference is believed to arise solely from an individual's acquired erotic responsiveness to stimuli with one gender or another (Kinsey, Pomeroy, & Martin, 1948; Kinsey et al., 1953). Patterns of erotic response are represented by an individual's erotic fantasies or "scripts," which develop out of various learning processes and experiences (Gagnon & Simon, 1973). Furthermore, any characteristics associated with sexual preferences other than actual erotic responses, such as gender role identity and gender role behavior, are merely secondary effects of social labeling, habits, or genuine preferences.

Fantasy and Sexual Preference

M. D. Storms (1980), a Kansas University researcher, has proposed a modification of the unidimensional model of sexual orientation, arguing that homosexuality and heterosexuality may be separate, orthogonal erotic dimensions rather than opposite extremes of a single, bipolar dimension. This researcher's investigation focused on the suppositions (1) that sexual orientation relates to a person's general gender role orientation, and (2) that sexual orientation relates to a person's erotic fantasies. Subjects were recruited from a college population, and subjects assigned themselves on Kinsey's seven-point scale ranging from exclusively heterosexual to exclusively homosexual. Subjects also assigned themselves to one of three common sexual orientation labels: "straight," "bisexual," or "gay." All subjects who marked the two most heterosexual values on Kinsey's scale also called themselves "straight," n = 107; all subjects who marked the three middle values called themselves "bisexual," n = 24; and all subjects who marked the two most homosexual values called themselves "gay," n = 54. Storms's subjects were divided into three groups based on their response to the label question. Subjects' gender role attributes were measured by Spence and Helmreich's (1978) Personal Attributes Questionnaire (PAQ), which contains a masculinity scale, a femininity scale, and a biopolar masculinity-femininity scale. Subjects' erotic fantasy experiences were measured by the Erotic Response and Orientation Scale (EROS), developed by Storms (1980) to measure eight basic types of erotic fantasy experiences. On one scale, each of the eight erotic items is described with men as the object of the fantasy (the androerotic scale); on the other scale, women are described as the object of the fantasy (the gynoerotic scale). On each item, subjects are asked how often they have had that erotic fantasy during the past year, on a seven-point scale from "never" (0) to "almost daily" (6). The items were written in Guttman scale format and covered a range of experiences from low-intensity fantasies (thinking someone is sexually attractive) through moderate-intensity fantasies (daydreaming about having sex with someone) to high-intensity fantasies (masturbating while fantasizing about having sex with someone).

The results of the Storms (1980) study clearly disconfirmed hypotheses derived from Freud's theory and other inversion theories of sexual orientation, that homosexual men are less masculine and/or more feminine and that homosexual women are more masculine and/or less feminine than their heterosexual counterparts. Homosexuals, heterosexuals, and bisexuals did not differ significantly from each other on any of the three subscales of the PAQ.

The second part of the study strongly supported the notion that a person's sexual orientation relates to the type and extent of his or her erotic fantasies. Homosexuals reported significantly greater heterosexual fantasy than heterosexuals reported homosexual fantasy. Bisexuals reported high levels of both homosexual and heterosexual fantasy.

The finding that homosexuals reported higher levels of heteroerotic fantasy than heterosexuals reported homoerotic fantasy is inconsistent with the belief that homosexual fear and reject sexual feelings toward members of the other gender. That bisexuals reported high levels of both hetroerotic and homocrotic fantasy strongly contradicts Kinsey's notion that sexual orientation is a single, bipolar continuum. According to the unidimensional view of sexual orientation, bisexuals should have reported moderate levels of each type of erotic fantasy. Instead, bisexuals actually reported just as much same-gender fantasy as homosexuals and just as much other-gender fantasy as heterosexuals. These data are better described by a two-dimensional model in which homoeroticism and heteroeroticism are viewed as separate variables and in which bisexuality is defined as scoring high on both dimensions and asexuality is defined as scoring low on both dimensions.

Storms uses the study cited above in his controversial new theory that predicts precocity is apt to contribute to a homosexual orientation. Storms argues that those reaching puberty at an early age are more likely to develop a homosexual orientation because they play partners during that time are of the child's same gender. Same-gender socialization is seen to be the major contributing factor— along with early maturation—to the development of a homosexual orientation. This theory has not been proven empirically, and there is evidence to the contrary; for example, the work done at Johns Hopkins University by John Money, and the empirical findings of John Green of the State University of New York at Stony Brook, indicate that effeminate prehomosexual boys play with girls, not boys.

Weinrich (1982b) argued that the mechanism of same-gender socialization in Storms's model of sexual orientation fails to explain the histories of adult gay men who were labeled as sissies when they were boys. This argument is based on prospective studies of boys seen for "serious gender identity disturbances," such as gender nonconformity and cross-dressing. The fact that many of these boys play with girls right into adolescence and later label themselves homosexual calls to question the mechanism of same-gender socialization for this group of boys, but does not question the prediction of precocity. The attitudes expressed by parents and other socialization agents regarding the relationship between gender non-conformity and homosexuality were not accounted for in Weinberg's (1982b) report of these prospective studies. However, it may be true that Storms's mechanism of same-gender socialization does not account for those cases where parents and others create a less than healthy homosexual identity and subsequent homosexual behavior by their own misguided behavioral expectations for sissy boys (and tomboy girls). In fact, Weinberg argues that the Storms model most accurately describes boys who share the same values for adventure and compete with one another. (Silverstein [1982] refers to boys with this friendship pattern as "comrads".) Weinberg brings us to an important point about theories of the paths to homosexual identity: These theories must be grounded in an understanding of the experience of social control and regulation during psychosexual development.

Weinberg, trained as a biologist, seems to depart from an understanding of the social control of the homosexual capacity in his own theorizing about homosexual acts, actors, and identities. He maintains that homosexuality runs in families and has its roots in biology. Weinberg argues that homosexuality is a familial trait on the basis of unpublished studies reporting that homosexual respondents declared more homosexual siblings than heterosexual respondents declared. Of course, "homosexuals" and "heterosexuals" as either index cases or family members may not be capable of reporting accurate information regarding the nature of homosexual capacity in themselves and their families. Moreover, what probably do "run in families" are relevant constellations of sexual beliefs, attitudes, and expectations. Consequently, these family studies may be carefully gleaned for data on the incidence and method of homosexual labeling among contemporary sociobiologists, index cases, and family members.

Thus far we have used the terms "homosexual," "heterosexual," and "bisexual" to describe patterns of sexual preference. Another relevant term is *ambisexual*, another word for bisexual. The definitions of bisexual and ambisexual vary. For example, they may denote no preference and a low response to both genders or no preference and a high response to both genders. A person who has little or no fantasy or sexual preference is termed asexual.

More recently, the terms *gay* or gay activist and *lesbian* or lesbian femininist have appeared. These terms are used primarily by homosexuals who have *come out*, or publicly disclosed themselves as "homosexuals." *This kind of sexual labeling represents the political reification of human sexuality.* Some of the homosexuals who publicly come out claim to reject the negative stereotype of the effeminate male or masculine female homosexual. Coming out has been described as the process of recognizing, accepting, and integrating one's sexual preference into one's personal and social life (deMonteflores and Schultz, 1978). The process of social labeling and affiliation will be explored in detail in the following chapters.

The perspective adopted here acknowledges the fact that neither prenatal nor adult hormone conditions are related to increased frequency in homosexual object choice. Contemporary endocrine research shows that the vast majority of "homosexuals" have testosterone levels within the normal range and that differences found between "homosexual" and "heterosexual" samples vary considerably (Ehrhardt, 1979). The genetic and hormonal theories of homosexuality (e.g., those of Lang, 1940; Glass et al., 1940; Dorner & Hinz, 1968) have been ably reviewed by Richardson (1981), Gartrell (1982), and Weinrich (1982a).

The goal of *Homosexual Acts, Actors, and Identities* is not intervention in some causal chain supposedly leading to homosexuality; such thinking is clearly wrong-headed. Others have argued that change-of-orientation therapy programs should be eliminated because they confirm professional and societal biases against homosexuality (see, inter alia, Davidson, 1982). Silverstein (1972) made the situation clear in his 1972 address at the Association for Advancement of Behavior Therapy convention:

> To suggest that a person comes voluntarily to change his sexual orientation is to ignore the powerful environmental stress, oppression if you will, that has been telling him for years that he should change. To grow up in a family where the word "homosexual" was whispered, to play in a playground and hear the words "faggot" and "queer," to go to church and hear of "sin" and then to college and hear of "illness," and finally to the counseling center that promises to "cure," is hardly to create an environment of freedom and voluntary choice. The homosexual is expected to want to be changed and his application for treatment is implicitly praised as the first step toward "normal" behavior.
>
> What brings them into the counseling center is guilt, shame, and the loneliness that comes from their secret. If you really wish to help them freely choose, I suggest you first desensitize them to their guilt. Allow them to dissolve the shame about their desires and actions and to feel comfortable with their sexuality. After that, let them choose, but not before. I don't know any more than you what would happen, but I think their choice would be more voluntary and free than it is at present (p. 4).

The focus achieved here addresses the interaction between theories about sexual orientation and the self-concept. *Homosexual Acts, Actors, and Identities* represents an emerging shift for practitioners in the direction away from a search for "etiology" and toward considering the meanings of behavior for the individual (see also Hart & Richardson, 1981; Paul et al., 1982).

"Sexual acts" is used here to mean erotic behavior *and* fantasy that may lead to orgasm. I have chosen the word "erotic" because any form of behavior may be eroticized. Observation and measurement of sexual acts may be made from behavior, self report, or physiological arousal. However, interpretation and meaning of sexual acts must be guided by personal descriptions and cultural constructs. Clearly, there is more to "having sex" than the manipulation and conjugation of the genitalia.

It is interesting to note that Kinsey and Storms found that "heterosexuals" can be categorized more readily than "homosexuals." Homosexuality appears more inclusive of *all* sexuality than heterosexuality. The less apparent truth is that the concept of *sexual identity* is derived from broader cultural meanings that interact with personal constructs. It is not assumed that *sexual* acts per se have a direct causal relationship to sexual identity. The emphasis here is upon sexual identity rather than sexual acts. This *social interactionist* perspective is described by Hart & Richardson (1981) as placing

> the emphasis . . . on homosexual identities rather than sexual acts. A homosexual identity, in this sense, however, is not assumed to be an inborn and permanent characteristic, although it may be construed by the individual in this way. Rather, sexual identity is considered to be socially construed and maintained through the process of social interaction. Within such an analysis, therefore, it is important to look at the social context in which homosexual acts occur and identities develop, and the individual meanings each person ascribes to these (pp. 35–36).

The beliefs that people have about their own and others' sexual preferences involve an extension from the sexual act to the actor. In this way, we assign ourselves and others social identities that are based on particular thoughts, feelings, or behaviors. Furthermore, peoples' theories of sexual preference are commonly of the either/or type; on one dimension, you are either homosexual or heterosexual.

The failure to separate the whole person from the specific act performed in a particular situation within a particular society is depersonalizing and alienating. This process of labeling others and the self may assist in categorizing and processing information about a complex world, but less chaos may mean less truth. Indeed, this extension of the act to the actor lays the foundation for stereotyping, prejudice, and assigning of "deviant" labels. In short, the unidimensional labels that we use to categorize human sexuality strip away human dignity and deny recognition of the variation in the sexual responsiveness of the human species.

SUMMARY OF CHAPTER ONE

Sexual identity has been traditionally conceptualized as having both biological and psychological components. The categories of sexual identity that the developing person chooses from are typically either homosexual or heterosexual. Biology affects sexual identity by way of physical development, body consciousness, and the experience of aggression. Actually, male and female are overlapping biological ranges, showing more in common than different. Gender differences in pejorative attitudes toward homosexual acts, actors, and identities are a product of social learning coupled with biological preparedness.

The psychological components of sexual identity are related to the development of socially structured choice. Gender identity is defined as self-acceptance of one's physical gender; it is thought to develop by the age of three. Adults who experience a conflict between biological gender and gender identity are termed transvestites when they cross-dress and transsexuals when they undergo surgery whereby biological gender is modified to suit the individual. Homosexuality is not viewed as an incongruity of gender identity; rather, gender identity is discussed as a cultural meaning that interacts with personal constructs. Hence, individuals receive a particular "reality" regarding sexual identity that is socially constructed.

Gender role identity and gender role stem from the development of "healthy" gender identity. These categories of sexual meaning adhere in socially valued ways and are presented as a cluster during the socialization of the young. The concept of social role was described as a set of social expectations or norms for behavior. Masculine and feminine categorizations of behaviors, traits,and mannerisms are clearly cultural constructs, traditionally analyzed as psychological constructs of the individual. Theories of gender role socialization were reviewed to show how social definitions of normal personality development are transmitted. Identification theory teaches parents to develop a unique emotional tie to their same-gender child so that the child will turn out just like the same-gender parent. Social learning theory teaches parents to reward and punish their children according to societal expectation; thus, normal identity is the product of internalized types and acquired attributes. Cognitive-developmental theories teach parents that cultural sex role stereotypes can be transmitted as soon as biological gender emerges as an important social category in the child's cognitive system; the child's behavior and attributes will reflect identification with the cultural stereotypes of the child's biological gender.

A difference in treatment of boys and girls during socialization does exist. There are lethal aspects of the male role, which include competitiveness; fear of homosexual acts, actors, and identities; and fear of personal vulnerability and openness to anyone. The relationship between neurotic behavior and gender role reveals that a strong sense of agency, unmitigated by a sense of communion, is destructive. The Type A coronary-prone behavior pattern is a result of internalizing the cultural expectations and categories of sexual meanings that are transmitted and acquired during childhood socialization, demanded and performed during adulthood.

The concept of androgyny permits us to break from the either/or formulation of gender role. It is possible, according to this view, to be both masculine and feminine. People are not androgynous because cross-gender behavior becomes motivationally problematic for the postsocialized individual.

Sexual preference has also traditionally been defined as a psychological component of sexual identity. Sexual preference is conceptualized as neither discrete nor static. Rather, sexual preference is characterized as a matter of learning and forced choice. Storms' study (1980) disconfirmed the notion that homosexual men are less masculine and/or more feminine than their heterosexual counterparts; sexual preference was shown to relate to the type and extent of one's erotic fantasy. Storms demonstrated that homoeroticism and heteroeroticism should be viewed as separate variables in which bisexuality is defined as scoring high on both dimensions.

The emphasis in this chapter was on the cultural meanings and categories of sexual identity definitions. Homosexual and heterosexual identities, like masculine and feminine identities, were considered to be socially construed and maintained through the processes of social interaction. The system of beliefs that supports the cultural construction of sexual identity involves an extension from the sexual act to the actor. Hence, we assign ourselves and others social identities that are based on the meanings given to thoughts, feelings, or behaviors. The origin and function of beliefs about homosexual acts, actors, and identities will be explored in detail in the next chapter.

CHAPTER TWO

BELIEFS AND SYSTEMS OF BELIEFS

Reality . . . is fragile and adjudicated—a thing to be debated, compromised and legislated. Those who succeed in this world are those who are most effective in having their interpretations ratified as the true reality.

G.J. McCall
J.L. Simmons

People struggle to transform dominant sexual meanings and definitions under determinate historical conditions. . . .

Frank Mort

COGNITIVE FEATURES OF BELIEFS

A belief system is a set of beliefs, convictions, or opinions about something or someone and/or about groups of either people or objects. Beliefs become stereotypes when they are overgeneralized and based on too limited a set of experiences. I will begin by describing some of the characteristics of belief systems. A main feature of a system of beliefs is that one belief is often the basis for another belief—that is, belief systems have a *vertical structure* (Bem, 1974a). For example, the quasilogical structure of a belief may be revealed when syllogisms are used:

The Bible says that homosexuality is a sin.

The Bible is a true source of knowledge.

Therefore, homosexuality is a sin.

Another feature of a belief system is that the second premise may be *nonconscious*, or unquestioned. Such a premise is called a zero-order primitive belief (Bem, 1974a). Most religious and quasireligious beliefs are based on some unquestioned zero-order primitive faith in an internal or external source of knowledge. When a belief has been derived from some logical process, it too has a vertical structure of beliefs underneath it. For example, the conclusion to the following syllogism is generated as a product of a higher-order quasilogical inference:

The Bible says that homosexuality is a sin.

Contemporary literal translations of the Bible do not consider historical context or original meaning.

Therefore, homosexuality may not be a sin.

Beliefs and systems of beliefs also have a *horizontal* structure. This means that the conclusion to one vertical pillar of reasoning is often the conclusion to more than one syllogistic chain of reasoning. Thus, one could conceivably alter the chain of reasoning in one syllogistic pillar without weakening the belief. A particular higher-order belief is thus the conclusion to more than one chain of reasoning. For example, Bem (1974a) cites the following structure using the example, "The Surgeon General believes that":

Smoking causes cancer.	Smokers drink more heavily than nonsmokers.	Statistics show smokers die younger than nonsmokers.
Cancer can cause death.	Heavy drinking can lead to early death.	These statistics are reliable.
Therefore, smokers die younger.	Therefore, smokers die younger.	Therefore, smokers die younger.

Thus, the individual who endorses this broad horizontal and deep vertical structure to derive a belief that smokers die younger will weaken that belief only partially if one of the syllogisms is faulty or one of the premises turns out to be false.

Another feature of beliefs and belief systems is the notion of *centrality*. The concept of centrality in belief systems refers to the importance of a belief in an individual's entire belief system. For example, many syllogisms may lead up to my belief that my senses tell me the truth, but few depart from it. It appears as a conclusion to many syllogisms. Our zero-order primitive belief in the credibility of our senses is an example of a central belief.

The last feature of beliefs and belief systems is that they may be cultural and institutionalized or they may be personal, as seen in personal likes and dislikes. For example, personal likes or beliefs may lead one to never fall in love with someone of the same gender; on the other hand, a cultural belief may prevent one from ever experiencing institutionalized legitimacy or protection for falling in love with someone of the same gender. Racism, sexism, and homosexual/homogender prejudice can be characterized as belief systems manifested both personally and culturally. As personal belief systems, they reflect the ideology of the institutions within the cultural superstructure.

In summary, a belief system is a set of beliefs that tend to cohere, or appear together. They are based on one another; they may be derived from more than one chain of reasoning; and some beliefs may be more central or important than others. Some beliefs are nonconscious or unquestioned, while others are derived from a higher-order process of quasilogical inference. Finally, beliefs and belief systems may be both personal and cultural.

BELIEFS ABOUT SEXUAL IDENTITY

Belief systems containing a constellation or set of beliefs and attitudes regarding sexual identity may be shown to support negative beliefs and fears of homosexual acts and actors.

Chapter One conceptualized sexual identity with four components: biological gender, gender identity, gender role, and sexual orientation. The beliefs we hold about these four aspects of our sexual identity—and the importance we assign to them—determine a considerable amount of our social life and thinking processes. The following syllogistic chain of reasoning exemplifies the rigidity and valuation contained in the belief systems relating the components of sexual identity:

All who are masculine identify as men.

Mary Jane is masculine.

Therefore, Mary Jane identifies as a man.

All who identify as men prefer sex with women.

Mary Jane identifies as a man.

Therefore, Mary Jane prefers sex with women.

All who prefer sex with persons of the same sex are homosexuals.

Mary Jane prefers sex with women.

Therefore, Mary Jane is a homosexual.

These syllogisms are particularly susceptible to three predictable types of errors in logic:

1. *Content errors*, in which the truth or desirability of the premises or conclusions influence the individual's deductions regardless of the logic involved.

2. *Undistributed middle term errors*, in which the individual may over-generalize the breadth of the middle term.

3. *Particular premises errors*, in which individuals may overgeneralize the breadth of "some" to mean "all" (Mayer, 1977, pp. 150–151).

These errors suggest that formal logic and human psychology are not the same. It is nonetheless important to study these errors, for content errors are shaped by cultural and personal beliefs, and for errors (the two latter kinds of errors) have practical value for propagandists and others who wish to affect public opinion.

The notion that underlies the syllogistic model of beliefs is that we strive to achieve internal consistency. However, in order to be consistent, one does not necessarily have to be rational or logical. Beliefs can be based on faulty evidence (inductive generalization) and false, nonconscious ideology. Furthermore, while one line of reasoning leads us to one conclusion, another line of reasoning leads us to a contrary conclusion.

Abelson (1968) provides a theory of nonconsistency to characterize beliefs. According to this theory, the individual has "opinion molecules," made up of (1) a belief, (2) an attitude, and (3) a perception of social support for them. Each opinion molecule contains a fact, a feeling, and a following. For example, "It's true that when my brother accepted his homosexual feelings he was happier" (fact); "I feel better about myself since I accepted his homosexual feelings" (feeling); and "a lot of people have told me they were a lot happier after accepting homosexual relationships" (following). The opinion molecule theory is a good charac-terization of conversational units. Such units do not necessarily have logical interconnections between them, and they are invulnerable to discon-firmation because of their isolated, molecular character.

There are three apparent cognitive and behavioral patterns observed among individuals in response to homoeroticism. They represent the focus of concern the individual has regarding homosexual acts and actors. The first, and most inclusive, is *gender role conformity*, defined as follows: An obsessive fear or worry over social rejection and deviant labeling for "unmasculine" behavior or a feeling of being "on stage" during inter-personal interaction. The essential feature of gender role conformity is behavioral and emotional restriction. Type A coronary pattern is invariably present.

The second pattern observed is most likely a product of gender role conformity but may be isolated for purposes of discussion. The term *ego-dystonic homosexuality* is chosen, and defined as follows: Negative feelings toward the fact of one's own homoerotic arousal; desire to increase heteroerotic arousal and relations. Accompanied by guilt, distress, and low self-esteem.

The third pattern is also likely to be a product of gender role conformity under a patriarchal system and has received considerable attention as an isolated component. *Homophobia* has been broadly defined as any pejorative attitude or action relevant to homosexual acts, actors, or life choice. It is defined narrowly here, as follows: Phobias with a common theme of homosexual acts, actors, or homosexual contamination. Essential features must include distress and disability due to the persistent fear. The fear must be out of the individual's control and not within the culture's norm of homosexual oppression.

The belief systems characterizing the aforementioned cognitive and behavioral patterns may be shown by syllogistic reasoning, opinion molecules, or belief, attitude, and feeling sets. Table 2.1 presents a partial list of the cognitive elements and affective states that may characterize these patterns of response to homoeroticism.

Additional insight is attained by considering the thematic content and linguistic implications of antigay arguments. Paul (1982) reviewed printed materials and classified them according to both category and theme. The *categories* of argument include, with an example of each:

Natural Law:	There is a natural order and this order is upset by homosexual people.
Personal Disorder:	Homosexuals tend to be neurotic, unhappy, unstable individuals leading disordered lives.
Morality and Religion:	Homosexuals are morally decadent and hedonistic, and they exert a generally bad influence on society.
Social Pathology:	Homosexuals are social psychologically deviant.
Social Utility:	Homosexual preferences may not be intrinsically bad, but bringing up the emotionally volatile issue may disrupt larger common concerns.

Table 2.1. *Belief Systems*

	Ego-dystonic Homosexuality	Homophobia	Gender Role Conformity
A.	Heterosexuality is better than homosexuality.	Homosexuals are dangerous.	Heterosexuals condemn homosexuals.
B.	I wish I were heterosexual.	Homosexuals should be locked up to protect society.	It is better to stay in the closet.
C.	I feel negative about my homosexual arousal.	I feel afraid of being near a homosexual.	I am afraid that, if I come out publicly, people will harass me.
D.	Homosexuality is an inherent disadvantage.	Homosexuals are contaminated with venereal disease.	Homosexuals have been killed for their sexuality.
E.	When I am sexually attracted to a person of my gender, I feel critical toward myself.	I am terrified of being contaminated by a homosexual.	I am afraid to come out publicly.
F.	Most of the members of my family feel critical toward homosexuality.	Most people I know believe homosexuals are filthy perverts.	Most of the homosexuals I know feel the same way.
G.	It is easier to be heterosexual than to be homosexual.	Homosexual men don't fulfill the social responsibilities of masculine provider.	There are no laws to guarantee my civil rights in homosexual relations.
H.	I wish I were heterosexual.	Homosexuality causes the downfall of civilizations.	I am afraid to be open about my sexuality.
I.	I want to increase my heterosexual arousal.	Homosexuality is to be feared.	I will always act like a heterosexual.

A = Belief statement
B = Attitude statement
C = Feeling statement

D = Fact statement
E = Feeling statement
F = Following statement of social support

G = If statement
H = Then statement
I = Therefore statement

The thematic elements in antigay positions reflect the general concerns, feelings, and assumptions or reactions of an individual. Paul (1982) lists the following ten elements of antigay arguments: contagion; pollution; gender role violation; abnormality; mystery and power; avoidance; danger; evil; victim blaming; and generalization.

Teachers often use themes in instruction. It is possible to transmit cues that elicit desired interpretations or completions of ideas or sentences (DeCecco 1968). In this way, thematic prompts serve as code words with hidden meanings (e.g., "flaunt"). Inductive prompts contain an implication, without explicitly describing the relationship between stimuli and context. Consideration of these thematic and linguistic facts points to a mind-control explanation of homophobia. Of course, peer exposure and education in a support group environment remain efficacious solutions.

In light of the above evidence, I offer the following list of propaganda techniques:

1. Repetition: Attempt to reinforce an idea or image by repeating it often enough.

2. Card stacking: Only present one side of an argument. Often, with this technique, no recognition at all is given of the existence of another point of view.

3. Battle of Good and Evil: Cast your cause as the hero and the opposition as the villain. Use stereotypes, generalities, emotional symbols, etc.

4. Show Biz: Produce testimonials for your cause and enlist as many famous people as you can.

5. Socialization: Aim propaganda at children.

6. Bandwagon: Give the idea that everybody's doing it.

7. Plain folks: Convince people that ordinary folks want and use what you're pushing.

8. Glittering generality: Associate an idea with a "virtue" word or thing and don't get too specific.

One way to fight imposed ignorance is to ask questions when interpreting information. For example:

1. Authorship: Who said it? Is the author an authority on the subject? What is the author's known bias?

2. Sponsorship: Who publishes, distributes, or sponsors a program or product?

3. Factual Content: How specific is the author?

4. Objectivity: Is a vested interest involved?

5. Verifiability: Can the data be checked?

6. Relevancy: Do the data support the conclusions?

7. Consistency: Does the information agree with the facts?

8. Plausibility: Does it sound reasonable?

STEREOTYPES

The process of generalizing characteristics or motives to a group of people is called stereotyping. According to Allport (1958), a stereotype is an exaggerated belief associated with a category. Its function is to justify (rationalize) one's conduct in relation to that category. The stereotype acts both as a justificatory device for categorical acceptance or rejection of a group, and as a screening or selective device to maintain simplicity in perception and thinking. Thus, stereotypes in general function to help people classify and process information.

According to Cantor (1977), people group both objects and people according to similarities in their essential features. People label these groupings "natural categories" and communicate about the similarity and differences in these "kinds" or "types" of objects or people. Thus, they use a system of shared names or category labels.

We move now to a content analysis of the primary features of the contemporary homosexual stereotype. A review of the contemporary psychological literature reveals considerable uniformity in the evaluative and descriptive content of the homosexual stereotype. For example, Simmons (1965) had subjects identify, from a list supplied by the experimenter, traits they associated with homosexuals. The traits identified were, for the most part, extremely negative. Examining content uniformity, 47% of the responses included the descriptions sexually abnormal, perverted, mentally ill, maladjusted, and effeminate.

Some attempts have also been made to examine the effects of homosexual status on estimations of elements of personality. Weissbach and Zagon (1975) compared responses to men having been introduced into a group as homosexuals with responses to those not introduced with that status. It was found that an individual homosexual status was judged to be more feminine, emotional, submissive, unconventional, and weak.

The psychological literature reveals a long-standing tradition in which homosexual males have been compared to the female gender. Researchers have commonly assumed that male homosexuality and masculinity are mutually exclusive states of being and that homosexual males suffer from an impaired masculine self-image (Bieber et al., 1962). This masculine deficiency hypothesis is frequently reflected in the etiological theories of male homosexuality, in which homosexuality has been variously defined as: "a result of insufficient proportion of the male sex hormone" (Karlen, 1971, p. 344); "a flight from masculinity" (Kardiner, 1963, p. 27); "a search for masculinity" (Socarides, 1968, p. 46); "a confession of masculine failure" (Ovesey, 1969, p. 129); "a primary feminine identification" (Freud, 1905/1953, p. 226); and, "a secret longing to play the female's less demanding role" (Ruitenbeek, 1963, p. 120).

Public acceptance of the stereotype of the homosexual male as a caricature of a woman, ill-disposed toward that sex, was recently demonstrated in an attitudinal survey on sexual morality. In a four-year investigation based on interviews with a nation-wide probability sample of over thirty thousand American adults, Levitt and Klassan (1974) found that nearly 70% believed that male homosexuals act like women, and 56% espoused the notion that all homosexuals fear the opposite gender.

The term "homosexual" evokes a certain image and triggers very definite social responses. Individuals are often called homosexual because they seem to fit a general concept of what a homosexual looks or acts like. Yet, it has become obvious that homosexuality is not caused by adopting an inappropriate gender role.

Historical and cross-cultural studies have shown that only certain societies believe that male homosexuals tend to act like women and that female homosexuals try to imitate men. In the ancient Greek city-states, for example, male homosexuality was associated with strength, virility, and heroism. The most famous of all Greek military elite troops, the "sacred band" of Thebes, is said to have consisted entirely of male lovers. In short, there is no homosexual personality, or condition with unmistakable symptoms; homosexuals are defined by the image that people have of them at any given period in history.

It is of interest to note that the term "homosexuality" was not even invented until the end of the nineteenth century. "Homosexuality" was introduced into the English language in 1897 by Havelock Ellis at a time when the full range of human sexual capacities was no longer tolerated. The terms "homosexual" and "heterosexual" have created an artificial dividing line between peoples.

A major problem with conceptualizing sexuality in history concerns the categories that most historians typically use to analyze sexual matters. For example, when we approach Greek antiquity with the predetermined categories "homosexual" and "heterosexual" real history disappears. The Greeks shared a common attitude that sexual passion in any form implied sexual passion in all forms. According to one historian, the important comprehension that sexuality, class, and politics cannot easily be disengaged from one another must serve as the basis of a materialist view of sexuality in a historical perspective (Padgug, 1979). In his discussion of ideology and sexuality, Padgug argues:

> In sum, the most commonly held twentieth-century assumptions about sexuality imply that it is a separate category of existence (like "the economy," or "the state," other supposedly independent spheres of reality), almost identical with the sphere of private life. Such a view necessitates the location of sexuality within the individual as a fixed essence, leading to a classic division of individual and society and to a variety of psychological determinisms, and, often enough, to a full-blown biological determinism as well. These in turn involve the enshrinement of contemporary sexual categories as universal, static, and permanent, suitable for the analysis of all human beings and all societies. Finally, the consequences of this view are to restrict class struggle to non-sexual realms, since that which is private, sexual, and static is not a proper arena for public social action and change (p. 8).

According to Padgug, the real issues to deal with in the historical study of sexuality are those that affect contemporary struggles:

> Through a better understanding of how capitalist societies developed, and are continuing to develop, the modern ideology of sexuality—including the struggles which have occurred around it, both between and within classes—we will better understand the specific role it plays in legitimating contemporary society and in defusing class struggle, as well as its contradictory potentialities for undermining the capitalist system. We can also begin to develop specific socialist strategies for political activity which combine economic and sexual struggle in fruitful ways. And, finally, we will be in a better position to examine the possible outlines of sexuality in a socialist society, with the useful comprehension that the sexuality of the future cannot be a simple unveiling of something which capitalism "repressed" or distorted, but must be an essentially new creation within the total configuration of the developing social relations of a future society (p. 19).

The social psychological influences that a homosexual stereotype has upon persons who have acknowledged homoerotic arousal and/or have been labeled homosexual are complex. The individuals may boast of it or may have a low opinion of themselves as a result of it. Recently, many have developed a positive self-image and call themselves gay: open, angry, and proud. These militant gays claim to be voicing their anger for daily assaults on their identity and integrity. It is nearly impossible for these people to remember that the divisions between them and "heterosexuals" are artificial. Most "heterosexuals" certainly do not think so. *Only by understanding ourselves and our culture in its totality can we discover the truth about human sexuality.*

Some gay political writers imply that defending homosexual behavior per se is indefensible and politically incorrect. Instead, they consider open involvement in the gay lifestyle and community to represent a solidarity front. In this way, gay identity and gay community appear to be political reifications born out of the human organism's urge to gain legal and social control of the human sexual response.

The ever-changing image of "gay male lifestyle" in the contemporary United States is illustrative. Gay subcultures contain a variety of role models, ideologies, tastes, fashions, and patterns of social interaction. The gay image for men in the 1960s and 1970s was quite different from the emerging image of the 1980s. The drag queen and effeminate male homosexual of the 1960s and 1970s have virtually disappeared. Today, the ultra-macho image is chic for gay men, while their androgynous look has been adopted by heterosexual men. In an attempt to angrily defy the oppressive stereotypes nongays have of them, gay men have become obviously masculinized.

Information-Processing Implications

The cognitive processes we are describing here were described centuries ago by Francis Bacon (1620/1902):

> The human understanding, when any proposition has been once laid down ... forces everything else to add fresh support and confirmation. ... it is the peculiar and perpetual error of the human understanding to be more moved and excited by affirmatives than negatives (pp. 23–24).

Biases in information processing have been demonstrated empirically. Snyder, Tanke, & Berscheid (1977) described four such biases. First, there is overestimation of the frequency of occurrence of confirming or paradigmatic examples of our stereotypes. This occurs because such instances are more easily noticed and retrieved from memory. Second, we may fill in the gaps in our evidence base with information consistent with our preconceived notions of what evidence would support our beliefs. For example, Chapman and Chapman (1969) demonstrated that both college students and professional clinicians perceive positive associations betweeen particular rorschach responses and homosexuality in males, even though these associations are demonstrably absent in real life. Third, once a stereotype has been adopted, a wide variety of evidence can be construed to support that stereotype. For example, in-group virtues ("We are sexually liberated") may become out-group vices ("They are sexually promiscuous") in attempts to maintain negative stereotypes about disliked groups. Fourth, by selectively recalling and reinterpreting information from the past, an individual supports current stereotype-based inferences. Thus, having discovered that Alan is a homosexual, it may be all too easy to recall a variety of behaviors and events that, taken together, will support the stereotyped inference that he is (as are all members of his group) effeminate and promiscuous. These behaviors and events are insufficient, one at a time, to support the inference, but taken together, they warrent the inference. This way of thinking involves the reconstructive memory process.

The reconstructive hypothesis of memory (e.g., Bartlett, 1932) assumes that remembering is not simply retrieving previously stored constructions; it is more like solving a problem. People remember only the general idea of what was presented, and then reconstruct the details according to their expectations of what "must have been true." *The major implication of the reconstructive memory process is that new information about a topic may affect one's memory of the topic by providing a different basis for reconstruction.*

Social stereotypes about homosexuals may influence memory and produce reinterpretations of previous experiences or information. Bransford (1979) argues that reconstructive memories reinforce social stereotypes. For example, Snyder and Uranowitz (1978) presented different groups of students with the same narrative, about the life of an imaginary woman named Betty K. The narrative provided information about Betty's birth, childhood, education, choice of profession, and so on. It also described her early home life, relationship with parents, and social life (for example, it stated that Betty dated occasionally). The crucial aspect of the study was the type of information students received *after* reading the narrative. Students in one group were told that Betty is now a lesbian; those in another group, that she follows a heterosexual lifestyle. This "after the fact" information was designed to activate different stereotyped assumptions about lesbians and heterosexuals.

One week later, the students were asked to remember as accurately as possible the details of Betty's life. Multiple-choice tests like the following were used to probe their memory for the events:

In high school, Betty

A. Occasionally dated

B. Never went out with men

C. Went steady

D. No information was provided

Results indicated that students' performance was strongly influenced by the degree to which earlier information was consistent with stereotyped beliefs about lesbian and heterosexual lifestyles. For example, although the original narrative stated that Betty dated occasionally, people who heard Betty is a lesbian were likely to believe they had read that Betty never went out with men.

Bem (1981a) proposes a gender schema theory that construes perception as a constructive process wherein what is preceived is a product of the interaction between incoming information and the perceiver's preexisting schema. The readiness with which a schema is evoked is referred to as its cognitive availability. This is a theory of organizing self-concept and behavior on the basis of gender. The first hypothesis explored by Bem was that sex-typed individuals do, in fact, organize information in terms of gender schema and thus will show more clustering of gender-relevant items in free recall than non-sex-typed individuals. The subjects were forty-eight male and female undergraduates at a West Coast university who were preselected on the basis of Bem Sex Role Inventory (BSRI) scores to form equal-sized groups of sex-typed, androgynous, cross-sex-typed, and undifferentiated subjects. In her procedure, subjects were presented with sixty-one words in random order, including sixteen proper names (half male, half female), fifteen animal names, fifteen verbs, and fifteen articles of clothing (one-third of each were rated by independent judges as masculine, one-third as feminine, and one-third as gender neutral). The words were presented at two-second intervals, and three seconds after presentation of the last word, the subjects were given eight minutes to write down as many as they could recall, in any order. The results indicated that sex-typed subjects clustered a significantly higher percentage of words on the basis of gender than the other three groups.

A second hypothesis was explored in a subsequent study reported by Bem (1981a). She predicted that sex-typed individuals have a readiness to encode gender relevant information that will be revealed in the individual's response latency when asked to make a dichotomous me/not me judgment about each of the sixty attributes on the BSRI itself. The subjects were forty-eight female and forty-eight male undergraduates at the same university as in the previous test who were preselected on the basis of a median split on the BSRI as sex-typed, androgynous, and undifferentiated. In Bem's procedure, sixty attributes from the BSRI were projected on a screen one at a time, and the subject pushed either the "me" or the "not me" button in front of them. Response latency was recorded for each judgment. Sex-typed subjects were faster than the other three groups when making schema-consistent judgments about themselves. They were also significantly slower than the others when making schema-inconsistent judgments.

Spence and Helmreich (1981) reveal a logical contradiction in Bem's gender schema theory. The nature of the contradiction is simply that the same set of measures (masculine and feminine scores on the BSRI of similar instruments) cannot simultaneously define a single, unitary continuum (gender schema, sex role orientation, etc.) and two independent continua, masculinity and femininity. These authors assert that their own Personal Attributes Questionnaire (PAQ), as well as the BSRI, are primarily measures of two orthogonal trait dimensions: expressiveness and instrumentality. Moreover, they argue that these personal qualities have implications for many kinds of socially important behaviors, only some of which are gender related.

Bem (1981b) argues in defense of gender schema theory that the fact that the BSRI has two dimensions rather than one is irrelevant. The BSRI has two dimensions identifying people who ought to be engaging in gender schematic processing; it is not a measure of gender schematic processing. Bem contends there is no theoretical reason that the instrument used to identify sex-typed individuals should be structurally isomorphic to the cognitive process that the theory implies sex-typed individuals are using. Moreover, when sex-typed individuals describe themselves on the BSRI, it is precisely the masculine-feminine connotations of the items to which they are responding. Thus, Bem concludes, the very act of describing oneself as sex-typed on the BSRI is, in part, a product of gender schematic processing.

The internalization of gender differentiated, patriarchal belief systems influences the behavior and perception, and the information processing, of individuals. The impact of the stereotypes of homosexuals contained in the belief system, when these are endorsed by homosexuals, includes stereotyping others as well as the self. In fact, homosexuals may use their internalized stereotypes to shape their concept of self in many of the same ways that prototypes influence the way they perceive others. The frequent consequence for homosexuals is the development of a complete identity that has been externally defined.

This dynamic has been previously referred to as internalized stigma, negative identity, or ego-dystonic homosexuality. Here we characterize the stereotypes' influence in terms of cognitive generalizations about the self, derived from past experiences, that organize and guide the processing of self-related information contained in the individual's social experiences. These self schemata function as selective mechanisms that determine whether information is attended to, how it is structured, how much importance is attached to it, and what happens with it subsequently (Markus, 1977).

In a study on schematic processing of information, Wright, Storms, and Duncan (1976) found that, if people focus on the presumed heterosexual nature of the typical male, a homosexual act becomes "understandable" and less abnormal. In this study, these two views were triggered by asking subjects questions designed to prime one schema or the other. However, when subjects were confronted with a schema implying homosexual potential not only in others but in themselves, they reacted negatively and defensively. The methodology elicited schemata simply by asking subjects to consider their preexisting beliefs about male sexuality. The study provides clear evidence that schemata existed a priori in subjects' minds (as indicated by their extremely high endorsement of the belief items).

The ways that perceivers create or construct the information that they process, as well as the ways in which they process that information, are relevant. It may be that events in our social world are as much the effects of our perceptions of those events as they are the causes of those perceptions (Snyder, Tanke, & Berscherd, 1977). In other words, through certain cognitive bolstering processes, a perceiver may create a cognitive reality to support traits erroneously attributed to an individual. Whenever this occurs, the stereotype-based attributions will guide the perceivers' behaviors toward a person. "This process itself," Snyder states, "may generate behaviors on the part of the target that erroneously confirm the predictions and validate the attributions of the perceiver." It has been shown (e.g., Bandura, 1977; Mischel, 1968; Raush, 1965) that how others treat us in large measure reflects our treatment of them. Thus, a major information-processing implication of endorsing a rigid gender differentiated belief system may be seen when we use our social preceptions as guides for regulating our interactions with others: *We may constrain their behavioral options. The ability of perceivers to shape the behavior of the perceived to fit their expectations has been referred to as behavioral confirmation of a social stereotype* (Snyder, Tanke, & Berscherd, 1977). When perceived persons see themselves behaving in stereotypical ways, they may grow to believe they are as they act; this is interpersonal confirmation of a social stereotype. Inter-personal confirmation occurs when individuals temporarily comply with situational expectations and, through a process of self-perception, conform their self-schemata to the social stereotype.

RELIGIOUS BELIEF AND TRADITION

In this section we examine the religious origin of pejorative attitudes toward homosexuals. The antihomosexual taboo is a part of the Judeo-Christian code of sexual morality, and, with the exception of Zoro-astrianism (a religion of ancient Persia), antihomosexual prejudice and repression have been limited to cultures under the influence of Judeo-Christianity (Lauritsen and Thorstad, 1974). With this in mind, we turn now to the scriptures.

The Bible

The primary source of the traditional condemnation of homosexual activity as contrary to the divine will has been the interpretation of certain texts in the Old and New testaments. The following texts have been understood as dealing with homosexuality: Genesis 19:4–11; Leviticus 18:22, 20:13; Deuteronomy 23:17; Romans 1:26, 4:18; I Corinthians 6:9; and I Timothy 1:10.

There is a theory that the interpretation given to the story of Sodom and Gomorrah (Genesis 19:4–11) has been perhaps the single most important factor in the Western Christian tradition condemning homo-sexual practices (McNeil, 1976). The "moral" of the story has been that homosexual practices are against the will of God, and they will bring a terrible divine wrath in the form of earthquakes, floods, famines, etc. This interpretation has been challenged by modern-day biblical scholars, who argue that the essence of the sin of Sodom and Gemorrah was primarily one of inhospitality towards strangers or the idolatry of the strangers in Sodom.

The New Testament also contains passages that have been selected for argument against homosexual activity. Romans 1:26 is often cited as evidence that homosexual behavior is intrinsically immoral, because the Greek words *para' phusin* are used. The English translation for the phrase is "against nature." When taken out of context, this verse gives rise to the "abnormal" medical model of homosexuality. As John Boswell (1976) notes: "The modern reader is apt to read into that phrase a wealth of association from later philosophical developments, scholastic theology, Freudian psychology, social taboos, as well as personal misgivings (p. 54).

McNeil (1976) points out that the same phrase is used in Romans 4:18 to express the idea that God is acting *para' phusin* in grafting a wild olive branch (the Gentiles) onto a cultivated tree (the inheritance of the Jews). The phrase itself does not imply a moral judgment on the action. A textual analysis finds seven different uses of the word *phusin* in the epistles of Paul, revealing a fusion on the concepts of custom and essential character (McNeil, 1976).

The creation account in Genesis also provides reasons that some moralists believe all homosexual activity is condemned in scripture as contrary to the will of God. The human male, apart from the human female, was not considered a full human being. "So God created man in his own image, in the image of God he created him, male and female, he created them." Thus, the divine purpose of sexual differentiation was procreation. God's first covenant with humanity reads: "Be fruitful and multiply." Many Christian ethicists read a condemnation of all homosexual activity into these texts with the assumption that the homosexual condition is the result of man's fall and is a deviation from the God-willed state of heterosexuality. From the moral position of heterosexual orientation as the divine image of man, psychologists Bieber, Dain, Dince, Drellich, Grand, Gundlach, Kremer, Rifkin, Wilber, and Bieber (1962) begin their book on homosexuality with, "We assume that heterosexuality is the biologic norm, and that unless interfered with, all individuals are heterosexual (p. 5)."

Several problems arise in the interpretation of these texts. The term "homosexual" used in English translations cannot be assumed to represent exactly the meanings in the mind of the biblical authors. Contemporary moralists keep in mind a distinction between homosexual activity and the homosexual condition (see Bailey, 1955; McNeil, 1976). These analysts have found ample evidence that in most instances, where scripture deals with homosexuality, the author probably had in mind what today we would call perversion, namely, the indulgence in homosexual activity on the part of those who were, by nature, heterosexually inclined (McNeil, 1976).

Another problem with the use of the scriptures is their historical and cultural limitations; that is, one cannot merely transpose a Biblical text to the temporary circumstances of life. Yet another limitation on the use of scripture is the selection of individual texts taken out of their contexts. For example, the New Testament writings against homosexuality are written by Paul, a Jew, who abides by the Holiness Code (Leviticus 18:22; 20:13), which specifically warns the Israelites against accepting the idolatrious practices of the Caramites, including homosexual activity, a part of religious rites. Furthermore, the profertility emphasis of the Old Testament writers was due to underpopulation and to the Hebrew stress on preserving the family name for progeny.

With these issues in mind, McNeil (1976) writes: "The only condemnation of homosexuality to be found with certainty in Scripture, is a condemnation of perverse homosexual activity indulged in by otherwise truly heterosexual individuals as an expression of contempt or self-centered lust and usually associated with some form of idol worship" (p. 66).

The contribution of the Bible to pejorative attitudes toward homosexuals is that homosexuality is against the will of God, unnatural and sinful. *These scriptures expose immoral treatment of gays when understood in light of the tradition in Western Christianity.*

Tradition and History

Historical evidence for the religious theory of pejorative attitudes toward homosexuals is available from three major sources. Western Christian tradition has pointed to contrasts in the cultural mores between Greek and Hebrew cultures, with the early Christian community (primarily the Jews of the diaspora) recording any variation of behavior in Greek culture as a deviation from divine law given to Israel. The second major source was an appeal to Thomas Aquinas's version of natural law (sin against nature). The third source of pejorative attitudes toward homosexuals in Western Christianity is evident in the prevalent version of the Sodom and Gomorrah story.

The homosexual interpretation of the Sodom story was not evident in the Old Testament, which rather portrayed the town's sin as false pride and inhospitality (McNeil, 1976). The earliest references giving a sexual nature to the sin of Sodom do not call it homosexuality, but emphasize a transgression of order, i.e., the sexual incompatibility of the angelic and human orders (see Palestinian apocrypha, Book of Jubilees V11. 20–22; XVI. 5–6; XX. 5–6) and mixed marriages. Jews and Gentiles who marry would be in defiance of the law and be cursed with sterility (Testament of Nephtali, second century B.C.).

The association of the wickedness of Sodom with the lawlessness of the Gentiles became particularly associated with the pederasty of an alien and hostile culture. The origin of the homosexual interpretation of the Sodom story can be explained as the Jewish reaction to a closer acquaintance with homosexual practices common in the Hellenic world during the century preceding the Christian era. The first writings to identify the sin of Sodom with homosexual practices in general were those of Philo, dating from the middle of the first century, and those of Josephus, from around the year 96 A.D. In Philo's *Quaest. et Salut.* in Genesis 4:31–37, *yadha* is interpreted as "servile, lawless and unseemly pederasty." This conception of Sodom and its offense had gradually established itself among the Jews of the diaspora during the preceding two centuries of their contact with Hellenic society. It became a rejection of Hellenic custom (e.g., fertility rites) and gave rise to the myths of effeminancy, man-woman role playing, and sodomizing children among male "homosexuals."

In his work *De Abrahamo*, Philo vividly captures the myths and prejudices already prevalent in his account of the Sodom story:

> The land of the Sodomites was brimful of innumerable iniquities, particularly such as arise from gluttony and lewdness.... The inhabitants owed this extreme license to the never failing lavishness of their sources of wealth.... Incapable of bearing such satiety... they threw off from their necks the law of nature, and applied themselves to deep drinking of strong liquor and dainty feeding and forbidden forms of intercourse. Not only in their mad lust for women did they violate the marriages of their neighbors, but also men mounted males without respect for the sex nature which the active partner shares with the passive, and so when they tried to beget children, they were incapable of any but a sterile seed. Yet the discovery availed them not, so much stronger was the force of their lust which mastered them, as little by little they accustomed those who were, by nature, men to play the part of a woman, they saddled them with the formidable curse of a female disease. For not only did they emasculate their bodies, but they worked a further degeneration in their souls, and, so far as in them lay, were corrupting the whole of mankind.

The fathers of the Christian church accepted the homosexual interpretation of the Sodom story. The history of the Christian church is well documented by Boswell (1980).

St. Augustine was influenced by the homosexual interpretation of the Sodom story in his writings regarding human nature and sexuality. In line with the Stoic philosophers he held that *logos* (God) was diffused through the cosmos, thus, God's material presence in the universe as cosmic biologic reason was the rational law of nature. The principle virtue of man was indifference—fighting against passions or affections.

Thomas Aquinas condemned homosexuals because their inordinate selfish seeking of venereal pleasure was a result of sin. Also, Aquinas wrote that homosexuals cannot serve the exclusive divine purpose governing use of all human sexuality—procreation.

There are many different Protestant churches today, and they present a rather varied picture in regard to their teachings on sex. Some more fundamentalist churches retain the strictest standards, condemning all sexual activity outside the marriage. Many of these church groups forbid fashionable clothing, facial makeup, movie-going, dancing, kissing, or any close physical contact between persons who are not married. Other, more modern churches view complete sexual fulfillment for everyone, regardless of marital status or sexual orientation, in a positive light. Some of these churches advocate women as ministers and perform marriage ceremonies between partners of the same gender. The United Church of Christ and the Episcopal Church have ordained openly homosexual clergy.

Today most of the Protestant churches take a less extreme position than the two mentioned above. Many acknowledge the erotic nature of humans as God-given, serving the purpose of procreation, and creating a strong physical and spiritual bond between marriage partners. Thus, masturbation, oral and anal sex, contraception, and sterilization are sometimes viewed as moral. Divorce has become a legitimate alternative to an unhappy marriage. Those who deviate from traditional sexual norms are sometimes viewed with compassion and understanding, providing they do not harm others. Indeed, the U.S. National Council of Churches has now officially demanded an end to persecution because of sexual matters, recommending full civil rights for all citizens, homosexual and heterosexual.

In conclusion, psychology can find evidence for a religious explanation of pejorative attitudes toward homosexuality from correlational studies. These psychological studies find consistently that conservative religious attitudes correspond to pejorative attitudes towards gays and sex guilt. The fundamental belief is a derivative of the notion that nonprocreative sex is a contagious disease that could result in all kinds of symptoms and disorders.

Morality and Law

Through a cultural and historical perspective this section considers the history behind present-day conflicts over homosexuals' civil rights and acceptance. The hostility of religious and secular institutions toward variant behavior is incorporated in current laws, religious doctrines, and the institutions of education, psychiatry, and psychology.

This was not, however, always the situation. Boswell (1980) notes that gay relationships have often been viewed as superior to nongay relationships:

> Many Greeks represented gay love as the only form of eroticism which could be lasting, pure, and truly spiritual. The origin of the concept of "Platonic Love" (which post-dates Plato by several centuries) was not Plato's belief that sex should be absent from gay

affairs but his conviction that only love between persons of the same gender could transcend sex. The Attic lawgiver Solon considered homosexual eroticism too lofty for slaves and prohibited it to them. In the idealistic world of the Hellenistic romances, gay people figured prominently as star-crossed lovers whose passions were no less enduring or spiritual than those of their non-gay friends. In Rome, Hadrian's undying devotion to his dead lover Antininous was one of the most familiar artistic expressions of erotic fidelity.... Even among primitive peoples some connection is often assumed between spirituality or mysticism and homosexuality. Only in comparatively recent times have homosexual feelings come to be associated with moral looseness (p. 27).

Religious and secular institutions have encouraged hostility toward variant sexual behavior and have created justifications for prejudice. Societies' prejudice and fear have been sustained by the belief that deviance from heterosexuality is either an abomination, a manifestation of mental illness, or an expression of criminality. As a result, widespread fear and ignorance of homosexuality persist despite today's greater acceptance of different lifestyles.

Most homosexuals concealed their sexual orientation before the advent of the gay liberation movement. Now, gays are coming out and demanding acceptance and equal rights. An understanding of Judeo-Christian tradition is useful for understanding some of the problems that homosexuals are confronting today.

Although homosexual religious rites were important in pre-Greco/Roman civilizations from the eastern Mediterranean to Sumeria, the Hebrews seem to have a tradition of homosexual hatred. Homosexuality may have been condemned by the Jews because it did not contribute to population growth. In addition, Jewish homosexual repression could have been a reaction to the variant sexual habits that existed in the surrounding hostile civilizations. The Jews were exiled in Canaan, where Atargatis, a goddess whose rites encouraged homosexual acts, was worshipped (Karlen, 1971). In an attempt to retain their distinctiveness as a culture, Jewish leaders promulgated laws that differentiated their followers from the Canaanites. Thus, the consensus is "that the Jews had a long-standing and strict prohibition against... homosexuality, which... came to be equated with ungodliness, heresy and moral subversion by neighboring enemies" (Karlen, 1971).

Western morality and legal control is described by Karlen (1971):

The church gave final definition and authority to these doctrines at the Council of Trent in 1563, in response to the challenge of the reformation. Questions on which there had been room for some conflict of opinion crystallized into dogma, so Augustine and Aquinas became unshakable law for the faithful: sex, even in marriage, shows a degree of moral abasement; the ideal state is freedom from impulse; the deepest and most dangerous impulse is sex.

This sort of attitude was not . . . anything new in the West; the Christian view of sex was a variation on an old theme. The traditional Western hostility to homosexuality went on with little change in rationalization. Christianity simply showed greater vengefulness and punitive fervor, as it did generally in moral controls (p. 77).

In England homosexuality remained an ecclesiastic offense until the sixteenth century. During the Middle Ages the usual punishments were exile, castration, flogging, or most commonly simple penance (Riley, 1975). Secular treatment of homosexuality changed in 1533, when Henry VIII made sodomy a felony. This law enabled temporal courts to inflict the death penalty for homosexual acts not connected to other crimes (Riley, 1975).

Prosecutions vary through history, according to rules for evidence and social pressures. For example, prosecutions (including executions) increase in times of war (Weeks, 1979). "Sodomite" emerged in the nineteenth century as the typical epithet of abuse for the sexual deviant. Even Oscar Wilde pleaded that he was "posing" as a sodomite during his libel case against the Marquis of Queensberry. It was not until 1861 that the Offences Against the Person Act removed the death penalty for sodomy, replacing it with sentences from ten years to life. This was the state of English law until July 27, 1967, when the recommendations of the Committee on Homosexual Offenses and Prostitution were enacted. Private homosexual conduct between consenting adults is no longer criminal in England.

The United States has not followed this approach. Most states still make criminal the practices by which homophiles manifest their physical love. These practices are described in penal codes as "abominable and detestable crimes against nature." However, a trend toward lesser penalties is evident in recent legislation, with some states moving toward the Moral Penal Code recommendations (Riley, 1975). There is a detailed analysis of homosexuality and the law, in Knutson (1980); this is an entire special edition of the *Journal of Homosexuality* devoted to the legal implications of morality and sex.

Cultural Difference in Belief

The impact of cultural experience and tradition on sexual behavior is most striking when we compare ourselves with people from other cultures. For example, Margaret Mead (1938/1961) analyzed Samoan and U.S. girls and concluded that the physiological disturbances and psychological tension that accompany the reaching of sexual maturity in the United States must be learned since they are absent in Samoa.

Cultural traditions of sexual conservatism influence the nature and intensity of pejorative responding to homosexual acts and actors. In a group of several thousand people on an island in Melanesia (Davenport, 1974) we see that sexual patterns in a Southwest Pacific society differ markedly from our own in the U.S.:

> There are two categories of homosexual relationships: those between young single men of the same age group, and those involving older men and boys from seven and perhaps eleven years of age. With young men of the same age, homosexual interaction occurs between persons who are merely good friends, sometimes between brothers. One partner assumes the passive role when the other requests it, and subsequently the favor is returned. Men who behave thus are not regarded as homosexual lovers. They are simply friends or relatives, who, understanding each other's needs and desires, accommodate one another thus fulfilling some of the obligations of kinship and friendship. The usual relationship between older men and young boys is quite different. The man always plays the active role, and it is considered obligatory for him to give the boy presents in return for accommodating him. A man would not engage his own son in such a relationship, but fathers do not object when friends use their young sons in this way, provided the adult is kind and generous (p. 200).

In this Southwest Pacific society, masturbation and anal copulation were substitutes for premarital heterosexual intercourse. After marriage to a woman, however, most of the men do not become exclusively heterosexual. This group of people believed that the homosexual capacity did not exclude the heterosexual capacity, but it was expected that after marriage the man desired and valued intercourse with his wife above all other sexual relations.

> However, he need not forego pederasty as long as this does not prevent him from giving sexual satisfaction to his wife. In other

words, this is a society that quite frankly expects and accepts some bisexual behavior in most men, although there is nothing odd or deviant about an exclusively heterosexual male. As a result these people have no concept to compare with our commonly accepted stereotype of the "psychological homosexual" (p. 202).

Another example of homosexual behavior in the Melanesian groups is puberty rites for boys. Each boy is initiated into anal intercourse by the older males and spends his first year playing only the passive role. According to Ford and Beach (1951), this practice is believed by the natives to be necessary for the growing boy. Though fully sanctioned by the males, these initiatory practices are supposed to be kept from the women.

In cultures where concern for appropriate sexual behavior is guided by a negative attitude toward sex in general, homosexuality may be condemned in any form. Churchill (1967) used the word "homoeroto-phobia" to describe the fear of erotic or sexual contact with members of the same gender. He gave particular emphasis to the extent various cultures placed restrictions on homosexual contact, according to the continuum defined by Ford and Beach (1951). In Churchill's study, the socialization practices of sex-negative cultures were found to include various attempts to repress homosexuality. He argued that contemporary U.S. society is such a sex-negative culture, because any behavior that is suggestive of homo-sexuality is strictly forbidden.

Sexual attitudes are clearly influenced by religious beliefs. This is true whether one looks at our own Western, Judeo-Christian civilization or Eastern civilizations. In Africa and Asia, however, the persecution of sexual deviants has seldom been as crazed as in Europe and the United States. For example, in Arabia and northern Africa, Muhammad's followers take a realistic and often liberal attitude toward sexual expression. Consensual sexual behavior suffers few restrictions, with temporary marriages, some forms of polygamy, and divorce permitted. Contraception and abortion have generally been prohibited in countries practicing Islam because these countries desired population increases. The scope of this book does not permit a thorough and detailed discussion of non-Western religions; the examples cited may serve as illustrations.

MODERN-DAY SCIENCE IN WESTERN CIVILIZATION

The most commonly quoted European writers on homosexuality in the mid-nineteenth century were Casper and Tardieu, the leading medico-legal experts of Germany and France, respectively. Karlen (1971) has indicated that both were "chiefly concerned with whether the disgusting breed of perverts could be physically identified for courts, and whether they should be held legally responsible for their acts." The same problem was apparent in Britain. Most of the thousand or so works on homosexuality that, according to Magnus Hirschfeld, appeared between 1898 and 1908 were directed at the legal profession. Even J.A. Symond's privately printed pamphlet, *A Problem in Modern Ethics*, was explicitly addressed to medical psychologists and jurists. Havelock Ellis' *Sexual Inversion* was condemned for not being published by a medical press and for being too popular in tone. The medicalization of homosexuality—a transition from notions of sin to concepts of sickness or mental illness— was a notable transition. The polarized values of scientific paradigms have stood for decades: Is homosexuality congenital or acquired, ineradicable or susceptible to cure, to be quietly if unenthusiastically accepted as unavoidable or to be resisted with all of one's will? The notions of the immorality or sinfulness of homosexuality did not die in the nineteenth century; they were inextricably entangled with "scientific" theories that formed the boundaries within which homosexuals had to begin to define themselves.

Szasz (1970) argued that his fellow psychiatrists involved themselves in a program of social control that has nothing to do with scientific medicine, and that they disguise their primitive interventions behind the semantics and social trappings of the medical practice. The following quote makes clear the moral position of psychiatry:

> Psychiatry's preoccupation with the disease concept of homosexuality conceals the fact that the homosexuals are a group of medically stigmatized and socially persecuted individuals. The noises generated by their persecution and their anguished cries of protest are drowned out by the rhetoric of therapy. It is heartless hypocrisy to pretend that physicians, psychiatrists or "normal" laymen for that matter, really care about the welfare of the mentally ill in general, or the homosexual in particular. If they did they would stop torturing him while claiming to help him. But this is just what reformers—whether theological or medical—refuse to do (p. 109).

On one level, the scientific and medical speculation surrounding the category "homosexual" can be seen as a product of the tendency of social sciences to differentiate traditionally execrated and monolithic crimes against nature into discrete deviations and to map their etiologies. On another level, the emergence of the concept of homosexual corresponded to the clarification and articulation of a variety of social categories: the sexual child, the hysterical woman, the congenitally inclined prostitute (or indeed, in the work of Ellis and others, the congenital criminal). Perhaps most significantly, the formation of public concepts of sexual identity was part of the contemporaneous debate over an ideological definition of the role of the housewife and mother (Weeks, 1979).

Freud thought that homophiles were basically bisexuals who experience some disturbance during the early stages of sexual development. Freud was not convinced that this disturbance results in a pathological condition or that variant behavior is degenerate.

The following letter was written by Freud (1935) to a mother whose son was labeled a homosexual:

Dear Mrs. _____:

I gather from your letter that your son is a homosexual. I am most impressed by the fact that you do not mention this term yourself in your information about him. May I question, why you avoid it? Homosexuality is assuredly no advantage, but is nothing to be classified as an illness; we consider it to be a variation of the sexual development. Many highly respectable individuals of ancient and modern times have been homosexuals, several of the greatest men among them (Plato, Michaelangelo, Leonardo da Vinci, etc.). It is a great injustice to persecute homosexuality as a crime and cruelty, too. If you do not believe me, read the books of Havelock Ellis.

By asking me if I can help, you mean, I suppose, if I can abolish homosexuality and make normal heterosexuality take its place. The answer is, in a general way, we cannot promise to achieve it. In a certain number of cases we succeed in developing the blighted germs of heterosexual tendencies which are present in every homosexual; in the majority of cases it is no more possible. It is a question of the quality and the age of the individual. The result of treatment cannot be predicted.

What analysis can do for your son runs in a different line. If he is unhappy, neurotic, torn by conflicts, inhibited in his coital life, analysis may bring him harmony, peace of mind, full efficiency, whether he remains a homosexual or gets changed. If you make up your mind he should have analysis with me—I don't expect you will—he has to come over to Vienna. I have no intention of leaving here. However, don't neglect to give me your answer (p. 786).

The man who more than anyone else brought about a radical change in scientific thoughts about sex was Alfred C. Kinsey. Kinsey and his associates gathered detailed sexual histories from 12,000 Americans of both sexes and of all ages, unmarried, married, and formerly married. The sample was drawn from every state and from every educational and socioeconomic status. His purpose was to learn what sort of sexual activities people engaged in, not to condemn or to define what was natural or unnatural. Kinsey upset many people with the data on homosexual activity: Thirty-seven percent of the total male population had at lease some homosexual experience to the point of orgasm between adolescence and old age (Kinsey, Pomeroy, & Martin, 1948).

In 1972, the National Institute of Mental Health's Task Force on Homosexuality, led by psychologist Evelyn Hooker, released its Final Report and Background Papers. The task force urged that sexual behavior between consenting adults be decriminalized and that discrimination in employment against those labeled homosexual or deviant be eliminated. One result of the recommendation was the elimination of homosexuality from the category of pathological illness by the American Psychiatric Association in December of 1973.

Recent conceptions of sexuality consider it to be relational; that is, sexuality consists of activity and interactions—active social relations—and not simply acts (Padgug, 1979). Each society is seen as creating all of the sexual categories and roles within which they act and define themselves. Thus, the shifts observed in the location of historical taboos on sexuality may be described according to the needs and interests of a culture at some given time. For example, the relations between sexual patterns and population size may be causally conceptualized. Furthermore, it does seem possible to theorize why some individuals acquire homosexual identities rather than heterosexual identities within an historical and relational paradigm. The mechanisms that operate within the relationships between the individual and society, the individual and his or her reference groups, and between the individual and other individuals. Support power relations such as economic class and access to knowledge. For example, Foucault (1976) implies that bourgeois society, far from excluding "sex," has actually incited an explosion of sexualities. The fact that sex has become a major organizing principle of society attests to the power of bourgeois society. Some of the social psychological processes involved in these power relations may be seen in the creation and propagandism of misinformation and mysticism surrounding sexuality, and in the economics of gender roles in class society. Clearly, the cultural power relations described do not totally suppress sexuality, but define and regulate it.

Scientific Paradigms and Social Values

Scientific paradigms do reflect social values. For example, his analysis of coming out, Weeks (1979) takes a Marxist approach, inter-preting events and personalities in the context of consciousness and social relations in flux. The new women's history has made "problematical three of the basic concerns of historical thought: (1) periodization, (2) the categories of social analysis, and (3) theories of social change," comments historian Joan Kelly-Gadol (1976, p. 809). Kelly-Gadol concludes that the relation between the sexes is a social and not a natural one.

McIntosh (1968) has documented the rise of the European view that homosexuality is a condition. Her scientific paradigm is designed to document the historical emergence of a homosexual role and rejects the assumption that homosexuality and heterosexuality are transhistorical or psychological phenomena. This paradigm is based on the view that scientific paradigms generated by antihomosexual values themselves deserve close study, because they produce different kinds of historical evidence than those generated by more egalitarian values.

Another example of scientific paradigms and social values may be seen in the work of Michel Foucault (1976). He argues that *sexual repression* is the historical apparatus used in the past few centuries by bourgeois power to create an *explosion* of sexualities. These sexualities are organized and "repressed." Foucault also developed research that located four kinds of power relationships between capitalism and sexuality that have been operating since the eighteenth century to develop specific apparatuses of power and knowledge in relation to sex. These include: the hysterization of the woman's body, the pedagogization of the sex of the child, the socialization of procreative behavior, and the psychiatrization of perversities. This scientific paradigm and the values that support it produced a historical analysis of the following four objects of knowledge in the nineteenth century: the hysterical woman, the masturbating child, the Malthusian couple, and the perverse adult. According to Jeffrey Weeks (1979), Foucault's theories may be central to any further theorization of homosexuality that values historical process and subjectivity.

Sampson (1978) develops the thesis that the concepts androgyny, mental health, and moral development contain a cultural value bias, termed *self-contained individualism*. He argues that self-contained individualism is an integral part of the dominant concept and definition of proper science. Sampson presents two contrasting paradigms of science. Paradigm I argues that something in science insofar as: (1) it is objective, eliminating the standpoint of the knower from the knowledge that is obtained so that a realm of pure facts is achieved, and (2) it seeks principles of psychological functioning that are abstract, general, and universal. Rosenthal's (1966) "discovery" of experimenter effects is cited to show the flawed nature of Paradigm I science, in that it uncovers facts that are constituted in the particular transaction between experimenter and subject. Paradigm I science is necessarily ahistorical and acontextual because facts and truths are defined in universalistic ways, disregarding any particular and concrete sociohistorical standpoint. In Paradigm II science, facts, and truths emerge within specific times and places. The idea that sciences have paradigms is the crux of Paradigm II science. That is, to argue that a concept such as a paradigm exists and governs scientific inquiry is already to locate such inquiry in its historical and social context. Hence, science is no longer seen as a transcendent enterprise, and scientific truths are not considered abstract, general, and universal. Sampson argues that the needs of a male-dominated, Protestant-ethic-oriented, middle-class, liberal, and capitalistic society initially helped found and are now reaffirmed by Paradigm I science. In his view, both science and Protestantism are emerging liberation movements of the seventeenth century emphasizing individualism. That is, both sought to detach themselves from any particularistic reference points or earlier social norms and sought laws that applied to all persons. Religion and science oriented themselves to cognitive domains, teaching people rather than appealing to their emotional needs. Rossides (1978) comments that with the development of industrial society the core values of individualism, private property, market economy, political-legal equality, and faith in progress were extended. Paradigm I science in social psychology affirms the existing social order by the empirical perception of givens as things that ought to be. Lichtheim (1967) notes that "empirical perception . . . fixed on isolated aspects of the totality . . . is ideological . . . in that it mistakes the reified structures of immediate experience for permanent constituents of reality." Kohlberg's approach to moral reasoning is cited as a case example of male bias. In Kohlberg's model, cognitive growth moves from the concrete to the abstract, where the abstract is a measure of mature, adult development. It is recommended that each paradigm be viewed as one pole of an antagonistic theory of nature and our knowledge of it. By granting both poles equal status, a partnership or dialectical synthesis will be attained; that is, each is said to enter as an element for a newly emerging synthesis.

SUMMARY OF CHAPTER TWO

The cognitive features of beliefs include that beliefs tend to cohere in meaningful systems. Beliefs are often based on one another (vertical) and are derived from more than one chain of reasoning (horizontal). Some beliefs may be more central or important than others. Beliefs may be derived from higher-order quasilogical processes, or they may be non-conscious in that they are internalized without question.

Beliefs about sexual identity demonstrate these rules or cognitive features. Syllogisms show that errors in the vertical structure of beliefs about the components of sexual identity are predictable. The errors in logic may be predicted from an individual's conception of "truth" and over-generalizations in beliefs. Abelson's theory of nonconsistency preserves the molecular character of opinions as invulnerable to disconfirmation because they do not necessarily have logical interconnections among them.

Three cognitive and behavioral patterns observed among individuals in response to homoeroticism were charted. Gender role conformity is basically avoidance of cross-gender behavior. Ego-dystonic homosexuality is a reversed cultural norm, normally observed as a psychiatric diagnosis: socialized individuals are *supposed* to have negative feelings in response to their own homoeroticism and to desire heterosexuality. Ego-dystonic homosexuality is derived from the pejorative values toward some essential sexuality located within the isolated individual. The apparently reverse logic is based on the idea that "homosexuals" are victims of a congenital disease and tormented with heterosexual desire; heterosexuals would not have ego-dystonic homosexuality because they are essentially immune to the fear of women symptomatic of homosexuality. Obviously, the categories of sexual acts, actors, and identities defined by socialization agents and given meaning through propaganda are value-laden. Homophobia is the extreme reaction of irrational and incapacitating fear of the mythical homosexual.

The thematic contents of antigay arguments were categorized, and linguistic implications were drawn. Mind control has been achieved through various propaganda techniques. Imposed ignorance sets the stage for thorough mind control. Questions that reveal the biases in propaganda were listed.

Stereotypes function to help people classify and process information. Homosexual stereotypes include the descriptions sexually abnormal, perverted, mentally ill, and effeminate. Yet homosexuals are defined by the image people receive of them at any given period in history. The ideology of sexuality is organized around stereotypes and categories, locating sexuality within the individual as a fixed essence. Gay identity is a political reification born out of the human organism's rage to gain legal and social control of the total human sexual response.

The information processing implications include four biases in processing information: (1) overestimation of the occurrence of confirming examples of our stereotypes; (2) filling in of gaps in our evidence base with information consistent with our stereotypes; (3) construction of information that is not consistent with our stereotypes to support our biases: and (4) selective recall of information about our past and reconstruction of memory around our stereotypes. Snyder and Uranowitz (1978) demonstrated reconstructive hypothesis of memory in the study of Betty K: Although the original narrative stated that Betty dated occasionally, people who heard Betty is now a lesbian were likely to believe they had read that she never went out with men.

The schematic organization of behavior and self-concept based on gender was demonstrated by Sandra Bem (1981a). Gender schema theory identifies people engaging in gender schematic processing. For example, the very act of describing onself on the BSRI is a product of gender schematic processing. These self-schemata function as selective mechanisms that determine whether the information is attended to, how it is structured, how much importance is attached to it, and what happens to it subsequently (Markus, 1977). The implications for people conscious of their homoeroticism include the development of a complete identity (a negative one) that has been externally defined.

Religious belief and tradition reveal that antihomosexual prejudice is limited to Judeo-Christianity. The scriptures that are most commonly cited include the Sodom and Gomorrah story and the creation account in Genesis. Several problems in the theological interpretations of these and other texts were discussed. According to McNeil (1976), the true meaning of the scriptures regarding homosexual activity is a condemnation of perverse homosexual activity indulged in by otherwise heterosexual people.

McNeil's argument is based on a differentiation between essential gayness and heterosexual perversity rather than a redefinition of nature to include all forms of sexual expression. Tradition and history, in this chapter, charts the use of scripture in establishing pejorative attitudes toward and hostile treatment of homosexual acts, actors, and identitites. The hostility of religious and secular institutions toward variant behavior was incorporated in current laws and religious dogma, as well as in the institutions of education, psychiatry, and psychology. Cultural differences in beliefs reveal a useful distinction between sex-negative and sex-positive societies.

Modern-day science attempted to differentiate traditionally execrated and monolithic crimes against nature into specific deviations. The causes of "mental illness" or degeneracy have been mapped by the new guardian of morality: medical science. Freud's, Kinsey's, Foucault's, and Weeks's theories of homosexuality were given to show the evolution of theorizing in modern-day science.

Clearly, scientific paradigms do reflect social values. Recent theories that honestly state their social value positions were described. Scientific paradigms may be classified according to their acknowledgment or denial of the idea that the sciences have paradigms. By granting both classes of theory equal status, Sampson (1978) argues, a dialectical synthesis will be attained. The newly emerging synthesis of scientific theory corresponds to transformations in individual consciousness. For example, stereotypes guide perception in the same way that paradigms guide scientific inquiry. Moreover, the principles of dialectical transfromation* that create an emerging sysnthesis in scientific theory are meaningfully applied to individual and cultural alteration. We do not need separate and antagon- istic relationships with self, others, and society. With this in mind, we turn now to sexuality and beliefs about sexuality in more detail.

---

*By dialectical transformation I mean a mechanism of change that describes how thesis and antithesis interact to synthesize themselves into a better idea.

CHAPTER THREE

Sexuality and Beliefs about Sexuality

A homosexual identity is not given in nature, nor is it imposed as a social control on a deviant minority; it is the product of a long social process involving both definition and self-definition. It is a crucial stage in the rejection of stigmatisation, but at the same time it works very much within the definition presented. And all these definitions, categorizations, regulations are social impositions upon the flux of sexual possibilities there in the human animal at the time of birth.

Jeffrey Weeks

Most of the research reported on attitudes and stereotypes toward homosexual acts and actors has been collected from heterosexual respondents (see MacDonald & Games, 1974; Millham, San Miguel, & Kellogg, 1976). These studies tend to assess global cultural beliefs about and fears of homosexual acts and actors and are generally discussed in the context of "homophobia." These studies reflect limited or no experience with homosexuals themselves. In fact, individuals who report having a homosexual friend or relative tend to score in the direction of positive attitudes on these scales. These research studies are explored in some detail in Chapter Six.

Individuals who have some awareness of homoerotic fantasy or arousal are likely to have a different assessment of homosexual acts and actors. Very little systematic scaling of attitude dimensions among homosexual-identified groups has been reported. An exploration of the identity implications of personal stereotyping among individuals who experience homoerotic fantasy and arousal is called for. The degree of not-me-but-the-other ego-dystonic response indicated by self-labeled homosexuals' beliefs and attitudes is apparently less, once the global, cultural myths are deprogrammed through homosexual contact and experience.

The gender role self-concepts of homosexual men and their attitudes toward both women and male homosexuality reveal that support for women's equality on the part of homosexual men is highly significant. One group of researchers has explored this relationship in a study of eighty-eight homosexual males drawn from a nonclinical sample. These men were asked to respond to a questionnaire that assessed their gender role self-concept and their attitudes toward both women and male homosexuality. Their results indicated that homosexual males who view themselves as androgynous (in terms of socially valued masculine and feminine characteristics) favor equality between the genders more than homosexual males who rate themselves as more masculine, less masculine, or "different" from their stereotype of the masculine gender role. These males held positive attitudes toward women, regardless of their masculine self-concept. Similarly, those homosexual men who supported equality between men and women also held more positive attitudes toward male homosexuality. In this respect, heterosexual males do not differ from homosexual males; the authors stress the importance of not relying on explanations gleaned from investigations sampling heterosexual males. To do so, they caution,

> would deny the unequal social treatment of women and homosexual men that is reflected in the negative attitudes toward women and homosexual males so prevalent in North American society. Since masculine characteristics are most highly valued in our society, and since homosexual men are commonly equated with women and femininity, support for women's equality on the part of homosexual men is highly significant, involving, as it does, attitudes related to the way in which these men feel about themselves, their own femininity, and their own reference group (McDonald & Moore, 1978, p. 12).

HOMOSEXUAL IN THE CONTEMPORARY UNITED STATES

People in the United States today live in a culture where homoerotic feelings are seldom spoken of, and if they are, it is usually in a pejorative way. Many individuals grow up with no understanding of *what* to call the vague stirring of homoeroticism. At some point in development, typically approaching puberty, a word is acquired for these feelings: *homosexual.* Oddly, along with this descriptive adjective (most often not yet translated in behavior) comes a person, also referred to as a "queer," "fag," or "homo." In other words, homosexual is both noun and adjective. Moreover, the homoerotic feeling apparently extends to the very character of the person having the feeling. That persons are what they feel, or do, is confusing to preadolescents, particularly when *doing* homosexual acts and *being* a homosexual person appear to be so discrepant. Individuals often feel that they could do homosexual things, but that being a homosexual person is incongruent with their image of self. An identity conflict is likely to occur. The child ponders, "how can I be me [the global self-concept already forming] if I am one of 'them'? I am not me—I am the other."

During this time, and throughout young adulthood, individuals learn an entire set of characteristics supposedly typical of persons who have the feelings they themselves have misunderstood and probably hidden. These individuals may begin to imitate mannerisms and character traits that have, for them, come to be definitive of the "homosexual." On the other hand, individuals may deny, repress, and/or condemn those homo-erotic feelings with some degree of success, conforming to their perceptions of the goals of reference groups or significant others, for example, heterosexual monogamy. When the latter pattern occurs, the individual will conform to the rigid gender role expectations, denying the validity or reality of his or her homoerotic feelings. These two reactions to the awareness of one's homoerotic feelings may be opposite ends of a deviance-conformity dimension, upon which individuals who are at some point aware of their homoerotic feelings variously place. Conformity and deviance may be two of the more common adaptations to homoeroticism in the contemporary United States. If a male adopts the negative stereotype of the homosexual, he will be a "screaming queen," blatantly effeminate. He has not questioned his acceptance of this sexual indentity and perhaps has lost some personal identity in this process of personal stereotyping based on a self-endorsed social prejudice. The conformist, on the other hand, may monitor behavior, appearance, and so on, obsessed with becoming everything that would appear to confirm heterosexuality. The conformist will not associate with homosexual persons or go places where homosexual acts are acceptable. This person may marry heterosexually and may experience sexual performance anxiety and symptoms of the Type A behavioral pattern, e.g., hard-driving competitiveness and a sense of time urgency. These two extreme reactions may characterize an authoritarian reaction to the awareness of homoeroticism and a general repression of all sexual impulses.

These are only two extreme variations in response to the awareness of homoeroticism. What these two responses have in common are the initially acquired beliefs about and fears of homosexual acts and actors. These conformity-deviance reactions to perceived social pressures may be more similar than social psychologists have theorized. Specifically, deviance—on a general social level—may be conformity to a particular group or subculture, rather than general social values. The deviance—conformity dimension may indicate a common "need to conform" and to enjoy a stress-free, simple environment that maximizes self-image. On one hand, the self-labeling deviants may have more opportunity to challenge their own beliefs and fears through contact with homosexual acts, actors, and communities. On the other hand, association of an individual labeled "homosexual," with a subgroup labeled "homosexual," may lead to a strengthening of stereotyped homosexual behavior (Farrell & Morrione, 1974; Ross, 1979).

This process of recognizing homosexual arousal and choosing to integrate this knowledge into one's personal and social life is called "coming out." There are many developmental paths taken in this process, and several critical experiences. For example, awareness of same-gender attraction, first homosexual experience, contact with other homosexuals and groups of homosexuals, and labeling oneself homosexual are early events in the coming-out process. Labeling oneself as gay and disclosing one's homosexual feelings and lifestyle to friends, family, and coworkers are events that may occur after initial awareness and acceptance of one's homosexual feelings. Developing a romantic homosexual relationship may also be a significant event in the developmental chronology of coming out.

The individual's self-image is influenced profoundly by an awareness of homoeroticism. The following quote from a client (aged 32) is a response to the question, "How have your homosexual feelings influenced your own view of yourself?"

> The way I view myself has changed a lot in the past 3 or 4 years, towards being less of a "homosexual," and more of a person. In my teenage years and throughout most of my younger adulthood I felt that my being a homosexual was a contradiction to my real self. I mean, my homosexual identity seemed incompatible with my true self. I have always been friendly, bright, eager and a hard worker— and very supportive of the people around me. My homosexual identity was negative contradicting the rest of myself. When I felt friendly, or ambitious, I would stop myself, or sabotage myself for a long time.

The effect of one's sexual preference on one's global self-concept may be indicated by the acceptance of a homosexual identity. The more salient homosexuality becomes to one's total image of self, the more personal stereotyping is likely to occur. The information-processing implications of heterosexual schemata among rigidly masculine and feminine heterosexuals have been demonstrated (Bem, 1981).

The function and propagation of an ideology that includes strong prohibitions against homosexuality have pervasive implications that command the attention of social psychologists. A major implication lies in the realm of the self-concept as an internalized representation of social norms and beliefs. This addresses the development of self arising in the process of social influence, experience, comparison, and activity.

Mead (1934) proposed that there are two stages in the development of self. In the first stage the self is simply an organization of the particular attitudes of other individuals toward it and toward one another in the specific social acts in which the self engages with them. During the second stage of self-development, the self is also constituted by the organization of the social group as a whole to which it belongs. Thus, the individual becomes a reflection of the general systematic pattern of social or group behavior in which that individual and the others are all involved (Mead, 1934).

One may accept that one is homosexual and internalize society's devaluation of homosexuality. Such an identity will be a negative identity. Erikson (1959) described a negative identity as "an identity perversely based on all those identifications and roles which, at stages of development, have been presented to the individual as most undesireable or dangerous . . ." (p. 131).

The study of "ego-dystonic homosexuality" (APA, 1980) may also reveal certain traits or ego defenses due to "victimization." In *The Nature of Prejudice*, Allport (1958) states, "One's reputation, whether false or true, cannot be hammered, hammered, hammered into one's head without doing something to one's character" (p. 138). Allport described several possible character traits the oppressed minority group member might develop. He believed that the development of these traits, e.g., identification with the dominant group (self-hate), passivity and withdrawal, clowning (acting outrageously effeminate to be considered amusing), obsessive concern, and denial of group membership, would depend on the individual's life circumstances, or how severe his suffering from persecution was and how detached his own philosophy of life was.

Ego-dystonic Homosexuality

The classification provided by the American Psychiatric Association (1980) in their *Diagnostic and Statistical Manual III* (DSM III) for negative homosexual identity is *ego-dystonic homosexuality*. The essential features are a desire to acquire or increase heterosexual arousal, so that heterosexual relationships can be initiated or maintained, and a sustained pattern of overt homosexual arousal that the individual explicity states has been unwanted and a persistent source of distress.

According to the *DSM III*, loneliness is an associated feature, as are guilt, shame, anxiety, and depression. The most common age at onset of this disorder is adolescence when the individual becomes aware of homosexual arousal and has already internalized negative feelings about homosexuality. The manual states that "there is some evidence that in time many individuals with this disorder give up the yearning to become heterosexual and accept themselves as homosexuals. This process is apparently facilitated by the presence of a supportive homosexual sub-culture" (p. 281). In addition, homosexuals who develop a major depression may then express self-hatred because of their sexual orientation (p. 282). The predisposing factors to ego-dystonic homosexuality are "those negative societal attitudes toward homosexuality that have been internalized." No information is reported regarding the sex ratio and familial pattern for this condition.

The critical gaps in our knowledge of ego-dystonic homosexuality are:

1.　The nature of internalized theories of sexual preference.

2.　Role models in the traditional family pattern.

3.　Learning processes especially relevant to stigmatized people.

4.　Differential socialization implications for lesbians and gay men.

The beliefs people have about their own and others' sexual preferences represent an extension or generalization from the sexual act or fantasy to the essence or character of the actor. In this way, we assign ourselves and others social identities based on particular thoughts, feelings, or behaviors—all three of which are influenced by social norms. Moreover, peoples' theories of sexual preference are commonly of the either/or type: on one dimension, you are either homosexual or heterosexual.

The failure to separate the whole person from the specific act performed in a particular situation within a particular cultural context is depersonalizing and alienating. This process of labeling others and oneself may function to aid in categorizing and processing information about a complex world, but less chaos may mean less truth. Indeed, this extension of the acts to the actor lays the foundation for stereotyping, prejudice, and the assignment of deviant labels on both a social and a personal level. In short, the unidimensional labels that we use to categorize human sexuality strip away human dignity and the integrity of human variation in sexual responsiveness. This is a central—even higher-order—factor for the study of ego-dystonic homosexuality. In order to deprogram the not-me-but-the-other ego alienation observed in ego-dystonic homosexuality we must explore the identity implications of personal stereotyping and schematic processing guided by sexual preference theory.

Information regarding the familial pattern observed among ego-dystonic homosexuals is another critical gap in our knowledge of the disorder. The conditions for acquisition of negative attitudes toward homosexuality may involve role models in the traditional family. In fact, one of the most common conditions under which beliefs about and fears of homosexual acts and actors are acquired occurs within the traditional family. This family structure ideally consists of a dominant father, a submissive mother, and obedient children. Parents are a major source for definitions of people and situations, as well as for interpretations of physiological arousal. With this in mind, it is not suprising that features associated with heterosexuality, such as having children and a socially sanctioned family life, may be viewed by the ego-dystonic homosexual as desirable and incompatible with a homosexual arousal pattern (APA, 1980, p. 282).

Research geared toward the processes and contents of familial role modeling may be productive in understanding ego-dystonic homosexuality. This research may utilize already existing literature on the factors affecting the modeling process, such as gender of the model, nurturance, and perceived power of the model (see Maccoby & Jacklin, 1974). It may be demonstrated that the traditional family is capable of transmitting the prejudice and fear toward homosexuals necessary for the development of ego-dystonic homosexuality.

The relationship between the family and society must also be addressed. The need and interest of individuals to maintain the existing order of social relations may help explain individual differences in these beliefs and fears. That is, the social value placed on gender appropriate behavior, and on producing children for the labor market, may support the maintenance of a lower-social caste homosexual. This degradation and social chastisement for violating the given social order is a powerful means of social control. In light of this line of reasoning, it is the family as a productive economic unit that is being protected. Propaganda pictures homosexuality as a threat to societal and familial values.

Research programs relevant to the issue would do well to focus on the role of guilt in inducing compliance. Religiosity may be a critical factor facilitating ego-dystonic homosexuality.

The learning processes of stigmatized individuals include at least three elements that may illuminate the study of ego-dystonic homosexuality. In general, according to Goffman (1963), stigmatized people learn the normal point of view and that they are disqualified according to it. Second, they learn to cope with the way others treat the stigmatized people they may be shown to be. Third, they learn to control information about the existence of their stigma.

Research on the development of ego-dystonic homosexuality might profit from the model Goffman proposes. Significant events in a developmental chronology may be revealed.

The differential socialization implications for lesbians and gay men represent another critical gap in our knowledge of ego-dystonic homosexuality. The gender role expectations for sexual activity differ for men and women in our culture in terms of age at onset and rate of occurrence. The age at onset may reflect these differences for men and women with ego-dystonic homosexuality. The strategies for coping with homosexual feelings may also reflect socialization. Specifically, women apparently avoid identifying themselves as homosexual by emphasizing their feelings ("I really loved her"), whereas men cope by denying their feelings ("I was really drunk").

The violation of prescribed gender roles may be more punitive for men than for women. We need to understand why men have more fear and avoidance of cross-gender behavior and mannerisms than do women. The differences in legal and economic penalties for male homosexuals and female homosexuals indicate that men may become ego-dystonic more frequently than do women.

Factors operating in the etiology of ego-dystonic homosexuality point toward a program of research exploring characteristics of the individual, such as personal stereotyping; characteristics of the situation or immediate environment, such as role models and learning processes; and characteristics of the cultural complex, such as socialized gender role expectations. The distress experienced by the ego-dystonic homosexual may be sufficient to indeed be termed pathological and to generate what some may term pathological behavior.

Yet the etiological factors are clearly imbedded in a cultural context. On this level of analysis, homophobia* among heterosexuals is similar to, or perhaps the counterpart of, ego-dystonic homosexuality among self-labeled homosexuals. Indeed, we would do better to research characteristics of individuals, such as sexual preference label and gender role behavior, as they interact with characteristics of situations and cultural complexes. The pathological labels assigned on the basis of sexual orientation (homophobia among heterosexuals, ego-systonic homosexuality among homosexuals) may reflect common etiologies but distinct symptomology. It is to be hoped further research will utilize a standardized test of attitudes about homosexuality to reveal the higher-order variables that account for variance in reaction to homoeroticism.

---

*Broadly defined as pejorative responding to homosexuals and homosexuality.

A Study of Attitudes about Homosexuality among Homosexual Males

One of the central issues sometimes explicitly but often implicitly raised by the theoretical models reviewed is the distinction between homosexuals who feel positive about themselves and about homosexuals in general and homosexuals who do not.

In an attempt to explore the constellation of attitudinal differences between individuals labeling themselves homosexual who feel positive about themselves and about the label and those labeling themselves homosexual who do not, an attitude inventory was developed for an exploratory study. Specifically, the study was designed to answer the question of whether males labeling themselves homosexual or gay differ in some consistent way in their evaluative attitudes toward: (1) their own homoeroticism, (2) other males labeled homosexual and/or gay, and (3) public disclosure of their own sexual preference.

A self-report measure of attitudes was constructed such that a person scoring high on this test feels positively about his homosexuality and other homosexuals and is not overly concerned or sensitive to the expressions and self-presentation of information regarding his homosexuality. In contrast, the low scorer has a negative homosexual identity, negative attitudes toward his own homosexuality and homosexual impulses, and negative attitudes and stereotypes of other homosexuals; is overly concerned with the appropriateness and consequences of the presentation and expression of his homosexuality; and controls his presentation to a greater extent.

The Nungesser Homosexual Attitudes Inventory (NHAI)* consists of a series of attitude statements generated from each of the following categories:

1. Attitudes toward the fact of one's own homosexuality.
   a. Reactions to one's own behavior or attraction: specific instances of behavior, thoughts, or feelings.
   b. Reactions to being a homosexual.
2. Attitudes toward homosexuality in general and toward other homosexual males.
   a. Negative traits of homosexuals or absence of positive ones.
   b. Attitudes concerning the legal status of homosexuality.

---

*I am indebted to Sandra Bem for assistance in the construction of the NHAI and to Philip Zimbardo for his advice in the research program reported.

    c. Attitudes concerning the morality, biology, and value of homo-
       sexuality: Is it good, bad, or natural? Better, worse, or just as good as
       heterosexuality?
3. Attitudes toward the fact of one's homosexuality being known by
    others.
    a. Reactions toward others' knowing.
    b. Expectations of oppression.

      After considerable refinement, when face validity and item reli-
ability were discussed and subjected to criteria put forth by Anastasi (1968)
for standardized test items, a set of twenty-eight items was selected from
each of the three categories. Individual items were scored in the direction
of positive attitudes. For approximately half of the items, agreement was
keyed as high positive attitudes; for the remainder, disagreement was keyed
as high positive attitudes. The three subscales were disguised by alternating
items from each scale in sequence. Thus, on the preliminary attitudes
inventory of eighty-four items in true-false format, items 1, 4, 8, and so on
were from Scale A (self); items 2, 5, 7, and so on were from Scale B (others;
and items 3, 6, 9, and so on were from Scale C (disclosure). The sequence of
true and false answers followed this eight-item pattern: TF FT FT TF.
      In order to maximize internal consistency, an item analysis was
performed to determine the power of items to discriminate between high
and low test scores and intermediate difficulty of responses. The per-
centages of persons in the top and bottom thirds who responded in regard
to having positive attitudes were determined. Then the percentage in the
bottom group was subtracted from the percentage in the top group. This
difference (D) serves as an index of item validity to discriminate total test
scores (Anastasi 1976). D is directly proportional to the difference between
the number of "correct" and "incorrect" total score discriminations made
by an item. D values are not independent of item difficulty and are biased
in favor of items of intermediate difficulty level. D, then, is an appropriate
criterion for selecting items according to both discriminating power and
difficulty level.
      The respondents were fifty homosexual men whose mean age was
25. They were identified in public cruising areas and at a gay activist
meeting at a West Coast university. The criterion used to determine sexual
preference was self-report, that is, these men described themselves as
homosexual or gay. The return rate of questionnaires was 85% (n = 50).

Results

      Thirty-four items were selected from the eighty-four-item pool for
the final inventory. They are presented in Table 3.1 with their corresponding D scores.

The reliability coefficient obtained for each of the subscales on the Nungesser Homosexual Attitudes Inventory is the unbiased maximum likelihood estimate of each subscale's parameters. The assumption in this reliability measure is that the subscales are measuring the same thing. The assumption of equal means is relaxed, but the same true score variance over the sets of subscale items, the same error variance over the sets of subscale items, and the same error variance over the sets of subscale items, and the same error variance over replication were retained. The unbiased estimates of reliability for the subscales were:

Subscale A (self):	.94
Subscale B (others):	.88
Subscale C (disclosure):	.91

Conclusion

This study demonstrates that there is a positive-negative distinction in the attitudinal constellations endorsed by self-labeled homosexuals. Criterion validity and internal consistency of items contained in the test suggest that the attitudes one has toward the fact of one's own homo- sexuality are highly reliable items indicating an ego-dystonic stage of homosexual experience. The items from the subscale showing attitudes toward others' knowing of one's homosexuality were also highly reliable. Negative self-view and a fear of public scrutiny combine to suggest ego- dystonic homosexuality. Self-acceptance is the critical measure. Interest- ingly, attitudes toward other homosexuals and toward homosexuality are the least reliable of the items, suggesting that these attitudes have not been internalized without some variable change.

A subsequent study, reported elsewhere (Nungesser, 1979), identi- fied two additional subject groups of self-labeled homosexuals and gays: at an urban gay organization's meeting (n = 25), and at a private party for faculty, students, and staff at the same West Coast university (n = 25). Likert scaling was used rather than the initial true-false rating, with high scores indicating high negative responding. The overall reliability (alpha) coefficient for the NHAI was .95. A multiple regresssion analysis of NHAI scores revealed that the frequency of passing for heterosexual, the average reaction of significant others, the months elapsed since accepting the label homosexual, and the frequency of socializing with other gay males account for most of the variance in NHAI scores, with beta weights of −.842, .847, .367, and −.322, respectively. That the NHAI includes disclosure as a subscale obviously contributes to the magnitude of the "frequency of passing for heterosexual" beta weight. Moreover, these data are correla- tional and therefore do not tell us whether disclosure brings about positive responding or positive responding facilitates disclosure.

Table 3.1. Items, Scoring Key, D Scores, and Subscale Assignment for the NHAI

Items	Key	D	Subscale
1. When I am in a conversation with a homosexual man and he touches me, it does not make me uncomfortable	T	60	A
2. I would not mind if my boss found out that I am gay.	T	75	C
3. Whenever I think a lot about being a homosexual, I feel depressed.	F	100	A
4. Homosexuality is not as good as heterosexuality.	F	100	B
5. Whenever I tell my friends about my homosexuality, I do not worry that they will try to remember things about me that would make me appear to fit the stereotype of a homosexual.	T	75	C
6. I am glad to be gay.	T	100	A
7. Male homosexuality is a natural expression of sexuality in human males.	T	80	B
8. When I am sexually attracted to a close male friend, I feel uncomfortable.	F	80	A
9. I am proud to be a part of the gay community.	T	100	A
10. Male homosexuals do not dislike women any more than heterosexual males dislike women.	T	60	B
11. Marriage between two homosexuals should be legalized.	T	60	B
12. My homosexuality does not make me unhappy.	T	100	A
13. Male homosexuals are overly promiscuous.	F	100	B
14. When I am sexually attracted to another gay man, I do not mind if someone else knows how I feel.	T	75	C
15. Most problems that homosexuals have come from their status as an oppressed minority, not from their homosexuality per se.	T	60	B
16. When women know of my homosexuality, I am afraid they will not be able to relate to me as a man.	F	75	C

17.	Homosexual lifestyles are not as fulfilling as heterosexual lifestyles.	F	100	B
18.	I would not mind if my neighbors knew that I am gay.	T	100	C
19.	It is important for me to conceal the fact that I am gay from most people.	F	100	C
20.	Whenever I think a lot about being a homosexual, I feel critical about myself.	F	100	A
21.	Choosing an adult gay lifestyle should be an option for children.	T	80	B
22.	If my straight friends knew of my homosexuality, I would feel uncomfortable.	F	100	C
23.	If men knew of my homosexuality, I am afraid they would begin to avoid me.	F	100	B
24.	Homosexuality is a sexual perversion.	F	100	B
25.	If it were made public that I am a homosexual, I would be extremely unhappy.	F	88	C
26.	If my peers knew of my homosexuality, I am afraid that many would not want to be my friends.	F	80	B
27.	Adult homosexual males who have sex with boys under eighteen years of age should be punished by law.	F	80	B
28.	If others knew of my homosexuality, I would not be afraid that they would see me as being effeminate.	T	75	C
29.	I wish I were heterosexual.	F	100	A
30.	When I think about coming out to a peer I am afraid they will pay more attention to my body movements and voice inflections.	F	75	C
31.	I do not think I will be able to have a long-term relationship with another man.	F	80	A
32.	I am confident that my homosexuality does not make me inferior.	T	70	A
33.	I am afraid that people will harass me if I come out more publicly.	F	88	C
34.	When I think about coming out to a heterosexual male friend, I do not worry that he might watch me to see if I do things that are stereotypically homosexual.	T	100	C

HOMOSEXUAL IDENTITY FORMATION

The process of homosexual identity formation has been discussed primarily in terms of static components, traits, or stages, e.g., ego-dystonic homosexuality. The works reviewed next represent homosexual identity development as a continuing process of dialectics between the individual and society. Writers with this viewpoint are not clear on their positions regarding the nature of human sexuality; they often foreclose the process of homosexual identity formation at acceptance of the label homosexual. Cass (1979) is an exception; she considers identity synthesis the highest stage of development. Dank's (1971) study of identity is based on interview data with a sample of male homosexuals. Plummer's (1975) scheme of identity levels is based on a symbolic interactionist perspective. Cass (1979) advances an interpersonal congruency model of development based on clinical observations of male and female homosexuals.

Dank (1971) reports a study of fifty-five self-labeled homosexual men in a large metropolitan area in the northeastern United States. He sets forth the view that at one point in their lives, male homosexuals might be best portrayed as being at a "primary stage" in which they begin to engage in "rule-breaking behavior," i.e., participating in homosexual acts. At this stage, individuals who have had sexual relations with persons of the same sex would consider themselves "normal" even though they had engaged in a form of behavior that they know most people in the United States would consider to be both illegal and immoral. At a later point, people may (or may not) reach the "secondary stage," when they engage in the same behavior but begin to conceive of themselves as being what they do—in the sense of an identity. The major contribution of Dank's work is his examination and description of those social contexts in which individuals reported they were first able to say, "I am a homosexual"—to themselves as well as to other gays. He found that information allowing males to arrive at homosexual self-definition is acquired in a number of situations: "Through meeting other self-defined homosexuals, by meeting knowledgeable straight persons, or by reading about homosexuals and homosexuality" (Dank, 1971, p. 183). Same-gender environments—parks where homosexuals are reputed to gather, branches of the armed forces, or gay bars—are the types of social settings in which his informants tended to meet self-defined homosexuals. The average time from initial recognition of homosexual attractions to arriving at homosexual self-definition was found to be six years. Dank has described the initial stages of personal stereotyping as they correspond to the significant events in one's social interactions.

Plummer (1975) outlines a theoretical account of the process of "becoming homosexual" in contemporary England and the United States.

He restricts his analysis to males for whom homosexuality is a way of life and suggests that the process of becoming homosexual involves four stages:

1. *Sensitization*: In many early social and genital experiences a foundation is laid for a subsequent sexual interpretation. Sex acts become sexual only when they come to be defined as such. The significance of childhood genital and social experience is thought to reside not in the events themselves, but in subsequent meanings that are attached to them.

2. *Signification and disorientation*: "Signification" refers to the process of heightened self-awareness and meaning about the experience of homosexuality; "disorientation" refers to a process of high anxiety and confusion in coping with one's life situation.

3. *Coming out*: The process by which individuals pass out of the moratorium of signification and disorientation and are reborn into the organized aspects of the homosexual community—a process during which they come to identify themselves as homosexuals.

4. *Stabilization*: An individual becomes committed to homosexuality as a way of life.

   Cass (1979), drawing data from clinical interviews with homosexuals, outlined a six-stage model of homosexual identity formation within the framework of interpersonal congruity theory. These stages are differentiated on the basis of individuals' perceptions of their own behavior and the actions that arise as a consequence of this perception. The person is seen to have an active role in the acquisition of a homosexual identity. This model is intended to be applied to both female and male homosexuals. The six stages are summarized below.

1. *Identity confusion*: The person suspects some difference and is able to label behavior as potentially homosexual. The burning question is, "Who am I?" Feelings of personal alienation are paramount.

2. *Identity comparison*: The person has moved from a heterosexual self-portrait and has accepted the possibility that his or her identity may be homosexual. Incongruency is increased, and the individual has a sense of not belonging to society at large as well as to specific subgroups such as family and peers. The summative statement made by persons at this stage is, "I'm different!"

3. *Identity Tolerance*: The person has turned the self-image further away from heterosexual and more toward homosexual. This increased

identity committment is commonly expressed in the statement, "I am probably a homosexual."

4. *Identity Acceptance*: This stage is characterized by continued and increasing contacts with other homosexuals. These contacts allow the person to feel the impact of those features of the subculture that validate and "normalize" homosexual as an identity and a way of life. The homosexual self-image is now accepted, rather than tolerated.

5. *Identity Pride*: The person enters this stage with an awareness of the difference (incongruency) that exists between his or her own concept of self as being totally acceptable as homosexual and society's rejection of this concept. In order to manage this incongruency, the person uses strategies to devalue the importance of heterosexual others to self and to revalue homosexual others more positively. There is a strong sense of pride in being gay, typified in slogans such as "gay is good" and "gay and proud." The combination of anger and pride energizes the person into action against the established institutions and creates an activist.

6. *Identity Synthesis*: The person is now able to integrate a homosexual identity with other aspects of self. With increasing contact with supportive heterosexuals, the person comes to trust them and to view them with greater favor. Unsupportive heterosexuals are further devalued. Feelings of pride are still present but are felt less strongly as the person comes to see no clear dichotomy between the heterosexual and homosexual worlds. Instead of the homosexual identity being seen as *the identity*, it is now given the status of being one aspect of the self. This awareness completes the homosexual identity formation process (Cass 1979, pp. 219–235.).

In addition to the delineation of these various stages, Cass also describes alternative paths of development within each stage. For example, at any stage, the person may not choose to develop further (this choice is called *identity foreclosure*). Individuals may also perceive differentness as desirable or adopt a "special-case strategy" in which they feel their behavior is due to the specialness of the person chosen for sex.

Dialectics and Homosexual Identity Formation

Dialectics is a world view of social and historical change. It involves the theme of a changing individual within a changing society where each is both a cause and consequence of the other (Buss, 1979; Riegel, 1976). The reciprocal interaction between the individual and society will at times include conflict and crisis. It is under these circumstances that new development and change is generated within the individual and society. Dialectics as a method of understanding change is based on the notion of a dialogue "where 'truth' is increasingly approximated through a clash of opinions, and conflict is resolved at higher levels of analysis" (Buss, 1979, p. 76).

In agreement with Minton (1980), I have chosen Habermas's (1979) model of ego development as a conceptual basis for interpreting the homosexual identity process. This theory of ego development integrates the interdependent development of cognitive, linguistic, and social interactive development with affective and motivational development. Habermas provides a general theory through his identification and elaboration of four stages of ego development: (1) symbiotic, (2) egocentric, (3) sociocentric-objectivistic, and (4) universalistic. These stages may not adhere to a strict progression of linear development; phases of regression may occur in the transition from one stage to the next, and foreclosure may halt the development in a stage.

Minton (1980) has reviewed the models of homosexual identity formation considered here. These models are presented in relation to Habermas's stages of development in Table 3.2.

1. *Symbiotic*: This stage lasts through the first year of life, and during this period the child has not as yet developed any consistent perception of its own coporeal substance as a body. The child has no sense of separateness of identity from its social and physical environment.

2. *Egocentric*: Children are able to differentiate between self and environment in this stage. The process of homosexual identity may begin

Table 3.2. *Correlation of Habermas's Stages with Stages of Homosexual Identity*

Habermas's Stages of Ego Development	Stages of Homosexual Identity		
	Plummer	*Dank*	*Cass*
1. Symbiotic (lack of identity)			
2. Egocentric (natural identity)	Sensitization		Identity Confusion
3. Sociocentric-Objectivistic (role identity)	Signification	Identification	Identity Comparison
4. Universalistic	Coming Out	Self-Acceptance	Identity Tolerance
			Identity Acceptance
	Stabilization		Identity Pride
			Identity Synthesis

Adapted from Minton (1980).

to emerge. "This child cannot perceive, understand, and judge situations independently of its own stand-point—it thinks and acts from a body-bound perspective" (Habermas, 1979, p. 101). Minton (1980) relates the initial stages considered by Plummer (1975) and Cass (1979) to the egocentric stage. Awareness of homosexual feelings occurs at an earlier age than understanding the meaning of the label "homosexual." During this phase, experiences of an erotic, emotional, or social nature serve as sources for interpreting oneself as possibly homosexual. The small boy who sees his frail body as incongruent with the cultural definition of masculinity, and who is labeled "sissy," or the girl who feels different because she wants to achieve in the work world and who is labeled "tomboy," may be especially vulnerable to homosexual labeling. These children are at high risk if their parents believe that sissies and tomboys are queer, that is, that cross-sex-mannerisms indicate homosexuality. Language acquisition reflects dominant thought structures and social patterns. Cass (1979) refers to this as "identity confusion." According to Plummer (1975), a heightened self-awareness and assignment of meaning to the experience of homosexuality based on a normative understanding of homosexuality will begin to emerge during the critical midadolescent period of sexual identity. Identity foreclosure may halt development at a neutralization of homoerotic awareness. Goffman's initial learning process of stigmatized persons, in which the normal point of view is learned and it is recognized that the individual is disqualified according to it, corresponds to this phase of ego development.

3. *Sociocentric-objectivistic*: This stage of development begins at about age seven, when generalized expectations of behavior are internalized. It becomes clear to the child that his or her subjective experience may be distinct from objective conditions in their social and physical environment. The child's behavior and identity, previously based on bodily capacity, is transformed into a behavior pattern and identity based on performing a social role. At this point of heightened self-awareness, and awareness of social and linguistic norms regarding homosexual behavior, any homosexual experience is as highly significant for the child as society renders. For both males and females, language perpetuates stereotypes and myths while limiting the options available for self-definition. According to Plummer (1975), this stage of "signification"

> Entails all those processes which lead to a heightened homosexual identity: subjectively, from the nagging inner feeling that one may be 'different' through to a developed homosexual identity, and objectively, from minor homosexual involvements through to the stage known as 'coming out.' For some these changes pass quickly; for others they groan through the life span. (p. 141).

Dank (1971) and Cass (1979) describe the phase of significant and heightened homosexual awareness along similar lines as does Plummer (1975).

4. *Universalistic*: The individual considers the notion that societal norms regarding role expectations and cultural prescriptions regarding need satisfaction are mere conventions that may be critically evaluated. The successful individual will be able to separate norms from principles according to which norms are generated. Values and judgments will emerge from principles, rather than norms. Information control regarding the existence of homosexual feelings may be learned as a means of halting social stigmatization (see Goffman, 1963). According to Habermas, identity will be transformed from role identity to ego identity, such that the person can present himself or herself "credibly in any situation as someone who can satisfy the requirements of consistency even in the face of incompatible role expectations and in the passage through a sequence of contradictory periods of life" (pp. 85, 86). "Coming out" represents the first major exploration of the homosexual community and provides the opportunity to interact with other homosexuals. Some individuals stabilize their homosexual identity by taking pride in having such an identity and at the same time devaluing heterosexual values. Others stabilize where their homosexual identity is no longer *the* identity, but instead is given the status of being merely one aspect of self (Cass, 1979). Such a stable integration requires support from one's interpersonal environment if it is to be maintained. The possibility of foreclosing diverse opportunities and relationships exists whether one is discussing heterosexual or homosexual identities. Clearly, compulsive exclusivity in one's choice of sexual partners represents a negative foreclosure.

Two contemporary British writers have argued that any number of factors may be significant in the development, maintenance, and meaning of a homosexual identity (Hart and Richardson, 1981). These psychologists characterize the construction and maintenance of *any* sexual identity as influenced by the individual's experience of the world, the way in which the meaning of such experiences affects the individual's self-constructs, and also the relationship of sexual identity to the other self-constructs the individual has. Therefore, sexual identification as homosexual, heterosexual, or bisexual has different meanings and significance for each individual and is a dynamic interactive process that allows for change over time.

According to Hart and Richardson (1981), it is important to distinguish between homosexual acts and homosexual identities because many people engage in homosexual acts without identifying as homosexual. For example, the "hustler" or male prostitute often maintains a macho heterosexual identity even though much of his sexual activity is with other men (Reiss, 1967). Also, heterosexually married men who identify as heterosexual have been found to frequent public restrooms for anonymous sex with other men (Humphreys, 1970).

Hart and Richardson's thoughtful and eloquent model of sexual identity development recognizes that "the cognitive awareness of oneself as homosexual, heterosexual or bisexual usually occurs during early adolescence, with the onset of the development of formal abstract thought and the capacity for self-reflection. After this, redefinition of sexual identity may occur at any stage in the life cycle, regardless of sex or marital status" (p. 73).

Hart and Richardson argue that sexual identity is experienced as static and stable inasmuch as an individual assigns sexual identity core construct status in the overall self. When individuals assign such a status to sexual identity, "the possibility of change in sexual identity would represent a serious threat to their experience of social reality in general, and in particular to the fundamental ways in which they construe themselves and others" (p. 91).

HOMOSEXUAL AS BEHAVIORAL ACT VERSUS SOCIAL CATEGORY

Bem's (1976) essay, "Probing the Promise of Androgyny," argued that we should begin to use the terms "homosexual" and "heterosexual" to describe acts rather than persons and should "entertain the possibility that compulsive exclusivity in one's sexual responsiveness, whether homosexual or heterosexual, may be the product of a repressive society which forces us to label ourselves as one or the other" (p. 49).

Pattison and Pattison (1980) also adopt the position, with considerable conviction, that homosexual is a social category rather than an immutable condition. At the same time, they argue that it is immoral and can be altered by ideological conversion. Theirs is a modern-day version of a long-standing belief that guilt and religious ideology work to induce conformity to heterosexual monogamy. In their article, "Ex-Gays," the Pattisons consider the problem of social deviance for the homosexual to be "well-known." They discuss two common "mechanisms" to approaching deviance: (1) changing social attitudes and reducing the definition of deviance, e.g., the women's liberation movement; and (2) reducing the deviant behavior of those considered deviant, e.g., by child abusers' and alcoholics' self-help groups. For the homosexual, patriarchal procreation as religious ideology and heterosexual monogamy as the sexual norm are advocated.

In order to maintain such a religious and scientific conviction, the

Pattisons marshal evidence to assert that homosexual is not a permanent condition:

> Bell and Weinberg's (1978) data indicate that a substantial number of homosexuals can perform heterosexual intercourse without difficulty but that the problem is their gender object choice.... Furthermore, it is not difficult to condition homosexual persons to heterosexual erotica. Feldman & McCulloch (1971) reported that with sophisticated behavioral conditioning they were able to change the arousal reactions in 35 or 43 homosexual men; the subjects' response to male eroticism was eliminated and replaced by a positive response to female eroticism. ... the homosexual returns to the preferred homosexual object choice after satisfactory heterosexual experience (pp. 1557).

There is a critical period during which the conversion to heterosexual is most probable. Troiden (1979) reports that the major period of critical evaluation about assuming a homosexual identity is between 21 and 24 years of age. Masters and Johnson (1979) report sexual treatment data that indicate that homosexuals who successfully change to heterosexuality are usually much younger than 35. A recent review by Bancroft (1974) concludes from available data that there is simply no evidence to support the belief that homosexual or heterosexual identity is an immutable and fundamental aspect of an individual's nature.

The Pattisons assert that reducing the social stigma by challenging society and adopting the gay identity is destructive to the "personal" identity. That is, while arguing that "homosexual" is a reified term, only a behavior or an act, they are also arguing that homosexual behavior might be effectively reduced by adopting the view that one is immature, immoral, and irresponsible as a person for behaving in this maldeveloped way.

Pattison and Pattison argue that the concept of homosexuality is a reification with no basis in reality; that is, the stereotype of deviant behavior becomes the personal stereotype of identity tied to a social label. As Sagarin (1975) observed, "Because [homosexual actors] want to believe they are not worthless (which they are not), and because they confuse the worth of a person with that of a characteristic, they go to the next step and say that gay is good (p. 4).

According to the Pattisons, the gay liberation movement reflects an inherent contradiction, and a gay identity is destructive to personal identity. Moreover, "homosexual tension" is cited as justification for the undesirability of homophile affiliation. Thus, the Pattisons assert that the continued ideological belief in identity via one's deviance reinforces the deviant role behavior. The solution proposed is to halt the homosexual identity formation process and induce the heterosexual identity formation process.

The Pattisons' "therapy" is a clear example of what Bem (1976) invited us to consider, that is, that compulsive exclusivity in one's sexual responsiveness, whether homosexual or heterosexual, may be the product of a repressive society that forces us to label ourselves as one or the other. This consideration involves the relationship between societal attitudes toward homosexual behavior and the process of homosexual identity formation. For example, Plummer (1975) suggests how changes in societal attitudes can affect identity formation:

> The recent signs of change in our sexual mores may well mean that in the distant future, the process of becoming homosexual will be a less significant one and a less painful one. This may result in a decrease of polarization so that individuals come to see themselves as simultaneously occupying homosexual and heterosexual roles, with an accompanying decrease in rigid, exclusive forms of sexuality (p. 153).

The dialectical world view proves to be more illuminating in understanding the process of homosexual identity formation, and its concomitant societal elements. This view considers "homosexuals" and their "movement" to be engaged in constant change resulting from conflict and crisis with the rest of the social system. The emergence of a gay liberation movement marks a transition in sociosexual history, manifested individually as gay and lesbian identities. The form of sexual identity is transient, reflecting the social prejudices that remain as well as the active process of interaction between the individual and society. The difficulty in maintaining an integrated identity that is experienced by persons who desire to express same-gender relations is attributed to the lack of a general social acceptance of such same-gender affections. Hence, in a society liberated of its sexual repression, bisexuality would be regarded as the norm. According to Altman (1971),

> This view would not mean that all persons would behave bisexually.... The non-repressed person recognizes his bisexual potential; he is not some ideal person midway along the Kinsey scale. People would still fall in love and form relationships, and those relationships would be homosexual as well as heterosexual. What would be different (in difference between the two) would vanish, and once this happened, we would lose the feeling of being limited, of having to choose between an exclusively straight or exclusively gay world (p. 94).

Summary of Chapter Three

The relationship between one's sexual nature and one's sexual *identity* is a complex one. Sexual identity is so thoroughly indoctrinated and embedded in primary belief systems that one's true sexual nature is a mystery. The focus of this chapter was the process of coming out as a homosexual. The transformation of existing categories and meanings of sexual identity was explored.

Homosexual identity is conceptualized as a developmental process of the emerging reaction to one's body and the subsequent interactions the maturing individual has with the social world. Emerging reactions to homoeroticism correspond to aspects of language acquisition. The American Psychiatric Association's classification of ego-dystonic homosexuality was reviewed, and further research on critical issues was suggested. An exploratory study was presented that provided reliability data on the initial construction of an inventory of attitudes about homosexuality. Contemporary theories of homosexual identity formation were presented in an examination of the relationship between societal attitudes toward homosexuality and the process of homosexual identity formation. A dialectic world view was engaged to interpret the reciprocal interaction between the individual and society. Cognitive, linguistic, and social interactive development were integrated interdependently with affective and motivational development in Habermas's (1979) theory of ego development. The implications of homosexual as behavioral act and as social category were discussed. It was suggested that compulsive exclusivity in sexual responsiveness, whether homosexual or heterosexual, is the product of a repressive society that forces us to label ourselves as one or the other (see Bem, 1976). A program of religious conversion as a means of mediating change in homosexuals demonstrates that homosexuality is not an immutable condition, but rather a behavioral act. The role of a gay liberation movement in the dialectical process of ego development was contrasted with the role that movement plays according to the religious view, which sees it as an inherent contradiction and destruction of personal identity. The dialectic view proves useful in understanding the difficulty in maintaining an integrated identity experienced by self-labeled homosexuals. In a society liberated from the categories of sexual meaning that now exist, an inclusive sexuality would be the norm.

PART TWO:

PEJORATIVE RESPONDING TO HOMOSEXUAL ACTS AND ACTORS

CHAPTER FOUR

ACQUISITION AND PERFORMANCE OF BEHAVIOR

We must suit our behavior to the occasion.

Cervantes

Believe that life is worth living and your belief will help create the fact.
William James

Sexuality is subject to sociocultural molding to a degree surpassed by few other forms of human behavior.

William Simon
John Gagnon

We begin this chapter by mentioning a fundamental distinction between the acquistion of behavior and the performance of behavior. For example, it has been argued that, at least in early childhood, the acquisition of most behavior learned through role modeling is not gender typed. According to some researchers (e.g., Macoby & Jacklin, 1974), gender typing is entirely the result of direct reinforcement for gender stereotyped behavior. Thus a child may learn a behavior and have it stored in memory even before a gender schema has developed, but not establish it as gender role behavior until the proper and sufficient conditions are present to produce the behavior.

The distinction between acquisition and performance promotes a situational specificity of behavior, involving the interaction between the person and the situation. The overall psychological atmosphere of institutions, for example, has been assessed by obtaining the perceptions of those who inhabit these settings (Moos, 1973), and it has been suggested that situations can also be characterized in terms of the behaviors they tend to elicit from the average person (Frederiksen, 1973). Block (1971) utilizes an "Environmental Q-Sort" to characterize an individual's past or historical environment. Craik (1976), in a study of the person-situation interaction, reports relationships between personality variables and the physical environment.

In an attempt to develop a language of description that could be used to characterize both persons and situations, Bem and Funder (1978) developed a "template matching technique." In this technique, situations are characterized as sets of template behavior pairs, each template being a personality description of an idealized "type" of person expected to behave in a specified way in that setting. The probability that a particular person will behave in a particular way in a particular situation is then postulated to be a monotonically increasing function of the match or similarity between that person's characteristics and the template associated with the corresponding behavior.

When people perform the behaviors they were shown or taught to perform, they might be said to be *modeling* their behavior after another. An operational definition of modeling might be the actual performance by the subject of an act concretely or symbolically similar to that previously exhibited by a model (Bronfenbrenner, 1970). In line with this two-phase process, then, we move now to a definition of modeling, observational learning, and reinforcement. In agreement with Bandura (1967), I will treat the terms "identification," "imitation," and "observational learning" as synonyms.

Much of the research bearing on the modeling process demonstrates that patterns of behavior are rapidly acquired in large segments or in their entirety, when a model is provided. In our daily experiences, we have seen the pervasiveness of this form of learning in childrens' play activities. Parents are surprised and often embarrassed to witness their child imitating, with great detail and accuracy, their voice, walk, and mannerisms.

One set of experiments was designed primarily to determine the extent to which aggression can be transmitted to children through exposure to aggressive adult models (Bandura, Ross, & Ross, 1961). One group of children observed an aggressive model, Bandura explains, who exhibited relatively novel forms of physical and verbal aggression toward a large inflated plastic doll; a second group that viewed the same model behaving in a very subdued and inhibited way expressed significantly less aggression.

There are three conditions affecting the modeling process: (1) characteristics of the individual, (2) characteristics of the stimulus acts, and (3) characteristics of the model. The major point to be made concerning characteristics of the subject concerns motivation. An obvious motivator is the subject's prior history of reinforcement for modeling behavior. Mischel and Grusec (1966) take a similar position, stating that the reinforcement history of the child, and the child's observations of the reinforcements delivered to models, will determine which actions a child selects out of its behavioral repertoire for performance. Another strong determinant of motivation may be found when the behavior exhibited is a salient feature in the actions of a group of which the child already is or aspires to be a member. The child will tend to adopt the patterns of behavior that are prominently engaged in by its family, its classmates, the neighborhood gang, and other groups of children and adults with whom it associates (Bronfenbrenner, 1970).

The second condition affecting the modeling process is the characteristics of the stimulus act. The major factor is the consequence of the exhibited behavior. If the model is praised or rewarded, the likelihood that the subject will imitate that behavior when in a similar situation is increased.

The third and final condition is the characteristics of the model. According to Bronfenbrenner (1970), the potency of the model increases with the extent to which the model is perceived by the subject as possessing a high degree of competence, status, and control over resources. This has been demonstrated by Bandura, Ross, and Ross (1963) in their experiment with two adult models whom they called the controller and the consumer. The controller, providing obvious control over resources by rewarding the consumer, proved to be much more powerful as a model than his low-status counterpart.

Another factor increasing the inductive power of the model is the degree of nurturance or reward exhibited by the model. Empirical support for the nurturant hypothesis was demonstrated experimentally by varying the quality of the rewarding interaction between a female model and nursery school children (Bandura & Huston, 1961). With one group of children the model was warm and nurturant, while a second group of children was given a nonnurturant model. After these experimental interactions the children engaged in game playing with the model. Measures of imitative responses performed by the children were taken. The results were in agreement with the nurturant hypothesis. Children not only displayed more imitative behavior after the nurturant interaction with the model, they showed an increased level of nonimitative verbalization.

The effectiveness of the model also increases with the degree to which the subjects perceive the model as similar to themselves. The research in this category has been extensive (Bronfenbrenner, 1970; Kohlberg, 1966).

The properties affecting the modeling process, particularly regarding sex typed behaviors, are: (1) characteristics of the child, such as age, that may determine the ability of the child to perceive or perform the behavior being modeling (motivation is affecting in that the prior reinforcement history of the subject serves as a great motivator; (2) distinctions of the stimulus act, especially the consequent of exhibited behavior; and (3) impact of certain pecularities of the model, including perceived power, nurturance, and similarity to subject, on the model's potency to induce imitative behavior.

The behaviors acquired through the modeling process are the major characteristics of the individual that interact with the reinforcement contingencies of the situation to determine behavior. For example, the social matrix provides situations in which homosexuals or homosexuality are considered deviant. If we formalize a procedure we use in everyday life, we may be able to assess the interaction between a person's learning and performance in a particular situation. Consider, for example, how we might answer the question, "Should Joe be openly gay when he attends Harvard?" This is a question about person-situation interaction. Joe needs to know how his own characteristic of being homosexual will mesh or interact with Harvard's characteristics. One way we can assist Joe in this decision is to describe Harvard in terms of how several hypothetical "ideal" types of persons function in that environment. "Students who are not stereotypically homosexual, who feel positive about their homosexuality, and who disclose it only after they get to know the person receiving this intimate information do tend to get above-average grades and have a lot of positive interaction with other individuals. However, those who see sexual overtones in most situations, who are stereotypically homosexual, and who feel negatively about their homoeroticism and disclose it indiscriminately at Harvard may get average grades and have a lot of conflict with faculty and other individuals." Now all Joe has to do to predict his success at Harvard is to match his own characteristics with the set of "templates" we have provided. Thus, we are better able to predict Joe's outcome by the fact that we have discribed the Harvard environment in precisely the same language system we would use to characterize Joe himself. In terms of the modeling process and behavioral acquisition and performance, this person-situation language system provides an adequate description of behavioral selection. It also allows for a sensitive account of one's behavioral repertoire.

We turn now to a clarification of the social processes related to one's goals of being correct, staying in the good graces of other people by living up to their expectations, and maximizing one's values.

THE PRESENCE OF OTHERS

The impact of the presence of others on individuals has been a central issue in social psychology since its beginning. Three general approaches have emerged to deal with these issues. The work of Asch (1952) on the study of social influences on judgments characterizes the first of these research traditions. The second research tradition focuses on group dynamics or the social influences arising from small-group interaction, e.g., Cartwright and Zander's *Group Dynamics* (1953). The study of social influences arising from persuasive communications composes the third research tradition, eg., Hovland, Janis, and Kelley's *Communication and Persuasion* (1953).

The development of social influence studies has made it necessary to make qualitative distinctions among types of influence. In general, *conformity* refers to a change in a person's behavior or opinions as a result of real or imagined pressure from a person or a group of people. For cxample, if I were in a situation in which I really loved someone of my own gender, but when I told my parents about it they told me to pack up and get out, I might: (1) decide to stay home, acquire a public girl friend, and keep my same-sex love private; or (2) decide to stay at home, denounce my same-sex love and value opposite-sex love, and attempt to develop a rigid hetero-sexual orientation both publicly and privately. If I choose the first option, I have changed my behavior in accordance with the social pressures around me—a type of conformity—but the change is a situational agreement or a compliance with the social norms set by someone who can control my destiny. On the other hand, the second choice represents a more permanent internalization of the conformance. This example elucidates two aspects of social influence. In one case, an individual is motivated by rewards and punishments or by a need to know how to behave in an unfamiliar setting. On the other hand, if the conformity is relatively permanent, the individual may have internalized it. In the first alternative, the mode of behavior appears to be motivated by a desire to gain reward or avoid punishment. Typically this conforming behavior is as long-lived as is the promise of the reward or the threat of the punishment. Public and private behavior and opinion will be discrepant. In the second alternative, the reward for the belief or behavior is apparently intrinsic. Thus, the value or belief accepted becomes internalized; it becomes a part of the individual's own belief system. This differentiation of reinforcement and permanence has been used to distinguish between types of public con-formity and private acceptance.

Thus, social influence may have qualitatively different kinds of change. The analysis of compliant behavior in the example above demonstrates a general finding in this field; that is, under some conditions social influence may result in public conformity, characterized by super-ficial changes on a verbal or overt level without accompanying changes in belief. In other situations it may result in private acceptance, a change that is more general, more durable, more integrated with the person's own values (Festinger, 1964). Still other investigators have found a motivational basis for changes due to social influence. That is, under some conditions influence may be primarily informational, with conformity resulting from utilizing a person or group as a source of valid information. Deutsch and Gerard (1955) found that the need for credible information motivated people to conform; in addition, they found that under some conditions a person may conform in order to meet the positive expectations of the influencing person or group.

A more useful and conceptually distinct classification of social influence includes three kinds of responses to social influence: compliance, identification, and internalization (Kelman, 1961). In compliance, a person agrees to behave in a particular way in order to gain reward or avoid punishment. The important component in compliance is the power of the influencer to parcel out rewards for compliance and punishment for noncompliance. It is important to note that the complying individual adopts the induced behavior not from believing in its content but because it is instrumental in the production of a satisfying social effect. In this way, the behavior should be observed only when the influencing agent is present.

Identification is the social process through which an individual adopts behavior or patterns of behavior from another person or group as a way of establishing or maintaining a desired relationship with that person or group. The relationship is self-defining in that it is a role relationship that forms a part of the individual's self-image.

Identification is similar to compliance in that the behavior adopted is not intrinsically rewarding. Identification is unlike compliance in that the individual actually believes in the behavior or role, and private behavior is congruent with public behavior. The manifestation of the behavior composing the self-defining role relationship will depend on the situational expectations for the individual's own role performance. In other words, the behaviors I exhibit with my mother may be different than those exhibited when I am with my father, because mother and father prime different self-defining role relationship scripts for me. Opinions or behavior adopted through identification are strongly tied to their external source and depend on social support. Thus, they tend to remain isolated from the individual's value system.

In the process of identification, an individual desires to be like another person. Continuous direct reward and punishment may not be necessary. For example, suppose you identify with your older brother because you like him and want to be like him—not necessarily in order to obtain a reward or avoid a punishment, as in compliance. As you grow up, you hear your brother announce his position against homosexuality on several occasions, and this position becomes a part of your own self-image in relation to him—neither because you thought it out and it seemed right to you nor because your older brother rewarded you for adopting or threatened you for not adopting this position. If your opinion of the person identified with changes, so can the beliefs you previously shared with this person. They can also change if a person or group of people who are more important to you, or more attractive to you, professes a different set of beliefs.

The process of identification, when delineated from compliance, reveals a reinforcement differentiation that may be misleading. Specifically, wanting to be like another person may contain some reward through social comparison. The important component here is the attractiveness of the person with whom the individual identifies. The esteem gained by the social comparison may be reduced, however, by endorsing incompatible beliefs. The process of identification may not be based entirely on direct rewards and punishments, but when the characteristics of the behavior, e.g., homosexual acts, do not mesh with the characteristics of the model, e.g., antihomosexual beliefs, the positiveness of the identification is reduced. By this process, self-labeled homosexuals may employ a strategy of devaluing heterosexual models in order to halt this process of social influence and thus defend their self-esteem.

A third process of social influence further develops our understanding of the presence of others. Internalization is the most permanent response to social influence. Motivated by the desire to be right, the individual seeks credible information and integrates this information into his or her own value system. Thus, the reward for the internalized belief is *intrinsic*. It is the content of the induced behavior and its relation to the person's value system that is satisfying. The manifestation of internalized values does not depend on the presence of the influencer, as in compliance, or on the activation of the relevant social role, as in identification. Rather, behavior depends on the extent to which the underlying values have been made relevant by the issues under consideration.

These three social processes may be distinguished by identifying the influencing agent's source of power and by the conditions required to change the induced response. For example, the influencer has power in inducing compliance if he or she has control over the means by which an individual might attain a goal. In identification, the influencer's power lies in his or her attractiveness. In internalization, the credibility of the influencer is that person's source of power.

The conditions under which some change may occur in the induced response further distinguish the three processes. In compliance, there must be a change in the individual's perception of conditions for social rewards before a behavioral change will occur. Similarly, altering identification requires changed perceptions of conditions for satisfying self-defining

relationships. In internalization, one must change the individual's perception of the conditions for value maximization to induce a change in the
internalized behavior. In other words, because internalized behavior is
imbedded in the person's value system rather than in the external demands
of a specific setting (compliance) or in expectations defining a specific role
(identification), the response must no longer be viewed as the best path
toward the maximization of the individual's values before change will
occur. Thus, the self-image may be changed by reorganizing its internal
structure; the process of values clarification and reorganization thus
induces change vis-à-vis the process of internalization. The self-image may
also be changed through identification by reshaping the social relationships
in which this image is anchored.

Experimental Demonstrations of Social Influence

If people do not conform to the norms of a group, one of the effects
is that they are usually not held in high esteem, at the time, by those people
to whose demands they refuse to conform. This observation was
demonstrated in an experiment by Schachter (1951) in which several
groups of students participated. Each member was given the case history of
a juvenile delinquent. After reading the case, each group was asked to
discuss it and to suggest a treatment for the delinquent on a scale that
ranged from "very lenient treatment," on one end, to "very hard
treatment," on the other. A typical group consisted of about nine
participants, six of whom were real subjects and three of whom were paid
confederates of the experimenter. The confederates took turns playing one
of three roles that they had rehearsed in advance: (1) the *model* person, who
took a position that conformed to the average position of the real subjects;
(2) the *deviate*, who took a position diametrically opposed to the general
orientation of the group; and (3) the *slider*, whose initial position was
similar to the deviate's but who, in the course of discussion, gradually "slid"
into a model, conforming position.

The results clearly showed that the person who was liked most was
the person who conformed to the group norm: the model person. The
deviate was liked least. Thus, these data indicate that the "establishment"
or model group tends to like conformists better than nonconformists.

Further demonstration of the presence of others as an external
pressure to comply was conducted by Asch (1956). Telling his volunteers
that his experiment was on perceptual judgment, he had five participants
enter a room at the same time. The experimenter showed all participants a
straight line (line X, below). Simultaneously, he showed three other lines
for comparison (lines, A, B, and C). Then he asked each participant to judge

which of the three lines was closest in length to line X. The four participants he asked first, however, were confederates whom he had hired to say line A was closest in length to line X. Then he asked the only "real" participant. When faced with a majority of their fellow students agreeing on the same incorrect responses in a series of twelve judgments, approximately three-quarters of the subjects conformed at least once by responding incorrectly. An average of 35% of the overall responses conformed to the incorrect judgments rendered by Asch's accomplices. In short, the public behavior exhibited by the subjects in the Asch experiment kept them in the good graces of their fellow students and kept them "right."

X   A B C

We are left to wonder, however, if public and private behavior correspond. I mean, was it really the presence of others that made these subjects conform? Suppose we repeated the experiment, but did not require the subjects to make their judgments in the presence of others. This has been tested on several occasions, and the results are consistent: the greater the privacy, the less the conformity (Aronson, 1980).

Another question raised by the conformity paradigm is as follows: What if another participant has given the correct response? For example, in terms of disclosing one's homosexual love relationship to one's siblings, is it easier to do so if another sibling has already done so? Asch (1951) also demonstrated that the presence of a fellow dissenter dramatically reduces the subjects' conformity. It may be easier, then, to disclose one's sexual preference if in the presence of another person of your same persuasion. Dank (1971) found that same-sex situations such as branches of the armed services or the presence of a self-defined homosexual allow one to more easily define oneself as homosexual. The presence of others is an important consideration in establishing a hierarchy of anxiety-producing stimulus-object characteristics of pejorative responding.

The impact of the presence of others in a situation is further demonstrated by some of the demographic correlates of "homophobia." Demographic studies show that those who are more negative in their attitudes toward homosexuality are more likely to live in a rural area than in an urban area (Levitt & Klassen, 1974). This indicates that the values of certain subcultures within the United States, such as those in mountain regions of the Southeast, are especially effective in inducing conformity.

SOME EFFECTS OF GUILT ON COMPLIANCE

Religiosity has been found to be an important ideological correlate of pejorative responding to homosexual acts and actors. The more traditional one is about religious doctrine and worship, the more antigay one is. Guilt, a feeling that is closely related to religiosity and the concept of sin, is also reported more frequently by individuals who espouse negative beliefs and fears of homosexual acts and actors. These findings raise some important questions about the effects of guilt on compliance.

It has become clear from much of the research stemming from dissonance theory (e.g., Brehm & Cohen, 1962; Carlsmith, Collins, & Helmreich, 1966; Festinger & Carlsmith, 1959) that in order to get maximal attitude change following compliance, it is important to have as little pressure for compliance as is consistent with obtaining the compliance. An interesting addition to this body of literature is a study by Carlsmith and Gross (1971), "Some Effects of Guilt on Compliance." This study provides convincing evidence that a very powerful technique for obtaining compliance is to first induce people to do something that they are convinced will harm another person. Guilt arising from this action is considered the mediating factor in producing the compliance, and this compliance need not be to the person who was hurt. The fact that the compliance need not be to the person who is responsible for initiating the guilt suggests that an interpretation based on bolstering the subject's self-image may be the most productive. All of the subjects in these experiments had been asked to comply by engaging in some behavior that was of fairly high social desirability—that is, helping another person gather names for a petition. Because of this, compliance is likely to give subjects positive information about themselves.

People can thus be manipulated to conform to heterosexuality by beliefs about the harmfulness of homosexuality. *The propagation of beliefs that say homosexuals are to be feared and are harmful to society, to their mothers, or to other people are among the most sinister and powerful of social controls.* An Opinion Research Center poll (1966) showed that more than 67% of the people contacted viewed homosexuality as "detrimental to society." The Harris Survey has been asking large cross sections of U.S. households whether they feel homosexuals (and other groups) do more harm than good to the country. In 1965, homosexuals were placed third (behind communists and atheists), with 82% of the males and 58% of the females thinking they were primarily a danger to the country. Levitt and Klassen

(1973) similarly found that 49% of their sample of U.S. adults agreed that "homosexuality is a social corruption which can cause the downfall of a civilization" (p. 32).

THE EXPERIENCE AND EXPRESSION OF EMOTION

We turn now to a discussion of the experience and expression of emotion. The theoretical and empirical literature on emotion reflects two general views. The first is that emotion is the product of nonemotional processes, usually a synthesis of cognitive and autonomic motor reactions. The second is that emotion is a real product of specialized biological mechanisms that are part of our evolutionary history. The synthetic positions view emotion as the product of social learning and are built on the rationalist conceptions of humans (James, 1884; Cofer, 1972; Schachter and Singer, 1962). The realist positions view emotions as a primary fact of experience and are built on an animal or impulse conception of humans (Izard, 1977; Plutchik, 1962, 1980; Tomkins, 1962, 1980).

The integration of emotion and cognition is observed in people's reactions to homosexual acts and actors. Obviously, both feeling and thinking influence the responses of preference or prejudice. These emotions are nested and integrated in meaning systems (Mandler, 1975). An emotion generator appears responsible for memory and action. Studies of memory and mood (Bower, 1981) demonstrate an emotion generator, with emotion tied to specific cognitive entities.

Some researchers conceptualize the affect-cognition mechanism as two parallel, sequentially staged processing systems that act as feedback systems for regulating emotion and for controlling noxious settings (see Leventhal, 1981). The separation of the two processes reflects the stage of emotion theory building more than it reflects any real independence. "Some type of perceptual process is always active along with—if not prior to—emotion," notes Leventhal (1980). Our understanding of emotion may improve from Leventhal's requirements for a perceptual-motor theory of emotion:

1. The system needs a primary mechanism to account for differences in the quality of emotional experiences. This primary mechanism should have the following secondary mechanisms:

    a. Operation early in life to allow for the perception of similarity and difference in emotional meaning across settings. In this way the growing child can learn to use social labels to identify emotional states.

   b. Selective responses to situational stimuli so that emotional feelings
   or meanings (e.g., fear, anger, joy) are appropriate to the adaptive
   needs of the setting.

   c. Some degree of independence from learned or acquired emotional
   reactions. This is essential to allow for change in acquired feelings
   and the capacity to experience emotion in situations that would
   seem impossible given the individual's history. An example would
   be a dying cancer patient who experiences joy when treatment
   reduces pain and immobility for even just a few weeks. Schachter
   and others . . . suggested that emotional qualities were determined
   by cognition because of the persistent failure to locate a primary
   mechanism in the autonomic system. There is no need to review
   once again the controversy surrounding autonomic differentiation.
   But it is important to recognize that people on both sides, Jamesians
   and Schachterians, assumed that the experience and behavioral
   display of turbulent emotions was impossible in the absence of
   autonomic activity. If this assumption is false, the search for a
   primary emotional mechanism need not be confined to the
   autonomic motor system. This does not mean, of course, that
   autonomic activity does not enter into emotional experience.

2. The system needs to contain a memory mechanism to account for the
connection of emotional experience and behaviors to perceptions and
to allow for the development of new affective ties to perceptions. More
specifically, this memory mechanism should:

   a. Combine subjective feelings and primary response components
   with perceptions of situations and actions (both autonomic and
   instrumental), so as to form emotional memory schemas.

   b. Allow for the blending of primary emotional meanings to form new
   and more complex emotional states.

   c. Be able to function automatically without the intervention of
   complex, intellectual evaluation.

3. The system must contain a mechanism for processing the abstract and
volitional aspect of emotion. This includes two types of processing:

   a. The abstract representations of emotional situations and experiences so we can think about, discuss, and evaluate their meaning.

   b. The voluntary control of the instrumental, expressive, and autonomic components of emotional responding.

4. The system must have an attentional mechanism to describe the effects

of changing the contents of consciousness on emotional processing and experience (p. 3).

Leventhal's theory of emotion is promising because it considers emotion as varying in position within self-regulating systems. The framework for relating emotion and cognition considers two systems underlying the observed behaviors.

> The behavioral mechanism consists of two simultaneously active, parallel systems, one cognitive, the other emotional. Each of these systems is made up of two stages, an initial perceptual or representational stage and a second action-planning or coping stage (Leventhal, 1970). The perceptual stage takes the form of a perception and an abstract representation of the objective system, and a feeling representation and its related expressive and autonomic reactions that is created in the emotional system. The action-planning or coping stage consists of response alternatives and their anticipated outcomes. The two systems, emotional and objective, function as self-regulating feedback mechanisms, one designed to control feelings, the other to control the objective features of these threatening situations. Because the two stages draw upon a common behavioral mechanism, the output of either system can be expected to appear in a sequence determined by features of the situation and the person (p. 3).

Lesbian Mother Studies

The beliefs and fears modeled by parents regarding homosexual acts and actors may be a major source of homosexual oppression, stereotyping, and prejudice. In order to better understand the acquisition of sex typed behaviors in children of lesbian mothers, Nungesser (1980) examined lesbian lifestyles and values through a review of several descriptive studies of lesbian mothers. In one of the studies reviewed, Bryant (1975) undertook to examine the characteristics of lesbian mothers as a population and to explore how they interact with their children and with society. She based her study on a forty-eight-item self-administered questionnaire. Bryant's sample consisted of 185 women who considered themselves to be lesbian and who had raised or were then raising children. Respondents in this study were generally less religious, better educated, more often professionally employed, and more involved with the women's movement than was the general female population. As Bryant points out:

> The findings of this study do not support the commonly held beliefs about lesbian mothers. Most respondents have been heterosexually

married and have male friends in the lives of their children. The majority of the respondents, furthermore, have no preference as to the sexuality of their children and believe it is their right to choose without pressure. The incidence of lesbian, gay or bisexual children in this sample is no larger than in the general population. The rewards of being a lesbian mother centered around no longer being in an oppressive marriage, developing more independence and pride in themselves than before, and being able to thereby share more love, openness, and affection with their children. The major concerns of this sample of lesbian mothers are coping with the economic hardships and having their children taken away. The difficulties in being a lesbian mother do not appear to be inherent in the role, but rather come from society's attitudes and discriminatory behavior (p. ii).

Bryant's study is particularly important because it addresses issues to which the courts frequently refer. Responding to the question of the child's sexuality, the mothers in Bryant's study supported overwhelmingly their children's right to make their own decision, free from persuasion. Bryant writes than 80% of the children had male role models in their lives. The majority of the children in Bryant's study were not conscious of society's prejudice against their mothers. Those children who were aware supported their mothers and rejected society's negative judgment.

The mothers often express worry that society's attitudes would make it difficult for their children to cope. In some cases, children are embarrassed for their friends or the general public to know their mother is a lesbian, but the majority of the children combine any embarrassment or initial uncomfortableness with an understanding that society has created the prejudice; that it is society, and not their mothers, that should re-examine its position (p. 73).

Research in the medical anthropology tradition does not support the usual concerns raised in family courts, which typically regard the homosexual as an unfit parent (Hotvedt & Mandel, 1982). These scientists have gathered data from two matched nonclinical samples of children of lesbian mothers and heterosexual single mothers. The findings were clear: "No evidence of gender identity conflict, poor peer relationships, or neglect was seen" (p. 285).

According to one group of researchers, adult lesbian relationships are best understood in light of similarities between the values and experiences of lesbians and those of *all* women. For example, Peplan and Amaro (1982) note that "childhood socialization experiences of girls in this culture often emphasize emotional expressiveness and love as central to close relationships, and these themes can be seen in the adult relationships of both lesbians and heterosexuals." The issues of dependency and power in intimate relationships are relevant to the potency of lesbian mothers as role models. Patterns of power and dependency may be shaped by the impact of children on lesbian relationships as well as heterosexual relationships. Other research suggests that single motherhood among both lesbians and heterosexuals gives rise to a single adaptive system that is unified by the salience of motherhood as a central organizing force (Lewin & Lyons, 1982).

It may be useful to apply the theoretical concepts of modeling and androgyny to the lesbian parenting situation in particular. Earlier, in the discussion of some of the characteristics of the subject, stimulus act, and model that enhance the potency of the modeling process, it was mentioned that the subject will be more motivated if the behavior exhibited by a model is a salient feature in the actions of a group of which the subject is or aspires to be a member. For example, we might find independence as the behavior exhibited and a lesbian feminist organization as the group to which the child aspires to belong. The possibility that sexuality will be modeled seems less likely than that feminism will.

The second condition affecting the modeling process is the characteristic of the stimulus act. The most important factor here is the consequence of the exhibited behavior. What would the consequence of this independent self-reliant behavior be for the model? In terms of reinforcement, it was apparently intrinsically rewarding to challenge male supremacy. Independence is also a socially valued trait. For women, however, it may also serve, in some situations, as an adversive social reinforcer.

The potency of the model is another important condition affecting the modeling process. The controller-consumer experiment by Bandura, Ross, and Ross (1963) cited earlier demonstrated that the model's degree of competence, status, and control over resources, as perceived by the subject, affected the process. It would seem, then, that the independent status of the lesbian mother would greatly enhance her potency as a model. Her lack of power in society would be a minor factor, as most of the children in the studies reviewed were either unaware of society's negative judgment or felt that it was society, rather than the mother, who had the erroneous attitude. The nurturant hypothesis discussed above also has relevance here. Women in general are socialized to be nurturant, and being a lesbian does not change that: Most lesbians were reared as nurturers and are very supportive of one another in matters concerning their lesbianism and status in society as women. This factor implies that women may be generally more powerful models than men are socialized to be. The female models in a child's life (particularly the child of a lesbian mother) would have a very strong impact on the child's socialization.

Finally, the ability of a model to induce imitative behavior is increased if the model is seen as similar to the subject. For example, a 4-year-old male may not "identify" with a female model out of an awareness of anatomical dissimilarity. Conversely, if the child is a female, she may identify with the female models to a higher degree.

BRAINWASHING WITH GOD'S BLESSING

The arousal of guilt was a major technique of brainwashing used by the Chinese Communists in the Korean Conflict. Individuals were encouraged to confess all their misdeeds, ranging from very small ones to extremely large ones. The individual was first induced to confess something small and then led to larger and larger confessions. Some prisoners were eventually pouring out their innermost secrets and were even confessing fantasies they had. Apparently, this procedure aroused an enormous amount of guilt, making it relatively easy for the Communists to elicit compliance. In a few cases, basic changes were evoked in an individual's views of the world.

Pattison and Pattison (1980) have recently reported a study relevant to this discussion. In their shockingly straightforward "Ex-Gays: Religiously Mediated Change in Homosexuals," these authors evaluated eleven white men claimed to have changed sexual orientation from exclusive homosexuality through participation in a pentecostal church fellowship. The term "ex-gay" was selected by the church to denote an ideological position in opposition to "gay liberation."

Two brainwashing strategies are demonstrated in their study. The first strategy is to reach maximal attitude change following compliance by having as little pressure for compliance as is consistent with obtaining the compliance; that is, they did not overdo it. When the homosexuals came to church, they were welcomed and presented with the invitation to commit their lives to Christ. No mention was made of changing their sexuality. It was only during later church fellowships that they came to believe that they were "psychologically immature and had poor interpersonal relationships." The homosexuals were "gently" exposed to an ideological expectational set demanding heterosexual growth in personal and interpersonal areas.

The second strategy used in this ideological conversion was the use of guilt. That these subjects were vulnerable to this strategy is evident in the following statement:

> Beliefs and values appear to play a significant role in changing sexual orientation. Our subjects were very religious and active in

religious practice. They believed that the practice of homosexuality was immoral. However, they believed that the condition of homosexuality was an emotional problem due to psychological maldevelopment. All regretted having been homosexual, and all had considered giving it up. They wanted to change to heterosexuality as a religious responsibility (p. 1558).

Pattison and Pattison go on to describe the processes involved in this self-blame model of "deviancy and rehabilitation":

They reduced the social deviancy of homosexuality by stating that homosexuality is only a behavior and not the identity of the person. Therefore, they shared a common concern to reduce the social hostility and social rejection of persons just because they were homosexual. In practice, our subjects were received into church fellowship as homosexuals. They did not accept homosexuality. . . . they . . . reduced deviancy through personally changing the deviant condition (p. 1561).

These men might have resisted mind control if they had carefully examined the inner pressure to be bonded to other people, the power of group norms to influence behavior, and the force of social rewards such as smiles, praise, and a gentle touch. Two social psychologists have recently charted the abilities and social commitment necessary to critically evaluate ideas, institutions, and our own behavior so that we can perceive options beyond those provided by convenient dogma and ostensibly inescapable circumstances. Anderson and Zimbardo (1980) give pragmatic advice interwoven with a conceptual analysis. For example, homosexuals who are under pressure to conform might:

1. Be willing to look foolish now and then, to accept being "different" as being "special" rather than being inferior.

2. Develop a concrete sense of self-worth, a sense of who they are, what they are interested in, and where their competencies lie, quite apart from the values, interests, and judgments of others.

3. No matter what the relationship, avoid getting sucked into unwanted confessions that may later be used against them.

4. Avoid making decisions when under stress, particularly in the presence of the person who has triggered the emotional reaction.

5. Learn to confront their frustrations and fears so as to avoid guilt feelings providing impetus for personal change. Keep from getting into situations where they feel indebted to other people.

6. Be sensitive to—and avoid—situations and people that put them on the spot, making them feel different, awkward, or inadequate.

SUMMARY OF CHAPTER FOUR

The acquisition of behavior was explored in this chapter. Models provide the developing child with a variety of behaviors and potentialities. The performance of those learned behaviors and subsequent identity formations depends largely on social influences. Some experimental demonstrations of social influence report the impact of group norm on conformity. Indeed, the very fact that "someone is watching you" is sufficient to induce compliance. Furthermore, individuals' assessments of their observers' social value judgments reveal the immediate demographic and historical context.

Power relations and preconditions to conformity were clarified. Goal attainment and the attractiveness and credibility of the influencer are sources of power. The processes of compliance, identification, and internalization were delineated. Implications for attitude change were discussed. Some effects of guilt on compliance were observed in the belief that homosexuals are harmful to their mothers, society, and so on.

The experience and expression of emotion includes a synthesis of cognitive and autonomic motor reactions. The impulse model views emotions are evolutionary facts. Leventhal's perceptual motor theory of emotion was presented as a model for understanding the dialectics of self-regulation systems.

Theoretical concepts of modeling were applied to the lesbian parenting situation. The children of lesbian mothers are likely to be highly adaptive, conscious persons. The characteristics of the lesbian model, such as control over resources, independence, nurturance, and similarity to the subject, determine her effectiveness.

An example of extreme special influence demonstrated the use of brainwashing techniques in a church fellowship. Homosexuals were "gently" exposed to an ideological expectational set demanding heterosexual growth in personal and interpersonal areas. These men felt guilty and wished to change their sexual preference. They reduced their deviancy by personally changing the deviant condition. Several tips for critically evaluating ideas, institutions, and our own behavior were presented: With certain abilities and social commitments we can perceive options beyond those provided by convenient dogma and supposedly inescapable situations.

CHAPTER FIVE

PREJUDICE

Knowledge is an ultimate enemy of prejudice. The restriction of knowledge, therefore—whether consciously so intended or not—is an agent of prejudice.

William Paul

For they conquer who believe they can.

Virgil

The struggle over definitions, which are actually struggles of power as to who should define . . . are going on all the time within the terms laid down by those who wield the power to define, and hence the power to control and oppress.

Jeffrey Weeks

In *The Nature of Prejudice* (1958), Gordon Allport observes that prejudice is a combination of unfounded judgment and an accompanying feeling tone. Allport defines prejudice as "an aversive or hostile attitude towards a person who belongs to a group, simply because he belongs to a group, and is therefore presumed to have the objectionable qualities ascribed to the group" (p. 12).

The content of prejudice against homosexuality is presumably based on a specific kind of act. However, the historical processes of persecution, ostracism, and prejudice extend beyond the act to the actor. Individual lives are controlled by the criminal justice system and by social sanction. Not only are specific acts and behaviors affected, the human dignity of the actors is destroyed. The deviant becomes a thing, not a person. In the words of Henry Steele Commager (1954), "It is becoming increasingly clear that it is respect for the dignity of the individual that most sharply differentiates democratic from totalitarian systems. Granted this basic principle, it follows that any conduct of the state that impairs the dignity of man is dangerous" (p. 5).

Prejudice against homosexual actors may thus be characterized by a set of unfounded negative beliefs and stereotypes about "the homosexual." These beliefs and stereotypes create and maintain the oppression of the group or caste labeled "homosexual." Each society socializes persons into gender role identities that are syntonic to the functions of that society, and gender role behavior that is not in agreement may be labeled deviant. The result is the creation of a social caste of deviant. *The role of homosexual deviant is not transhistorical, but evidence of real history.*

The sources of prejudice against homosexuals have been listed by Weinberg (1972). They are: (1) the Judeo-Christian religious taboo on homosexuality, (2) the secret fear of being homosexual, (3) repressed envy of perceived homosexual ease in life, (4) the idea that homosexuality is a threat to societal and familial values, and (5) the reawakening by homosexuals, as persons without children, of fears of death. Weinberg used the term "homophobia" to describe prejudice against homosexuals because he considered the fear component to be the most significant. According to Weinberg, the fear mediated prejudice and hostility. Because Weinberg did not elaborate on prejudice, but on phobia, his ideas will be discussed again in the next section on fears and phobias. In this section we consider the support for the sources of prejudice he listed. The following discussion reports data confirming sources 1 and 4 and clarifies problems with source 2. There are no data supporting sources 3 and 5.

Prejudice and Authoritarianism

There is some evidence to support the notion that there are individual differences in a general tendency or predisposition toward being prejudiced. Theodor Adorno and his associates refer to these individuals as "authoritarian personalities." The authoritarian personality tends to have rigid beliefs, to possess "conventional" values, to be intolerant of personal weakness and weakness in others, to be highly punitive and suspicious, and to be respectful of authority to an unusual degree. The instrument developed to determine authoritarianism is called the *F* scale. A major finding of studies using the *F* scale is that people who are high on authoritarianism do not simply dislike Jews or dislike blacks but, rather, show a consistently high degree of prejudice against all minority groups.

Negative beliefs about and fears toward homosexual acts and actors have been reliably indicated by a set of beliefs and attitudes that support the traditional family ideology, i.e., dominant father, submissive mother, and obedient children (Morin & Wallace, 1976). It is interesting to note that the following item measures authoritarianism on the *F* scale: "Obedience and respect for authority are the most important virtues children should learn." Moreover, the families of the subjects whose prejudices were studied with the *F* scale, especially those of the male subjects, tended to be father-dominated, and there is a tendency in such families toward a dichotomous conception of the gender roles and a relative separation of males and females within the family. In addition, people who hold negative beliefs about homosexual acts and actors have been found to support the double standard between males and females (MacDonald & Games, 1974) and may endorse a rigid, bipolar view of the four components of sexual identity reviewed in Chapter One. Individuals who are prejudiced toward and fearful of homosexual acts and actors have been found to be rigid in their thinking, conventional in their values, and authoritarian in personality (MacDonald & Games, 1974). Lastly, religiosity and the belief that Christ should be worshipped in the church are ideological correlates of negative beliefs about and fears of homosexual acts and actors (Morin & Wallace, 1976).

The defensive mechanisms used by authoritarian personalities are the instruments of rejection of those tendencies that the subject is not ready to face and to incorporate. In *The Authoritarian Personality* (1950), Adorno et al. found that prejudiced personalities relied on the repression of sex and aggression, overemphasis on cleanliness, and various forms of defense against their own passivity. "Again and again," they wrote,

> it became evident that the difference between the ethnocentric and the non-ethnocentric extremes hinges more on the rejection vs. the acceptance of such depth factors on homosexuality, or aggression, or passivity ... than it does on the mere presence or absence of one or another of these tendencies. In other words, it was not primarily the relative strength of such tendencies that seemed to matter, but rather the way in which these tendencies were handled in the motivational dynamics of the subject in question (p. 442).

The prejudiced person does not utilize information that might serve to disconfirm his or her prejudiced beliefs. The individual has a low tolerance for ambiguity. Numerous studies indicate associations between authoritarianism and person perception. For example, authoritarians are likely to minimize their own anxiety and to assume that others are similar to them, and to demonstrate intolerance of trait inconsistencies in impression formation (Warr & Sims, 1965). The logical opposite of authoritarianism and prejudice, openmindedness, is thought to result in more complex impression formation (White, Alter, & Rardin, 1965), the search for a greater utilization of additional information (Long & Ziller, 1965), and reduced use of stereotyped and conventional schemata in thinking (Plant, Telford, & Thomas, 1965).

Authoritarian beliefs may be particularly deleterious when they are internalized and operating to limit one's perception of options in life. For the gay and lesbian identified individual, the residual effects of growing up in an authoritarian household may include medical complications. A psychologist specializing in behavioral medicine and psychoneuroim-munology had the following to say about belief in the family and religiosity among his gay and lesbian clients:

> So often in my work with gay medical patients, especially those with chronic illnesses, I see the strong effects of internalized stigma on the disease process. Unresolved conflicts or unfinished business with family members about gay issues often underlie chronic patterns of stress. This indirectly links internalized stigma to a range of illnesses from classical psychosomatic disorders, to illnesses resulting from drug abuse, to conditions mediated through the immune system. I am constantly struck by the clinical presentation of patients (more recently AIDS patients) who come from strongly religious families. Almost invariably, they describe their relation-ships to family members as close and intimate, yet they have not "come out" to these family members. What must happen under such conditions of long-term isolation and suppression of parts of one's self? Are there physiological or immunological correlates to such psycho-social posturing? I think such factors may play a role in the immune suppression we hypothesize as necessary for full incubation of infectious agents (such as may be responsible for AIDS) eventually leading to fulminant or chronic disease (Jeff Mandel, personal correspondence, July 7, 1983).

Attribution and Prejudice

If a person performs an act, such as a homosexual act, observers will make inferences about what caused the act. These causal inferences are called *attributions*. Attributions are made according to characteristics of the situation in which the act occurs. For example, if a heterosexual (self-labeled) observes a prisoner engaging in a homosexual act, the individual observing may attribute the cause of the act on the basis of both the fact that the act took place in a prison and the observer's own schema of beliefs about the carnal sexual nature of humans.

Attribution theory suggests that the perception and evaluation of an individual are in part a function of the personality of the perceiver and the social situation in which the perception takes place (Shaver, 1975). Heider (1944) stressed the notion that people perceive the behavior of others as being caused and that they attribute the cause to either the person, the environment, or a combination of the two. For example, if I am told that a homosexual male prepared a successful dinner for six last night, I might conclude that he is effeminate (called a personal attribution or dispositional attribution or that he has been required to learn how to prepare dinners, as well as how to perform other domestic chores, due to his self-reliant lifestyle (environmental or situational attribution) or that he enjoys his domestic self-reliance and practices it frequently (combination of dispositional and situational attributions).

One of the basic principles of attribution theory is that actors are more likely to attribute the causes of their behavior to the situation, whereas observers are more likely to attribute the responsibility for the same behavior to personal dispositions. The implications for maintaining prejudice, and blaming the victim of prejudice, are obvious: The toxic impact of oppressive climates is attributed to the oppressed. "Actors" do have a more detailed knowledge of their own circumstances, history, motives, and experiences. Perhaps more importantly, the observer's tendency to attribute cause to the situation is the result of the different salience of the information available to the actor and to the observer (Jones & Nisbett, 1971). For the observer, behavior is figural against the ground of the situation. For the actor, it is the situational cues that are figural and that are seen to elicit behavior.

Scapegoat Theory

A dynamic orientation of prejudice is that of the frustration-aggression theory. Sometimes people respond to frustrating circumstances with anger (Allport, 1958; Dollard, Doob, Miller, Mower, and Sears 1939). It has also been demonstrated that some persons take an "extrapunitive" attitude, placing blame not on themselves, but on their problems of living specifically in available "out-groups" (Allport, 1958).

The theory of scapegoating assumes three stages: (1) frustration generates aggression; (2) aggression may become displaced upon relatively defenseless "goats"; and (3) this displaced hostility is rationalized and justified by blaming, projecting, and stereotyping.

This theory of scapegoating does not say anything about the choice of scapegoats. However, it seems plausible that homosexuals can become scapegoats against whom aggression can be directed without guilt; in the view of the aggressor, they are, as a group, engaging in behaviors that are judged morally reprehensible. Furthermore, homosexual males may be chosen as scapegoats when viewed by their aggressor as "gender role violators" whose violation lies in the direction of the less desirable and less powerful gender role.

The scapegoat theory of prejudice explored by contemporary psychologists is not altogether unlike Hebrew custom. To reconcile God and man and restore harmony, a sacrifice was made. During the days of atonement, a priest placed his hands on the head of a goat while reciting the sins of the people. This symbolically transferred the sin and evil from the people to the goat. The goat was then allowed to escape to the wilderness, thus clearing the community of sin. The animal was called a scapegoat (Aronson, 1980).

In contemporary times, the term "scapegoat" has been used to describe a relatively powerless innocent who is made to take the blame for something that is not his fault. Unlike the Hebrew scapegoat, the modern scapegoat is not allowed to escape into a wilderness but, rather, is usually subject to cruelty or even death. As Aronson (1980) says,

> If an individual is unemployed, or if inflation has depleted his savings, he can't very easily beat up on the economic system—but he can find a scapegoat. In Nazi Germany, it was the Jews: in the rural South it was the black people. Several years ago, Sears found that, in the period between 1882 and 1930, they could predict the number of lynchings in the south in a given year from knowledge of the price of cotton during that year. In short, as people experienced an economic depression, they probably experienced a great number of frustrations. These frustrations apparently resulted in lynching and other crimes of violence (p. 212).

Violent crimes against homosexuals may be motivated by economic and social threat. However, displaced aggression for one's own insecure sense of sexuality may also explain a portion of these violent acts. Legislation to decriminalize and destigmatize homosexual acts and relationships appears to be up against at least three forces. They are: (1) fear and hostility stemming from insecurity of sexual orientation, (2) social and economic threat stemming from gender role violation, and (3) selective religious or moral injunctions.

The ideal society would equally acknowledge and value homosexual and heterosexual relationships and social roles. Clearly, what is needed to alleviate prejudice against homosexual acts and actors is an absolute alteration in the prevailing point of view regarding natural sexuality. Legal protection for relationships on the basis of gender composition may not be desirable. Rather, law and custom in the good society would be impartial with regard to the gender of one's beloved. According to this view, it may be argued that "rights" for a legally defined sexual minority of congenital homosexuals reaffirm the oppression of homosexual nature and perpetuate a fundamental misconception about human nature. The existence of "gay rights" may serve to bolster antihomosexual prejudices that might have atrophied under an absolute redefinition of the prevailing point of view.

Defensive Projection

People's beliefs about and fears of homosexual acts and actors may be seen in the psychological process involved when individuals first believe they may have homosexual feelings. When individuals who have developed heterosexual identity—as all are socialized to develop—are subsequently convinced either by experiencing physiological arousal or by experimental manipulation that they are homosexual, they will—if they cannot accept homosexual acts and actors due to social values and comparison—begin to perceive homosexuality in respected others. This is a process of social comparison and defensive projection.

The process of social comparison—that is, of comparing and evaluating oneself in terms of others in the social groups in one's environment—related to the process of psychologically projecting unacceptable thoughts, motives, or needs onto others, reveals the psychological function of prejudice. The social caste, race, sex, or other factor that an individual chooses to be prejudiced against may reveal the particular needs, motives, and social values of that individual. Specifically, by examining the projected content related to beliefs and fears of homosexual acts and actors, we may delineate the extension of beliefs and fears from the act to the actor, revealing the process of social stigma and prejudice.

In an experiment to explore the process of defensive projection and social comparison, Bramel (1960) demonstrated that when people are exposed to a self-referent cognition that is dissonant with their self-evaluation (especially self-esteem) and that they perceive as negative valence, there is an increased likelihood that they will then attribute the dissonant trait to other people. Bramel also proved that one type of projection—for social comparison—resulting from this state of discomfort is more likely to be directed toward positively valued than negatively valued persons (Bramel, 1960).

The subjects were eighty-four undergraduate men in an elite private university. These men had very high scores on the MMPI Manifest Anxiety scale and low scores on the MMPI K (defensiveness) scale. The procedure employed by Bramel involved four steps, which will be reviewed in detail below. The assumptions guiding this research were in the following way guided by cognitive dissonance theory: Two cognitions are said to be dissonant when the obverse of one follows from the other according to the logical and experimental expectations of the cognizer. The focus of this study was to examine discrepant relations involving beliefs about the self and some of the means by which people attempt to reduce the resulting dissonance.

First, individuals were differentially prepared for the unfavorable cognition, so as to make one group experience more dissonance when it was introduced to the unfavorable cognition. To accomplish this result, subjects in one group (designated the favorable group) were temporarily convinced that they possessed a large number of "very desirable" traits; those in the other group (the unfavorable group) were temporarily convinced that they possessed a large number of "very undesirable" traits. Thus, the unfavorable information to be introduced about the self would itself produce more dissonance in the favorable than in the unfavorable group.

Subjects were prepared by taking a battery of personality tests and then receiving false information about the results in order either to boost their self-esteem (according to socially valued traits) or to lower it. The subjects were interviewed after the test and asked to describe themselves— an insight test—so the experimenter could act as a mere vehicle of transmission of the results to make it quite clear to the subject that the report was directly relevant to the important personality dimensions and that it often showed evaluations quite at variance with the subject's own self-evaluation.

Second, the two groups of undergraduate men were asked to judge—or to form an impression of—another target person. It was explained that the subject would be given the opportunity during the second hour of the experiment to form a first impression of another person, to make some personality ratings of him, and to fill out a personality questionnaire in order to study what a person thinks of himself and the impression he forms of others. The subjects were introduced to each other, sat down, and were told they had a period of time in which to form an impression of one another and to fill out a self-concept questionnaire. The experimenter "broke the ice" by asking each subject some questions about himself and his attitudes toward various issues and current events unrelated to the to-be-introduced unfavorable cognition.

Third, the unfavorable cognition was introduced. Bramel (1960) states, "We suspected that informing a male undergraduate that he is deficient in masculinity would be sufficiently threatening under certain conditions to provoke defensive behavior. In selecting homosexuality as the content area, we were reminded of Freud's . . . classic analysis of projection in the Schreber case, in which it was shown that an early form of

Shreber's delusion was the attribution of his own feared homosexual impulses onto his physician" (p. 31).

Having received the "results" of their personality tests, the two subjects were brought together into a room containing a seven-foot-long table, an opaque slide projector, and a projection screen. They were seated about four feet apart along one side of the table, facing the screen. A one-cubic-foot plywood box with a dial facing the subject was placed immediately in front of each subject, situated so that it would illuminate in the dark and not be seen by the other subject. The subjects were instructed not to speak to one another, although they could glance at one another, and were asked to make additional personality ratings of their partners and themselves.

Next, the experimenter sat opposite the subjects and read a set of deceptive instructions. These explained that psychologists were interested in whether or not people could estimate "deeper and more personal aspects of the personality" on the basis of first impression and that this part of the experiment was concerned with the perception of sexual arousal. It was explained that sexual arousal would be measured by the activity of the sweat glands, indicated by variation in the passage of current through a galvanometer. It was then explained that the task of each subject was to estimate the extent to which the other subject was sexually aroused by each of a series of photographs of male figures. In addition, the subjects were to observe their own levels of sexual arousal as indicated on the needle of the "psycholgalvanic skin response apparatus."

Then the experimenter strapped a pair of electrodes to a wrist of each subject. Lights were off, camera on, and the action began with the experimenter seated behind and between the subjects, but unable to see their dials.

Of course, the electrode wires were not at all connected to the galvanometer. Rather, the subjects' galvanometers were remotely controlled by the experimenter. The experimenter gave subjects high arousal readings consistently for those slides depicting "handsome men in states of undress" (p. 37).

It was hoped that the instructions would be so impressive to the subjects that denial of their homosexual arousal would not be a defensive strategy employed. The subjects were assumed not to differ in their negative evaluation of homosexuality.

Lastly, the projection was measured. In order most accurately to reflect the subject's comparison between himself and his partner, the differences between own and attributed scores were summed across fifteen photographs. This summary score would be positive if the subject attributed (on the average) higher needle indications to the other subject than to himself. It would be zero if there was no difference, and negative if the subject attributed lower needle indications to the other subject than to himself.

Following the photographs and the measure of projections, the subject was again asked to rate the other on the basis of the impression he had formed. This measure was closely related to the one used before the slide presentation, and included the adjective pair masculine-feminine. Then each subject rated the other person and himself as to the extent of possessing homosexual tendencies on a seven-point scale extending from "not at all" to "very strongly."

Results indicated that the unfavorable and favorable groups were equal in the accuracy with which they recorded their own needle indications. The groups differed in their attributions of homosexuality, with the favorable group projecting more homosexual arousal onto the target person than the unfavorable group projected. In addition, the self-esteem manipulations were effective in producing a mean difference between the two groups on the self-esteem variable.

These subjects were given information regarding homosexual arousal—that is, regarding the *act* of homosexuality. The results indicated that the more socially desirable traits a person—the actor—believes he has, the more upsetting the thought of having homosexual arousal is.

Let us consider the extension of beliefs about the homosexual act to the actor. Bramel (1960) discusses the halo effect, referring to a tendency to perceive other persons as possessing traits consistent with one's general evaluation of those persons. This process appears to be the hallmark of social stereotyping. He explores this phenomenon by hypothesizing that the more negative the initial personality ratings and impression formations are, the more likely it is that homosexuality would be attributed. Findings reveal that for relatively negative and moderate levels of evaluation of the other person, the favorable group and the unfavorable group attributed homosexuality consistent with the halo effect (Bramel, 1960). When the social object was evaluated quite favorably, the unfavorable group attributed very low homosexuality to the object—thus following the halo effect. However, the favorable group exhibited no decrease of attribution when confronted with favorably evaluated objects. Bramel suggests that defensive projection, a force contrary to the halo effect, is operating here. An alternative explanation is that the favorably evaluated partner is utilized as a comparison person and serves as a means of changing the subject's attitudes toward homosexual acts and actors.

This study, if extended another step, could examine the halo effects in such a way as to clarify further the attribution of sexual act to the actor. This may be accomplished by analyzing the adjective pairs endorsed by subjects on personality assessments of the other person and their own self-concept before and after the self-esteem manipulation.

Several assumptions were inherent in the design of this experiment, such as the masculine deficiency hypothesis of homosexuality. This experiment appears to be a clear example of cognitive consistency as social conformity: Homosexual arousal is inconsistent with the heterosexual self-concept internalized during socialization. It would be interesting if measures of authoritarianism, antihomosexual feelings and beliefs, inequality between the sexes, gender role, and sexual preference had also been obtained from these subjects. Furthermore, a close examination of the adjective pairs used to measure and manipulate self-esteem would conceivably reveal the dissonant elements between homosexual stereotypes and heterosexual self-concepts. The analysis of the constellation of prejudice may reveal that specific group prejudices are not substitutable. In other words, homosexual prejudice may not be substitutable for prejudice against blacks. The interrelationships of types of intergroup prejudices may reveal that different psychological needs and insecurities determine the particular prejudice expressed.

PERSON-SITUATION DEVIANCE

In situations where an individual is characterized as deviant, the person-situation language is facilitated by labeling. Labels are assigned to individuals in social settings, and these labels influence the acquisition and performance of pejorative attitudes, as well as avoidant and/or aggressive behavior. We begin this section with a discussion of social stigma. Second, the learning processes of stigmatized individuals are explored. Third, the interpersonal confirmation of social stereotypes is described.

Social Stigma

On December 16, 1950, the *New York Times* headlined a page 3 story with the title "Federal Vigilance on Perverts Asked." The following is an exerpt from that article:

> A Senate investigation group labeled sexual perverts today as dangerous security risks and demanded strict and careful screening to keep them off the Government payroll. It said that many Federal agencies had not taken "adequate steps to get these people out of government." Stressing the risks that the Government takes in employing a sex deviate or keeping one on the payroll, the subcommittee said: "The lack of emotional stability which is found in most sex perverts, and the weakness of their moral fiber, makes them susceptible to the blandishments of foreign espionage agents."

an example of the situation in which an
n full social acceptance due to an attribute
son comes to be viewed by "normals" as a
not quite human. That person becomes

According to Goffman (1963), there are three kinds of stigma. The first two are abominations of the body, such as the various physical deformities, and blemishes of individual character, such as a weak will, unnatural passions, treacherous or rigid beliefs, and dishonesty. These blemishes or attributes are inferred from a known record of mental disorders, imprisonment, addiction, alcoholism, suicidal attempts, unemployment, and homosexuality. The third kind of stigma described by Goffman is the tribal stigma of race, nation, and religion.

Through an interaction process with a partially structured world, we establish the means of categorizing persons and assign attributes felt to be ordinary and natural for membership in any of these categories. First appearances of social settings are likely to enable us to anticipate an individual's "social identity." We lean on these anticipations, transforming them into normative expectations and then into righteously presented demands (Goffman, 1963). Within these established categories of persons, there are certain properties that are shared by all of the members and serve to distinguish those persons from members of the other categories. The "as if" strategy is employed when we have typed a new person and then expect a certain set of behaviors and attributes of that person. We behave as if that individual had the attributes we expect of the type.

Goffman (1963) continues by discussing our awareness of the demands we make on people:

> Typically, we do not become aware that we have made these demands or are aware of what they are until an active question arises as to whether or not they will be fulfilled. It is then that we are likely to realize that all along we had been making certain assumptions as to what the individual before us ought to be. Thus, the demands we make might be better called demands made "in effect" and the character we impute to the individual might be better seen as an imputation made in potential retrospect—a characterization "in effect" a *virtual society identity*. While the stranger is before us, evidence can arise of his possessing an attribute that makes him different from others in the category of persons available for him to be, and a less desirable kind—in the extreme, a person who is quite thoroughly bad, dangerous, or weak. He is thus reduced in our minds from a whole and usual person to be a tainted, discounted one. Such an attribute is a stigma, especially when discrediting effect is very extensive; sometimes it is called a failing, a

short-coming, a handicap. It constitutes a special discrepancy between virtual and actual social identity. Not all undesirable attributes are at issue, but only those which are incongruous with our stereotype of what a given individual should be (pp. 2–3).

The expected relationship between virtual and actual social identities is one of harmony. The listener will complete the evidence base with information consistent with preconceived notions of what evidence would support the listener's beliefs. The listener adopts an "as if" strategy in the social interaction, and unless an attribute that opposes the personality type assigned arises, this strategy will eventually confirm the perceiver's belief.

Homosexuality constitutes a social stereotype and even a personality type to many researchers, clinicians, and lay people. People fail to see homosexuality as a simple behavior congruent with many personality types. Stigmatized individuals are disqualified from social acceptance and discredited; thus, they are not accorded the respect or recognition that nonstigmatized individuals are given. Rather, another prototype is enacted, and the "as if" strategy is continued. Using this critical feature, or stigma, a family of attributes is assigned to an individual. Thus, a prototype or stereotype of homosexuals may be used to process information about the individual.

Learning Processes of Stigmatized Individuals

The learning processes of stigmatized persons include at least three extraordinary elements. These individuals learn the normal point of view and that they are disqualified according to it. Second, they learn to cope with the way others treat the stigmatized people they are perceived to be. Third, they learn to control information about the existence of their stigmas.

The male role is internalized by kindergarten age, and the normative concept of masculinity already governs much of the young child's behavior. An identity based on an undesirable and central attribute—homosexual feelings—is likely to develop during early adolescence if homosexual feelings reach awareness. Many male homosexuals believe that they are disqualified from the status of their gender. Interestingly, the later in life one learns of one's stigma, the more likely one is to develop a negative view of self (Goffman, 1963).

Stigmatized persons cannot ever be sure of how the nonstigmatized will identify and treat them. This uncertainty often leads them to feel that they are "on stage" during mixed contact, having to be self-conscious and calculating about the impression they are making. They learn that their chosen mechanism of coping may be seen as a failing, rather than a strength, and that certain other incidental personality flaws are seen as direct expressions of their stigmatized differentness. Goffman (1963) cites the following example: "Ex-mental patients are sometimes afraid to engage in sharp exchanges with spouse or employer because of what a show of emotion might be taken as a sign of" (p. 15).

Thus, stigmatized people eventually learn to prefer interacting with people who do not see their stigma as a negative and central attribute for processing information about them.

Learning to control information about the existence of stigma is a central concern for the individual:

> When there is a discrepancy between an individual's social identity and his virtual one, it is possible for this fact to be known to us before normals contact him, or to be quite evident when he presents himself before us. However, when his differentness is not immed- iately apparent, and is not known beforehand, when in fact his is a discreditable, not a discredited, person, then the issue is not that of managing information about his failing. To display or not to display; to tell or not to tell; to let on or not to let on; to lie or not to lie; and in each case, to whom, how, when and where (Goffman, 1963, pp. 41–42).

The male homosexual is discreditable, and his ability to pass for heterosexual puts him in many uncomfortable situations. For example, he must listen quietly to fag jokes, and he must hide his feelings of attraction for male friends for fear of being rejected. A psychological consequence of passing can be acceptance of a negative concept of one's own right and worthiness to full social acceptance.

Learning to control one's expressive behavior is at the heart of passing; Goffman (1963) cites an example: "The strain of deceiving my family and friends became intolerable. It was necessary for me to watch every word I spoke, and every gesture that I made, in case I gave myself away" (p. 90).

Gay-oriented psychotherapists currently cite the reclaiming of self- expression as one of the most common needs of their clients. Two of the feelings that homosexual males have learned to control through self- monitoring are anger and erotic-affectional feelings (Clark, 1977).

The progression of disease may be fueled by the coping styles of masculine training:

> We are so well acculturated as men to keep our feelings to ourselves. Even more guardedly kept are our affectionate or homo-erotic feelings towards other men. How stubbornly independent we can

be at times, a precarious "self-confidence" born of long years of hiding in adolescence, being misunderstood by family, or needing to appear to the world as "masculine" to hide from others (and ourselves) the effects of our own internalized prejudices. Such coping styles, although adaptive and necessary to protect a fragile sense of self from a hostile culture, may be maladaptive as they affect the progression of some diseases (Jeff Mandel, personal correspondence, July 7, 1983).

Interpersonal Confirmation

In person-situation interactions where potentially stigmatized individuals are confronted with a stigmatizing situation, they sometimes behave according to the expectations of their social stigma. This template behavior pair reflects a process referred to as intrapersonal confirmation of a social stereotype.

Intrapersonal confirmation of a social stereotype is the process by which an individual internalizes a perceiver's belief about him or her. The individual may look for examples in his or her own behavior and character that would confirm the social stereotype or stigma. It is often the case that the homosexual male will internalize others' irrational fears and distrust of homosexuals or of a homosexual. This internalization sometimes has the profound effect of creating self-hate, self-denial, and an overall fear of trusting one's emotions. An indication of this intrapersonal confirmation is often a negative attitude toward the fact of one's own stigma—a negative reaction to being a cripple, a black, or a homosexual.

During periods of low self-esteem, the stigmatized individual may focus inwardly on these attributes and find supportive evidence for a negative self-view. The biases the person employs are similar, if not identical, to those biases in information processing (especially in retrieving and restructuring information) employed by "normals" in the bolstering of "deviant" social stereotypes. In fact, the stigmatized person will use those same biases when supporting social stereotypes of other minority groups. In this way, a stigma operates like an internalized stereotype, functioning to shape one's concept of self in many of the same ways prototypes influence the way we perceive others. The frequent consequence for the homosexual is the development of a complete identity that has been externally defined.

Intrapersonal confirmation of a social stereotype is a process of compliance, furthered by perceiving ourselves as behaving stereotypically. The self-perception is like identification and may mediate compliance and internalization. *Because stigmatized individuals begin to believe that their character is as the stereotypic behavior reflects, they come to internalize the perceiver's belief. The perceiver, by adopting an "as if" strategy, is able to create their reality: This is the nature of the self-fulfilling prophecy.*

Passing as a heterosexual when one is a self-labled homosexual has been found to correlate with a negative identity or internalized stigma. In particular, passing as a heterosexual may be a case of situational compliance, motivated by obtaining rewards and avoiding punishments. In such a case, it is not always damaging to self-esteem. *It is through the process of self-perception and identification with reference groups that compliance results in interpersonal confirmation of the social stereotype; from this comes negative identity or internalized stigma.* The process of identification renders a somewhat different analysis of passing. In this case, the individual grows up in presumably heterosexual self-defining role relationships that do not allow any choice in sexual styles. The process of identification, as understood in the context of socialization in the United States, may reveal the most important sources of oppression. We may be able to understand how sexuality has been shaped, defined, and regulated by medical, judicial, psychological, and family forces to repress choices, especially the freedom to express homosexual desire. A questioning of the naturalness of the categories of sexuality we have inherited can begin. This analysis supports a study about choices, about what constitutes us as individuals and the changes that are really essential: the way in which we relate to each other. Furthermore, the process of internalization makes possible a complete study of personality development and change.

Some of the immediate questions that arise are: (1) What is the relationship of passing as heterosexual to one's negative reactions to homosexuals and homosexuality? (2) What is the relationship of the support group or reference group a person chooses to that person's degree of negative reaction to homosexuals? These questions were explored in the empirical study described in the next section.

A Correlational Study

This study was designed to examine the social situations and personal variables that distinguish self-identified homosexual males with positive sexual identities from other homosexual males. In addition, it examined the learning processes and environmental antecedents of positive sexual identities among homosexual males. The Nungesser Homosexual Attitudes Inventory (NHAI) was administered. The Environmental Factors Questionnaire (EFQ) was developed and administered as an assessment of the environmental antecedents of positive homosexual identity; the environmental factors measured were psychosocial, with the emphasis on the nature and intensity of personal relationships, and functional, with the emphasis on reinforcement contingencies of behavior.*

The two subject groups were identified at an urban gay organizational meeting, n = 25, and at a private party near a West Coast university, n = 25. All subjects were male. The NHAI, the EFQ, a demographic data form, the Bem Sex Role Inventory, and the Snyder Self-Monitoring Scale were administered. A reliability analysis was performed on the NHAI revealing an alpha of .95 for the NHAI. Eleven variables were correlated both with the NHAI total score and among themselves. In addition, selected items from the EFQ and the demographic data form were correlated with the NHAI total score.

Results demonstrated the impact of environment on homosexual identity. It was shown that the participant's pejorative responding depended on the number of significant others to whom he had disclosed his sexuality, his feelings about "camping it up," the attitudes of his social support group, the number of gay experiences he had had, and whether the participant described himself as "primarily in the closet" or "primarily out of the closet."

Method

Subjects

Group A: Twenty-five homosexual males whose mean age was 30. Their mean disclosure score (where high scores indicate high disclosure) was taken as a measure of "closetness"; it was 28. These subjects were identified at a gay activist meeting.

Group B: Twenty-five homosexual males whose mean age was 22. Their mean disclosure score was 9.4. Subjects in this group were identified at a party for the university's gay faculty, students, and staff.

Apparatus

The thirty-four-item version of the NHAI was administered. A second inventory was developed for this exploratory study; it is called the Environmental Factors Questionnaire (EFQ), and its sources are interpreted in the same manner as those for the NHAI. In addition, as I have mentioned, this study administered a demographic data form, the Bem Sex Role Inventory, and the Snyder Self-Monitoring Scale. Two subscales of the EFQ are particularly descriptive:

---

*Special thanks to Daryl Bem of Cornell University for advice and direction on the construction of the EFQ.

Gay Experiences: A set of items describing positive gay experiences such as marching in a gay pride parade and creating a new mental category for thinking of one's sexuality. The subject is asked to indicate the number of experiences he has had in each area.

Gay Age: A number computed for each subject by subtracting the age at which the subject labeled himself homosexual from the subject's age at test date, thus deriving the number of years elapsed since the subject labeled himself homosexual.

Results

Reliability Analysis
We turn now to the reliability analysis of the NHAI and its component parts. Two reliability coefficients were obtained: Cronbach's alpha and standardized item alpha. Coefficient alpha is the maximum likelihood estimate of the reliability coefficient. It is also a member of the Guttman family of coefficients. The standardized item alpha is obtained by dividing the observations on each item by the standard deviation of the item. As can be seen in Table 5.1, the range of reliability coefficients is .67 to .95. In addition, item-subscale correlation coefficients were computed.

These statistics reveal the amount each item on the NHAI correlates with the item's total subscale score. As can be seen in Table 5.2, the range of correlation coefficients is .14 to .82.

Correlations of Variables with Total NHAI Score
Table 5.3 shows the correlations of variables with the total NHAI score. The first line of the table indicates that the less pejorative the subject's response pattern, the more likely he is to disclose his sexuality to others: $r = .61, p < .001$. As can be seen on the second line of this table, the less negatively an individual responds, the higher his number of positive gay experiences: $r: = .65, p < .001$. On line 3 we see a significant correlation between the number of years since the participant labeled himself homosexual and his degree of pejorative responding: $r = .27, p = .030$. Line 4 of Table 5.3 reveals a moderate correlation between one's degree of pejorative responding and one's masculine gender role attributions: $r = .20$, $p -.08$. Line 5 indicates a moderately significant negative correlation between the participant's degree of pejorative responding and his degree of feminine gender role attributes: $r = -.22, p = .06$. As can be seen on line 6, there is little correlation between the participant's income and degree of pejorative responding: $r = .16, p = .14$. Line 7 of Table 5.3 reveals a significant correlation between the participant's degree of pejorative responding and the amount of time he socializes with gay males: $r = .50$, $p < .001$. As can be seen on line 8, the lower one's pejorative responding,

Table 5.1. *Reliability of Full NHAI Scale and Subscales*

Scale	Number of Items	Alpha	Standardized Item Alpha
Full Scale Total	34	.95	.94
Subscale A (Self)	10	.88	.89
Subscale B (Others)	10	.67	.68
Subscale C (Disclosure)	14	.93	.93

the more likely one is to be out of the closet: $r = .69, p < .001$. Line 9 shows the strong negative correlation between a low degree of pejorative responding and a high degree of passing as heterosexual: $r = -.66, p < .001$. Line 10 indicates a significant correlation of the participant's positive feelings about camping it up and a low degree of pejorative responding: $r = .31, p = -.1$. As can be seen from line 11, the more positive the reactions to a participant's sexuality by significant others, the more apt he is to also react positively to himself and to other homosexuals and future disclosure: $r = .22, p < .001$.

Correlations Among Variables

Correlations among variables were also obtained. Four of these variables revealed a high degree of association with the others. These four variables—frequency of attempting to pass as a heterosexual, being in the closet or out of the closet, frequency of socializing with gay males, and the participant's number of gay experiences—run like threads through the other variables. Results show that, if a participant frequently or always attempts to pass as a heterosexual, the number and degree of his negative attitudes toward his own sexuality will be high, $r = -.57, p < .001$; the number and degree of his negative attitudes toward other homosexuals and homosexuality will be high, $r = -.47, p < .001$; and the number and degree of his attitudes toward others' knowing of his homosexuality will be high, $r = -.64, p < .001$. In addition, if a participant frequently or always attempts to pass as a heterosexual, he will have disclosed his sexuality to few significant others, $r = -.70, p < .001$; he will have had few gay experiences, $r = -.59, p < .001$; he will socialize infrequently with other gay males, $r = -.59, p < .001$; he will be in the closet, $r = -.54, p < .001$; he will monitor many of his self-expressive behaviors, $r = -.22, p = .06$; and he will feel negatively about camping it up, $r = .27, p = .09$.

If a participant reported that he is out of the closet, the number and degree of his negative attitudes toward his own homosexuality will be low,

Table 5.2. *Item-Subscale Correlation Coefficients*

Item	Key	r
Subscale A (Self)		
1. When I am in a conversation with a homosexual and he touches me, it does not make me uncomfortable.	T	.53
3. Whenever I think a lot about being a homosexual, I feel depressed.	F	.80
6. I am glad to be gay.	T	.80
8. When I am sexually attracted to a close male friend, I feel uncomfortable.	F	.63
9. I am proud to be a part of the gay community.	T	.75
12. My homosexuality does not make me unhappy.	T	.73
20. Whenever I think a lot about being a homosexual, I feel critical about myself.	F	.76
29. I wish I were heterosexual.	F	.80
31. I do not think I will be able to have a long-term relationship with another man.	F	.65
Subscale B (Other)		
4. Homosexuality is not as good as heterosexuality.	F	.75
7. Male homosexuality is a natural expression of sexuality in human males.	T	.63
10. Male homosexuals do not dislike women any more than heterosexual males dislike women.	T	.40
11. Marriage between two homosexuals should be legalized.	T	.14
13. Male homosexuals are overly promiscuous.	F	.42
15. Most problems that homosexuals have come from their status as an oppressed minority, not from their homosexuality per se.	T	.46
17. Homosexual lifestyles are not as fulfilling as heterosexual lifestyles.	F	.68
21. Choosing an adult gay lifestyle should be an option for children.	T	.64
24. Homosexuality is a sexual perversion.	F	.47
27. Adult homosexual males who have sex with boys under eighteen years of age should be punished by law.	F	.47
Subscale C (Disclosure)		
2. I wouldn't mind if my boss knew that I am gay.	T	.74
5. When I tell my friends about my homosexuality, I do not worry that they will try to remember things about me that would make me appear to fit the stereotype of a homosexual.	T	.68
14. When I am sexually attracted to another gay man, I do not mind if someone else knows how I feel.	T	.76

Table 5.2 *(continued)*

Item	Key	r
16. When women know of my homosexuality, I am afraid they will not relate to me as a man.	F	.76
18. I would not mind if my neighbors knew that I am gay.	T	.76
19. It is important for me to conceal the fact that I am gay from most people.	F	.82
22. If my straight friends knew of my homosexuality, I would be uncomfortable.	F	.78
23. If men knew of my homosexuality, I am afraid they would begin to avoid me.	F	.78
25. If it were made public that I am homosexual, I would be extremely unhappy.	F	.80
26. If my peers knew of my homosexuality, I am afraid that many would not want to be friends with me.	F	.80
28. If others knew of my homosexuality, I would not be afraid that they would see me as being effeminate.	T	.53
30. When I think about coming out to peers I am afraid they will pay more attention to my body movements and voice inflections.	F	.53
33. I am afraid that people will harass me if I come out more publicly.	F	.65
34. When I think about coming out to a heterosexual male friend, I do not worry that he might watch me to see if I do things that are stereotypically homosexual.	T	.61

Table 5.3. *Correlations of Variables with Total NIIAI Score*

	Variable	r	p
1.	Degree of disclosure score	.61	<.001
2.	Gay experiences score	.65	<.001
3.	Gay age	.27	.03
4.	BSRI masculinity score	.20	.08
5.	BSRI femininity score	−.22	.06
6.	Income	.16	.14
7.	Socializing with gay males	.50	<.001
8.	In the closet (0) or out of the closet (1)	.69	<.001
9.	Frequency of passing for straight (1-1/6 = always)	−.66	.001
10.	Feelings about self camping it up*	.31	.01
11.	Mean reaction of others who know	.23	<.001

*Camping it up: Exaggerated effeminate mannerisms so outrageously artificial or affected as to be considered amusing.

$r = .65, p < .001$; the number and degree of his negative attitudes toward other homosexuals and homosexuality will be low, $r = .37, p = .004$; and the number and degree of his negative attitudes toward others' knowing of his homosexuality will be low, $r = .72, p < .001$. In addition, if a participant reported that he is out of the closet, he will have disclosed his sexuality to many significant others, $r = .60, p < .001$; he will have had several gay experiences, $r = .62, p < .001$; and he will have labeled himself homosexual several years before the test date, $r = .33, p = .01$. The third variable showing high degrees of association with other variables is the frequency the participant socializes with gay males. If a participant very frequently socializes with gay males, the number and degree of his negative attitudes toward his own homosexuality will be low, $r = .55, p < .001$; the number and degree of his negative attitudes toward others knowing of his homosexuality will be low, $r = .53, p < .001$; the number of significant others he has disclosed his sexuality to will be high, $r = .42, p < .001$; and he will have had a high number of gay experiences, $r = .42, p < .001$. Results also show that if a participant had a high number of gay experiences, the number and degree of his negative attitudes toward his own homosexuality will be low, $r = .55, p < .001$; the number and degree of his negative attitudes toward other homosexuals will be low, $r = 45, p < .001$; and the number and degree of his negative attitudes toward others' knowing of his homosexuality will be low, $r - .66, p < .001$. In addition, if a participant had a high number of gay experiences, he had disclosed his sexuality to high numbers of significant others, $r - .70, p < .001$, and several years had elapsed since the participant labeled himself homosexual, $r = .28, p = .03$.

Let us now examine selected items from the Environmental Factors Questionnaire (EFQ) and demographic data form. These items have significant correlations with the participant's degree of pejorative responding. Results show that, if a participant is part of a social support group that places a positive value on being homosexual, his degree of prejorative responding will be low: $r = .59, p < .001$. If a participant is not isolated from other gay people, his degree of pejorative responding is low: $r = .58, p < .001$. If the participant is very involved in the gay rights movement, his degree of pejorative responding is low: $r = .61, p < .001$. The older the participant, the lower his pejorative response, $r = .47, p < .001$. Findings indicate that, if the concept of gay community or gay culture is important to a participant, his degree of pejorative responding is low: $r = .44, p < .001$. If straight friends to whom the participant has disclosed his sexuality have had very positive reactions, the participant's degree of pejorative responding is low: $r = .53, p < .001$. Results also show that, if schoolmates to whom the participant has disclosed his sexuality have had positive reactions, the participant's degree of pejorative responding is low: $r = .40, p < .01$. Several items on the gay experiences subscale show high degrees of association with the participant's degree of pejorative responding. If a participant had given money to a gay cause, his degree of pejorative responding was low: $r = .52, p < .001$. If he had disagreed openly when a fag joke was made, it was low: $r = .30, p = .01$. If the participant had rejected the notion that there are only two kinds of gender roles, those that are masculine and those that are feminine, his degree of pejorative responding was low: $r = .63, p < .001$.

In order to predict a homosexual male's degree of pejorative response to homosexual acts and actors, by using his scores on several variables, a multiple regression was performed. This analysis reveals the amount of variance in the total NHAI score that can be accounted for by each variable. A summary of the multiple regression analysis may be seen in Table 5.4.

Conclusion and Discussion

It was shown that the participant's degree of pejorative responding depended on the number of significant others to whom he had disclosed his sexuality, his feelings about "camping it up," the attitudes of his social group, the number of gay experiences he had had, and whether he described himself as primarily "in the closet" or primarily "out of the closet." These findings reveal the impact of environmental factors on the development and maintenance of pejorative homosexual response among homosexual males. The findings suggest that the reinforcement contingencies for positive homosexual identity, as well as the nature and intensity of one's personal relationships, influence the degree of pejorative beliefs endorsed by the individual.

Validity

Concurrent criterion-related validity was obtained for the construct of pejorative homosexual response among homosexual males, indicating a negative pattern that may be termed ego-dystonic. Age differences and developmental changes suggest a sequential stage of development in positive homosexual identity. Behavioral references directly and independently measured pejorative responding among homosexual males. Correlation of the total NHAI score with other test scores provided additional construct validity.

Reliability

A maximum likelihood of reliability was computed for the NHAI subscales. These reliability coefficients manifest the attitudes one has

Table 5.4. *Multiple Regression Summary Table*
(Dependent Variable: Nungesser Homosexual Attitudes Inventory Scores)

Independent Variables:	Multiple R	R Square	RSQ Change	Simple R	Beta
1. Frequency of passing for straight	.53	.28	.13	−.53	−.842
2. Mean reaction of significant other	.64	.42	.03	.23	.487
3. Gay age	.67	.45	.06	.18	.367
4. Self camping it up	.71	.51	.04	.20	.302
5. BSRI femininity score	.74	.55	.04	−.01	−.269
6. Socializes with gay males	.76	.58	.04	.15	−.322
7. Gay experiences	.79	.62	.02	.28	−.306
8. Label (i.e., homosexual or gay)	.80	.64	.03	.16	.187
9. Self-monitoring score	.82	.67	.003	.40	.238
10. Lifestyle (i.e., in closet or out of closet)	.82	.67	.002	.36	−.067
11. Annual income in dollars	.82	.67	.001	.07	−.046
12. BSRI masculinity score	.82	.67	.001	.06	.027
13. Parents' annual income	.82	.67	.001	−.11	−.042
14. Degree of disclosure (number out to)	.82	.67	.001	.31	.049

toward others' knowing of one's homosexuality as the most reliable items measuring pejorative responding to homosexual acts and actors among homosexual males. Attitudes toward the fact of one's own homosexuality were the next best indicator of the pejorative homosexual response. Attitudes toward other homosexuals and homosexuality were the least reliable items.

Positive Homosexual Identity

The development of a positive homosexual identity is a continuous function. There appear to be milestone events indicating significant points in a developmental chronology. Finding an average age when each milestone is reached may enable us to begin to establish a model of the developmental process of positive homosexual identity. The model suggests that the amount of social mind control one must overcome, the reactions of significant others, the values expressed by one's social support group, and certain societal responses may in turn modify one's developing positive homosexual identity. This model does not preclude a covert-overt model, as private coming out experiences may occur before more public experiences. Clearly, homosexual identity formation is a dialectical process, just as heterosexual identity formation must also be. This study has revealed some of the personal, situational, and social variables that contribute to this process of dialectical transformation.

SUMMARY OF CHAPTER FIVE

Prejudice toward homosexual acts, actors, and identities was characterized as pejorative beliefs and negative anticipations and feelings. Antihomosexual prejudice is evidence of real history, and changes form by altering the stereotyped image of "the homosexual" propagated by the family, church, state, and school. Homosexuals are granted, rather than earn, a reputation; the fact that many individuals are conforming to homosexual deviance proves the historical construction of homosexual identity.

The authoritarian personality was described as showing a consistently high degree of prejudice against all minority groups. These individuals were described as defensive and repressed. Authoritarian personalities are closed-minded and intolerant of ambiguity.

Attribution theory was reviewed to distinguish dispositional from situational attributions of cause. Observers tend to attribute cause to the observed, whereas the observed individual utilizes self-knowledge to attribute cause to the situation.

Negative dispositional attributions may be made by frustrated individuals. The scapegoat theory of prejudice provided examples of how economic and social frustrations can lead to aggressive and hostile treatment of relatively defenseless "goats."

A psychological function of prejudice was demonstrated by social comparison and defensive projection. In this study, unacceptable homosexual thought, motive, and need were projected outward by a group of heterosexual college students. These men began to perceive homosexuality in respected others after being convinced that they were homosexual. Prejudice is characterized as a reflection of psychological needs and insecurities that are created and maintained by social comparison and cultural norms.

The immediate level of human consciousness and awareness was considered in a discussion of the learning processes of stigmatized persons. Interpersonal confirmation of a social stereotype comes about through the process of self-perception and identification with reference groups that hold negative views of homosexuals. The impact of passing as heterosexual was considered potentially deleterious.

A correlational study was presented to gain a phenomenological appreciation of the self-perceptions, actions, and cognitive processes of homosexual males. The social situations and personal variables that distinguish homosexual-identified males with positive sexual identities from other homosexual-identified males were pinpointed. The reinforcement contingencies for positive homosexual identity (albeit foreclosed), as well as the nature and intensity of personal relationships, influenced the subject's degree of pejorative responding. Sexual identity formation and foreclosure may be understood in light of the personal, situational, and social variables contributing to the process of dialectical transformation.

CHAPTER SIX

FEARS AND PHOBIAS

Fear is the main source of superstition, and one of the main sources of cruelty. To conquer fear is the beginning of wisdom, in the pursuit of truth as in the endeavor after a worthy manner of life.

Bertrand Russell

A decade has passed since the United States' formal introduction to a mental illness so broadly defined that it included nearly the entire nation. The psychologists making the introduction of "homophobia: the irrational fear or dread of homosexuals" considered the common belief that "sissies are queers and queers are sissies" to be one evidence of this phobia. That is, the common cultural beliefs that homosexual males are not fully masculine and that being not fully masculine is an indication of homosexuality were taken as proof of the United States' pervasive fear of homosexuals (see Smith, 1971; Morin & Garfinkle, 1978). However, the cultural belief that homosexual males are stereotypically effeminate—or that they are untrustworthy or dangerous and thus to be avodied—does not provide data to prove the incidence of those individual cases where the criteria for a *phobia* would actually be met. For example, many people (approximately 20%) express a fear of snakes, but few (approximately 2%) have a symptom picture warranting a phobic diagnosis, according to Marks (1969).

The definition of homophobia as an irrational fear of homosexuals represented a shift in the study of the "homosexual problem." Specifically, studying the homosexual was considered a victim analysis that did nothing to prevent homosexuals and homosexuality from becoming as defined: sick, perverted, or criminal. Until recently, the assumption that heterosexuality was superior to homosexuality or more natural than homosexuality has been paradigmatic of most research on lesbianism and male homosexuality. Indeed, the assumption of pathology is exemplified by the past era's research focusing on assessment, etiology, and adjustment (Morin, 1977). The shift from the perspective of unquestioned cultural assumptions about homosexuality is both social and psychological. Now lesbianism and male homosexuality are being viewed in sexual minority terms, rather than as a sexual deviation (see MacDonald, 1974; Minton, 1980). Research in the minority paradigm may focus on the social action dimension of changing pejorative attitudes toward homosexuality that are held by the majority (Morin, 1977).

However, contrary to what some critics of traditional psychological approaches have supposed, the study of homophobia among hetero-sexuals, or among some homosexuals who may be said to be on the oppressor's side, does not represent a shift away from the methods or results of a victim analysis paradigm. The victim simply gets redefined as the curable heterosexual who fears and dreads homosexuals—and who has learned the U.S. language structure so evident in the contemporary sexual lexicon, including such words as "queer," "dyke," and "sissy." Homo-sexuals, in the "nonvictim analysis" view, experience social oppression imposed by heterosexuals and by some homosexuals. Perhaps this is a personal advance for some homosexuals, who have viewed themselves as victims of a demented sexuality. Indeed, the concept of homophobia may have gained popularity among homosexuals with this appeal. But an analysis that ignores broader societal context still remains one that blames the victim rather than the system.

The concept of homophobia was enthusiastically received by most gay activists and gained popular usage in the gay press and lexicon. Heterosexuals could be spontaneously labeled sick if they made homo-sexuals uncomfortable. Some gay activists were misled with the implicit power of the homophobia concept to "flush gays out of the closet." Publicly disclosed gays could label as sick those gays who made them uncomfortable, too! Hence arose the differentiation of closet queens as self-loathing perverts and gay activists as society's healthy homosexuals. In some ways homophobia appeared a notion that would serve its time; indeed, perhaps it has. The study of homophobia seemed to promise, more than to represent, the essence of a new social movement of transformations in sexual consciousness.

Today the word "homophobia" frequently appears in the gay press and occasionally in the dominant culture's media. However, homophobia doesn't seem to be seriously considered a meaningful clinical diagnosis. It also doesn't appear to be very effective as a strategy for political or social change. Homophobia has become a convenient reactionary term to the United States' pervasive bigotry against homosexual acts and actors.

Hencken (1982) cautions progay writers that prejudging people with antigay prejudices is prejudice, too; moreover, it represents a form of identification with the aggressor.

The validity of such a clinical diagnosis is unclear. A phobia must be a persistent irrational fear that is not within the cultural norm (Marks, 1969). Phobias cannot simply be reasoned away with persistence. Furthermore, fears of homosexuals and anxiety about gender role appropriateness are within the United States' cultural norms. That is, most individuals think they should feel guilty and/or anxious if they do not fulfill the highest social values and goals prescribed for adults of their gender. Indeed, it is rigid gender role conceptualizations that dynamically correspond with pejorative affect and attitudes toward homosexual acts and actors (see MacDonald et al., 1973). Moreover, education and revolution have created a change in many peoples' attitudes about homosexual actors and in their attitudes about gender role behavior. These appear to be normal fears motivationally related to gender role conformity that the U.S. public is coping with in various strategic ways.

A critique of the theoretical foundations for the scientific construct homophobia and its supporting data is in order. The following analysis will highlight the most influential psychological and sociological reports within the twofold framework that includes analysis from both a personal and a cultural perspective. The central issues of definition, validation, reliability, classification, and diagnostic criteria will be carefully examined.

THE PERSONAL PERSPECTIVE OF HOMOPHOBIA

The first question that arises from this perspective is: Does the homophobia construct meet the criteria for a mental disorder, specifically a phobia? One is at odds to answer the question because the diagnostic criteria used to develop the research and theory on homophobia are so fuzzy. The reliability of the diagnosis is questionable. The need for structured interviews is obvious. If diagnosis is not reliable, it cannot be valid. Construct validity is basically what needs to be demonstrated. The nomological network of lawful relations in which the homophobia construct is embedded must therefore be examined in this level of analysis.

This source of theory and data emphasizes the characteristics of individuals that influence the personal manifestation of homophobia. Early homophobia theorists (e.g., Weinberg, 1972) used the psychodynamic interpretation of phobias. The psychodynamic view stresses that phobias generalize through complex symbolic cues of special significance to the patient, e.g., morality seen in childlessness. Psychodynamic defenses against homoerotic arousal include reaction formation and paranoia. This analysis generally tests individuals' performances on measures of pejorative attitudes and avoidant behavior in regard to homosexual labelees. The content of the test items reflects cultural beliefs, e.g., the Judeo-Christian religious taboo on homosexuality and the "scientific" theory of homosexual deviance. The findings, however are generally used to describe an internal personality dynamic or profile manifesting in certain individuals.

The research generated under the term "homophobia" has raised several issues central to the definition and classification of homophobia as a discrete mental disorder. The definition of homophobia, to be valid, should be narrow and specific; it should meet the criteria of irrational fear, of phobia, and of mental disorder.

Criteria for Phobia

The word "fear" comes from the Old English word *faer*, meaning sudden calamity or danger; that word was later used to describe the emotion of uneasiness caused by the sense of impending danger (Marks, 1969). Fear is a normal response to active or imagined threat in higher animals, and it comprises an outer behavioral expression, an inner feeling, and the accompanying physiological changes (Landis, 1964). Marks (1969) considers a normal fear to be one within the cultural norm; such a fear does not lead to total avoidance and can be overcome with persistence and explanation. According to these criteria, it is inaccurate and discouraging to consider individuals abnormal because they express a socially taught apprehension. Furthermore, the criteria for classifying a culture or an institution as "phobic," which have been delineated (see Churchill, 1967), are necessarily different from those for an individual.

Phobias are a special kind of fear. The term "phobia" derives from the Greek work *phobos*, meaning flight, panic-fear, and terror, and from the deity of the same name, who could provoke fear and panic in one's enemies (Marks, 1969). The Greeks made fear masks by depicting the likeness of Phobos on weapons such as shields; examples of these appear on vase paintings (Errera, 1962).

Definitions of "phobia" in the psychological literature show remarkable uniformity:

Jaspers (1923)   an irresistible and terrifying fear of perfectly natural situations and performances.

Ross (1937)   a specific fear which the patient himself knows is ridiculous, but which he cannot overcome.

Terhune (1949)   a strong unreasonable fear of specific situations inhibiting the person from entering or remaining in them.

Laughlin (1956)   a morbid fear out of proportion to the apparent stimulus... fear which is inappropriate and unreasoning. It is beyond voluntary control, and cannot adequately or logically be explained by the pateint.

Errera (1962)   a persisting fear of an object or of an idea which does not ordinarily justify fear.

Marks (1969)   a special kind of fear which (1) is out of proportion to the demands of the situation, (2) cannot be explained or reasoned away, (3) is beyond voluntary control, and (4) leads to avoidance of the feared situation.

Phobias achieved a separate diagnostic label in the International Classification of Disease only in 1947 and in the American Psychiatric Association as late as 1952. Even by 1959 only three out of nine classifications used in different countries listed phobic disorder as a diagnosis on its own (Stengel, 1959), and some textbooks still group phobias together with obsessive-compulsive disorders (see, e.g., Scott, 1966; Curran & Partridge, 1963; Henderson & Batchelor, 1962). Subdivision of the phobic disorders themselves has only just begun. Marks (1969) divides phobic states into two distinct classes. Class I phobic states are fears of external stimuli, e.g., animal phobia and social phobia. Class II phobic states are fears of internal stimuli, e.g., hypochondriasis.

Criteria for Mental Disorder

The criteria that must be met for the classification of a mental disorder, according to the American Psychiatric Association (1981), include two that contribute to the specific criteria outlined above. In addition to the fear's having an abnormal quality, as described above, the patient should suffer distress and some disability in one or more areas of social or occupational functioning. Thus, the APA's Diagnostic and Statistical Manual III defines the basic concept of mental disorder as "a clinically significant behavioral or psychological syndrome or pattern which occurs in an individual and is typically associated with either a painful symptom (distress) or impairment in one or more areas of functioning (disability)" (p. 5).

Criteria for Homophobia

We now have a guideline for the necessary criteria for classifying homophobia as a mental disorder. They are:

1. The existing fear of persons believed to be homosexual must be out of proportion to the demands of the situation.

2. The fear cannot be explained or reasoned away and must be beyond voluntary control.

3. The fear must lead to *total* avoidance of the feared.

4. The fear and avoidance must create distress in the individual; having the fear response to a homosexual labelee must be subjectively experienced as painful and undesirable.

5. The fear and avoidance must impair the person in major life spheres, i.e., social/occupational functioning and private/personal well-being, causing disability.

Definitions of the Homophobia Construct from a Personal View

We turn now to an analysis of contemporary definitions of the scientific construct homophobia. There are a number of personal and political implications carried by each person's definition. The content and structure of the attitudes operationally defined as predictors of individual manifestations of this phobic disorder have taken several forms. The attitudes themselves have been referred to as the disease of homophobia. The central issue is, Can you legitimately label a pejorative attitude a mental disorder, that is, call a prejudice a phobia? The answer to this question will be sought through an analysis of the validity of the scientific construct homophobia and its lawful relation to pejorative attitudes toward homosexuals.

The term "homophobia" was popularized a decade ago, when in 1972 George Weinberg published a book called *Society and the Healthy Homosexual*. Weinberg is a psychotherapist who reports having seen two types of homosexuals: his friends and acquaintances in the gay liberation movement, and those who are properly seeking therapy for their own homophobia. He makes no mention of the personality or demographic profiles of this sample. Weinberg uses the term "homophobia" to describe the personal dynamic of irrational fear on the part of heterosexuals of being in close proximity, in general, to people they believe to be homosexual. When the homosexual internalizes others' irrational fears, the result, Weinberg postulates, is self-hatred. In the preface to his book, he states that the book is in part an examination of a disease called homophobia—an attitude held by many nonhomosexuals and perhaps by the majority of homosexuals in countries where there is discrimination against homosexuals (p. xi). Then Weinberg comments, "I would never consider any patient healthy unless he had overcome his prejudice against homosexuality" (p. 1). Hence comes his classification of prejudice as mental illness, specifically a personal phobic condition.

The personal perspective of homophobia is used by Morin and Garfinkle (1978) to "describe a specific phobic condition, rather than an internalized cultural attitude" (p. 32). Their description borrows from Weinberg's popular book, and from Smith (1971), who conducted the first published empirical study of homophobia. Additional findings are interpreted from attitude studies as being personality correlates, suggesting that "those people who are afraid or intolerant of homosexuals are afraid or intolerant in a great many other social and interpersonal situations as well" (p. 32). For example, these people are more cognitively rigid (MacDonald, 1974) and more sexually rigid (Berry & Marks, 1969) than are people who are tolerant of homosexual actors and their alternative lifestyle. Morin and Garfinkle conclude that all of these personality characteristics might be expected of any highly prejudiced group of people. The convergent validity suggested by these lawful relations among test scores indicates a prejudiced disposition—not an isolated phobia of the mythical homosexual. Furthermore, the method of contrasting groups has been used both as a basis for the selection of items and as evidence of test validity.

In an article that Steven Morin and I wrote (1980) during my early undergraduate years at Stanford, we defined homophobia in terms similar to those used by Morin and Garfinkle. The emphasis of our article was that the social stigma "homosexual" discredited men from the status of their gender and that the fear of being labeled homosexual prevented most male-male intimacy. At that time I considered these *homophobia symptoms*, caused by an attitude of prejudice toward homosexual acts and actors. I also believed that cognitive restructuring and behavioral intervention were sufficient cures for dimorphic gender identifications. Many of the observations we made in that article were correct; for example, dimorphic gender identifications appear to be the source of most social and personal conflicts in this area. However, we did not challenge the criteria for phobia used by early homophobia theorists.

Classic Fear Response

The classic fear response of the homophobic male, according to Morin and Garfinkle (1978), is a shrinking of the penis among heterosexual males when confronted with a nude homosexual male. They provide "ample evidence" of this "classic fear response" by the use of data from an experiment conducted by McConaghy (1967). The data are presented to make three assertions:

1. Heterosexual men do fear homosexual men.

2. Homosexual men respond no differently to female stimulus pictures than to neutral pictures.

3. Heterosexual men have a fear of their own sexual impulses toward other men.

These assertions may be true. However, the experiment cited cannot provide "ample evidence" needed for such confirmation. Let's take a close look at it to see why.

McConaghy (1967) employed a method derived from Freund (1963) to measure penile volume change in response to moving pictures of male and female nudes. The nudes were presented in moving pictures of ten seconds' duration, carrying out activities such as hair combing, "Designed to be non-sexually provocative, as it was considered this could limit the type of person to whom the film could be shown" (p. 43).

The subjects in McConaghy's experiment were twenty-two homosexuals, aged 18 to 41, all of whom had been referred for aversion therapy; they were aware of homosexual feelings and wished to have them reduced or eliminated. Ten said they were attracted to women; twelve had been arrested at least once for their homosexual behavior. The heterosexual control group was composed of eleven medical students who "were informed that they were to act as controls for homosexual subjects, and only subjects who were not conscious of any homosexual feelings were asked to volunteer" (p. 45).

The findings McConaghy (1967) considered to be important will be considered first.

> Statistically significant differences between the responses to male and female nudes were found in the majority of subjects. The sexual orientation indicated by the test was heterosexual for all the completely heterosexual subjects and homosexual for fourteen of the subjects conscious of homosexual feelings (p. 43).

Thus, the method was considered successful for indicating sexual preference.

We move now to a discussion of the findings relevant to Morin and Garfinkle's three assertions. Clearly, the first assertion is unrelated to this experiment. That is, the moving picture stimuli were designed to be nonspecific in regard to sexual orientation. These heterosexual men may have had some fear response (if one accepts that penile detumescence to nonpreferred stimuli is an indicant of fear) to men, but these data cannot support assertions about the subjects' responses to homosexual men. Moreover, the fact remains that the heterosexuals were told that they were controls in a study of homosexuality. In other situations like locker rooms penile shrinking probably doesn't occur.

Assertion 2, that homosexual men respond no differently to female stimuli than to neutral stimuli, is simply inaccurate. The experimental design did not include a neutral stimuli condition. (A later experiment conducted by Freund et al., 1973, used the same method but included this control procedure; it was these findings that Morin and Garfinkle described.) In the McConaghy results, six of the homosexual subjects had significantly negative mean responses to female nudes.

Assertion 3, that heterosexual men have a fear of their own sexual impulses toward other men, is not supported by the data either. Actually, it was not tested. To do so, an experimenter would have to induce sexual arousal and see if that led to fear.*

There are two further sources of experimental effects. The first is seen in the demand characteristics of the experimental instructions. Specifically, the experimental instructions may increase normative responding; the heterosexual subjects were told they served as controls for homosexual subjects. The second is the fact that all of the homosexual subjects had presented themselves for aversion therapy because they wished to reduce or eliminate their homosexual feelings. These people may have responded less to homosexual stimuli than a less troubled group of homosexuals would.

One way to examine the original data produced by these two contrasted groups would be to compute their standard deviations based on the sampling distribution of differences between the two group means. The results of this statistical test on the original data indicate that the magnitude of responding to preferred stimuli, i.e., heterosexual preferred to heterosexual stimuli and homosexual preferred to homosexual stimuli, differed significantly (^{t}obs = 2.65 > ^{t}crit = 2.57, < .01 for a two-tailed test). The significance of the difference in group responding reflects both of these experimental confounds.

One last point that deserves mention concerns normal responding to nonpreferred stimuli. For individuals who have a stated sexual preference (and perhaps for some who do not have), a self-report of revulsion and penile detumescence may be a normal conditioned response

---

*I am grateful to John O'Neale at the State University of New York at Stony Brook for this point.

of compulsive exclusivity to nonpreferred stimuli. The fact that homo-sexuals report less revulsion and demonstrate less penile detumescence than heterosexual males report to nonpreferred stimuli may also be an experimental artifact. In any case, this search for a common underlying personal aberration to serve as the classic symptom of such a broadly defined construct of homophobia is not meaningful.

Homosexism and Gender Role Conformity

Lehne (1976) argues that homophobia functions on an individual level as an underlying motivation in maintaining traditional gender roles. He asserts that the irrational fear of homosexual acts and actors is not an isolated trait or prejudice, although it is characteristic of individuals who are generally sexist or racist. Thus, rigid gender role conformity may exist in homosexuals and others not personally afraid of homosexuals. According to Lehne, in these cases, "homosexism," defined as sexism between members of the same gender, although they may differ in sexual preference, "is related to homophobia only in so far as homophobia is a social norm." Lehne includes, in his "motivation" definition of homo-phobia, the force it has on homosexuals. He asserts that homosexuals with homophobia feel they must work twice as hard as heterosexuals to avoid being labeled homosexual and suffering subsequent discrimination. In addition, these homosexuals may aggressively defend traditional gender roles to avoid suspicion of being gay; thus, according to Lehne, homo-phobia does not function as a motivation for publicly disclosed homo-sexuals.

Lehne's "normalized" homophobia is characterized by "symptoms" of supporting traditional gender roles aggressively and working twice as hard as the next person. However, it is apparently a fear of discrimination and hostility that serves as the motivational force for the discreet self-labeled homosexual, rather than a fear of homosexuals. These motivational dynamics require a very ethical and sensitive analysis. For example, gender role restrictions may remain problematic for the individual who discloses homosexual relations; accepting—even publicly disclosing—one's sexual preference is not the same, but rather is a part of, one's gender role experience in various situations over time.

In conclusion, the definitions of the homophobia construct re-viewed appear to have only equivocal support. Homophobia may be spuriously related to pejorative attitudes toward persons labeled homo-sexual, contributing to confusion about the construct homophobia. Pejorative attitudes towards homosexuality are generally within cultural norms for appropriate gender role behavior.

The irrational fear of homosexuals cited as homophobia may have more validity as a religious or superstitious construct.* Patriarchal pro-creation and gender differentiation as a religious ideology promote a male-dominated and highly gender segregated style; herein lies a powerful demonstration of emotional conformity. Nonetheless, neither religious belief nor cultural belief may be currently considered a mental illness (APA, 1981). *Real homophobia, however, may be an example of magical thinking, whereas the oppression of homosexual nature is an example of real history.*

Social Perceptions of Situational Demands

Individuals base their behavior on internalized scripts containing rules for the behavioral demands of a situation. That is, we often behave according to how we believe we are expected to behave. In this way, our social perceptions guide our behavior toward others. Therefore, when a fear is out of proportions to the demands of a situation, it may be considered *irrational.* Actually, in this case, it is the social stereotypes guiding perception selectively that influence both the perceiver and the perceived. It is to the rationality or correctness of these social perceptions that we now turn.

The classification of homophobia as irrational appeared initially in the theoretical writings of Weinberg (1972) and was advanced by Morin and Garfinkle (1978). Neither of these works considers the necessary criteria for such a classification. This is perhaps the greatest weakness in the theory of homophobia. Greater clarification and delineation of the characteristics of immediate situations arousing fear would strengthen the theories' diagnostic reliability.

The issue of mental illness classification rests on one's evaluation of homosexuality. The diagnosis of mental disorder was applied to persons who considered homosexuality a mental disorder or a religious violation. Lehne (1976) has made this argument clear. He asserts that homophobia is irrational because it embodies misconceptions and false stereotypes of male homosexuality. These belief systems, or prejudices, are considered ration-alizations supporting homophobia, he contends, not causes of homo-phobia. Lehne carefully examines the following beliefs and presents disconfirming evidence for each:

1.   Homosexual males dislike women.

---

*An interesting analysis of scriptural tradition, early Christian opinion, and theological objections to homosexuality can be found in Boswell (1980).

2. Homosexual men are similar to women in psychological functioning and appearance.

3. Only some professions are appropriate for homosexual men, e.g., beautician, artist, florist.

4. Homosexual males molest children.

5. Homosexuality is unnatural.

Public acceptance of the stereotype of the homosexual male as a caricature of women, ill-disposed toward that sex, was recently demonstrated in the attitudinal study on sexual morality. In a four-year investigation based on interviews with a nationwide probability sample of over 30,000 U.S. adults, Levitt and Klassen (1974) found that nearly 70% believed that male homosexuals act like the opposite sex, and 56% exposed the notion that homosexuals fear the opposite sex. It appears that stereotypes of homosexuals are disproportionately generalized. In many cases stereotypical behavior may be sought out and reinforced by prejudiced people. In any event, it can be argued that these stereotypes are inaccurate, not necessarily irrational. In fact, errors in logic may be predictable and based on cultural myth.

In the social sciences stereotypes have become the language of prejudice. However, the presence of stereotyped thinking has not been shown to accompany distress, disability, or even total avoidance. Moreover, stereotyped thinking can minimally be reasoned away.

We turn now to review findings of attitude research bearing relevance to the influence of misconceptions and false stereotypes of the "homosexual" upon interpersonal relations. The first published report of "homophobia . . . negative or fearful responding to homosexuality" was that of Smith (1971, p. 1091). The method Smith used to measure homophobia was a questionnaire.

Smith's subjects were 130 undergraduates in psychology classes at an eastern State University. The 93 questionnaires returned (77 percent) were scored for homophobia (maximum of 9, minimum of 0); the 21 highest and 21 lowest scores were selected for further data analysis. The composite attitude responses (all 24 attitude statements) were considered by Smith to reflect a working profile of the homophobic personality. The actual measurement of fear or of any affective response is reflected in the content of the following four labels in four of the items: upsetting, disgusting, nervous, and afraid. The only item questioning fear was, "I would be afraid for a child of mine to have a teacher who was a homosexual" (p. 1093). The scores for men and women were combined in the analysis, and no data were presented concerning the scale's reliability or validity. However, Smith did conclude from the results obtained from face-valid items that those who hold negative attitudes toward homosexuals are authoritarian, status conscious, and sexually rigid.

In a paper by Millham, San Miguel, and Kellogg (1976) the attitudes of 795 male and female heterosexual college-age students' attitudes were factor analyzed. Factor analysis is of particular relevance to the construct validation of homophobia. According to Anastasi (1976), "In the process of factor analysis, the number of variables or categories in terms of which each individual's performance can be described is reduced from the number of original tests to a relatively small number of factors, or common traits" (p. 154).

The six factors identified in the Millham study were as follows:

1. The belief that homosexuals (especially males) are dangerous and should be repressed.

2. A feeling of personal anxiety in the presence of homosexuals.

3. Preference of female homosexuals to male homosexuals.

4. The belief that homosexuals manifest certain characteristics of the opposite sex.

5. The belief that homosexuality is sinful and morally wrong.

6. Preference of male homosexuals to female homosexuals.

These investigators found that the greatest proportion of variance in responding to male homosexuality was related to differences among subjects in advocating social and legal repression of male homosexuals. In responding to female homosexuals, however, the question of social and legal repression was secondary in importance. This finding is in accord with our society's general lack of legal harassment and prosecution of female homosexuals and its often intensive legal repression of male homosexuals. Responses on the social and legal repression factor were independent from beliefs in the morality of homosexuality and from the existence of personal anxiety with respect to homosexuality. Individual differences in authoritarianism or a general repressive style with respect to deviance, e.g., from socially prescribed gender roles, may account for advocacy of legal and social repression of homosexuality. The results also indicated that persons express significantly more personal anxiety with respect to same-gender homosexuals than to opposite-gender homosexuals and that persons express preference for opposite-gender over same-gender homosexuals. Males advocated more repression than females against male homosexuals, and females attributed more cross-gender mannerisms to male homosexuals than males attributed to female homosexuals.

In an attempt to refine and operationally define homophobia for empirical measurement, Hudson and Ricketts (1980) presented a measure of homophobia called the Index of Homophobia (IHP). These authors viewed homophobia as but one dimension (the personal anxiety factor of Millham et al. study) among many that collectively refer to the larger domain of "homonegativeism." Their 25-item IHP was administered to 300 heterosexual college students to examine the reliability and validity of the scale. The study produced a reliability (coefficient alpha) of .90.

The content validity of the IHP was the central thrust of the study. These investigators take the position that homophobia is not cognitive but rather is purely affective and that cognition and emotion are contradictory terms. They define homophobia as an affective response of disgust, anxiety, aversion, discomfort, fear, anger, or dread toward homosexuals. They contend that homophobia excludes judgments concerning the morality of homosexuality, decisions about personal or social relationships involving persons (what one should or should not do), or any other responses concerning beliefs, preferences, legality, or social desirability. The closeness of the anxiety-producing situation or stimulus is referred to as both proximal and distal. The content of test items does appear to cover a representative and face-valid sample of the behavior domain to be measured.

Hudson and Ricketts (1980) claim that combining items that measure evaluative and attitudinal responses with those that measure more affective responses significantly reduces conceptual clarity. Thus, they eliminate social anxiety items and reduce socially desirable responses." Apparently they have successfully constructed a measure of negative anticipation by cognitive labeling of physiological arousal, that is, affect on a psychometric self-report instrument. Hudson and Ricketts have not yet demonstrated that high scorers on the IHP would meet the clinical criteria for a phobia. Further research may successfully demonstrate diagnostic reliability of the IHP.

Recall that one clinical definition of phobia includes that it is an irrational feeling of uneasiness caused by the sense of impending danger. Thus, it may be measured by physiological arousal, self-report, or behavior. Any of these methods is valid, and their intercorrelations would provide much-needed construct validity. The view that feelings of fear are distinct from cognitions of unfounded judgments creating the sense of impending danger suggests that multiple indicators of homophobia would not render convergent and discriminant validity. This remains to be shown. The correspondence between various measures of fear may be confounded by the fact that fear is reduced first physiologically, then behaviorally, and finally subjectively. Acknowledgment of the foregoing may improve future research designs in this area.

Avoidance of the Feared

We turn now to an examination of the criteria of total avoidance of the feared. The social distancing experiences are important to the validity of the homophobia construct because performance on a test, e.g., Smith's homophobia questionnaire, can be checked against a direct and independent measure of what the test is designed to predict, i.e., avoidance of homosexual labelees. These social distancing experiments provide a test of concurrent criterion-related validity. They are relevant to tests employed for the diagnosis of one's existing homophobia status.

In an attempt to experimentally isolate and determine the effects of the label homosexual upon the perceptions and behaviors of the social audience toward men so labeled, Karr (1978) asked college-age participants to rate three different experimental confederates, each labeled homosexual in three groups and not labeled homosexual in three groups. The results revealed that participants who endorsed attitudinal items that were negative in content from the questionnaire designed by Smith (1971) to measure homophobia sat significantly farther from the labelee than did low questionnaire scorers. Homosexual labelees were perceived as being significantly less masculine and less preferred as fellow participants in any future experiment by participants who endorsed negative attitudes toward homosexuals and homosexuality. Labelees were viewed as "appropriately masculine" in the control condition, yet the attribution of "femininity" was made to these same labelees by "homophobic" participants.

The reliability of the test designed by Smith has been discussed. The test should predict general prejudice and social distancing from any minority or social deviant. The test has not been proven a reliable diagnostic tool for homophobia.

Furthermore, Karr does not report any precaution taken to make sure that test scores themselves did not influence any individual's criteria status. That is, if the experimenter knows that a particular individual scored highly on the homophobia test, such knowledge might influence the rating assigned. What is considered "sitting significantly farther" from the labelee? This possible source of error in test validation is known as criterion contamination, since the criterion ratings become "contaminated" by raters' knowledge of the test scores (Anastasi, 1976).

The criterion of total avoidance has not been demonstrated by the research on homophobia. We are left with questions regarding the characteristics of the situations provoking the fear response and the characteristics of individuals such as their beliefs and preferences as they relate to the avoidance of homosexuals. Where avoidance can be demonstrated, it must be more than social distancing based on prejudice or preference.

Education and Homophobia

We turn now to a discussion of the notion that homophobia is so isolated a fear that it is not subject to the reason and logic of the adult ego. There is evidence that education eradicates stereotypes and fears toward homosexuals. The extent of change that is brought about is poorly documented, and the self-fulfilling nature of social stereotypes poses problems. Morin (1974) outlined a program of eduation that proved effective in alterning negative attitudes toward homosexuals. The subjects were nine male and nine female senior or graduate students at a West Coast college. The seminar (treatment) was a discussion of homosexuality as an alternative lifestyle. A reading list for the seminar included books with affirmative views on homosexuality, and a discussion format was used throughout. A semantic differential questionnaire was administered in a pretest and posttest procedure. Adjectives reflected evaluative, potency, and activity dimensions. Morin concluded that the effect of the course was significant in changing the pattern of attitudes.

The course described by Morin (1974) was attended by gays and non-gays alike, and was taught by a gay activist. This confounds the main effect of education with the simple effects of a diagnostic label, perceived social pressure, and consequences (motivation) of nonconformity. However, the situation described by Morin as "treatment," reminds us of this fact about changing bigoted attitudes: changes brought about by teaching are most effective if the contingencies for behavior and attitude change are favorable yet challenging to the learner. Evidence from the social psychology literature demonstrates that one of the most effective ways of changing the "hearts and minds" of men is to change their behavior first. For example, Lieberman (1956) demonstrated how roles and attitudes are correlated in a study in which officers scored more "favorable" votes toward the Army than did enlisted men, as scored on a favorable/unfavorable attitude study. The Lieberman study shows a cause-effect sequence, in which behavior change caused attitude change. In addition, racial surveys have shown that attitudes toward integration on the part of black and white Americans are more favorable in those who have experienced it, and least favorable in those who have had no interracial contacts (Pettigrew, 1969). Prejudice is best resolved by addressing an individual's thinking (for example, stereotypes), feeling (for example, fears), behaving (for example, approach-avoidance), and interacting with others (for example, expectations and confirmations). In short, the absolute eradication of hostile barriers to homosexual expression must consider the cognitive, emotional, behavioral, and social foundations of these pejorative beliefs and attitudes. Allport (1954) gave us good advice in the following quote:

> Prejudice may be reduced by equal status contact between the
> majority and minority groups in pursuit of common goals. The
> effect is greatly enhanced if this contact is sanctioned by institu-
> tional supports ... and provided that it is of a sort that leads to
> perception of common interests and common humanity between
> members of the two groups (p. 181).

Another way to examine the effect of education on antihomosexual
attitudes is to consider that the *restriction* of knowledge about homosexual
acts and actors creates popular myth and reinforces group mandates. For
example, Moore and Tumin (1964) argue that the social functions of
ignorance about the nature and extent of norm violation include preservation of stereotypes supporting sexual taboo. In this way, the restriction of
factual knowledge by academics and policymakers is institutionalized
prejudice.

The study of homophobia would benefit greatly by taking account
of the precondition for public misunderstanding. Taboo reinforcement
necessarily restricts sources of factual information. In a study of the
taxonomy of categories and themes in antigay arguments, Paul (1982)
concludes:

1. Widespread institutional avoidance and outright discrimination
   seriously inhibit open research and education about homosexuality, and Lesbians and Gay men as people.

2. There is powerful support and enforcement in educational
   institutions for implicitly approved sets of ideas that amount to
   quasi-official doctrines of homosexuality.

3. These conditions comprise a form of thought control that
   inhibits the free flow of ideas and information, thus restricting
   and censoring free public access to accurate knowledge on these
   issues and thereby distorting public understanding and communication about the issues (p. 50).

The everyday observation regarding attitude change in this area
leads us to answer a qualified "yes" to the question about education and
homophobia. Two qualifications concern the motivation or desire of
learners to alter their attitudes about gays, and their ability to tolerate the
ambiguity that might be created by questioning these and their supporting
beliefs. Moreover, the search for confirming evidence to support negative
stereotypes may *create* the negative stereotypic behavior in the educators
attempting to disconfirm the stereotype. Attitude change programs geared
toward cognitive restructuring are limited in their effectiveness. (Abelson

and Zimbardo [1970] provide an effective method of canvassing for peace that may be of interest.)

Voluntary Control

A criterion related to the ability to reason away an irrational fear with a nice-guy approach is the degree to which the fear is beyond voluntary control. It does seem plausible that people clinically diagnosed as "homophobic" could learn to reduce or control their heart rates, fearful cognitions, and other reactions of fear. In group therapy situations, for example, relaxation techniques and systematic desensitization might prove effective, as learned fears are most responsive to behavioral therapy (Rachman, 1974).

A most interesting consideration in the self-control of outward expressions of this fear arises when one considers the varying responses of the tolerant liberal. It is often the case that behind an intellectual, liberal facade there lurks a raging bigot. Moreover, just as a homosexual actor can often pass through the heterosexual world unnoticed, so may a "fag basher" who fears and despises homosexual acts and actors interact with known homosexuals yet remain unidentified as potentially murderous. Motivation is the key in understanding self-control of fear and aggression toward homosexual acts and actors.

Distress

The distress dimension is also central to the diagnosis of a mental disorder, especially a phobia. For example, fear and avoidance may both be present, but the individual must be subjectively distressed over the unreasonableness of the fear. The distress should reflect some disruption or impairment in social and occupational functioning. Clearly, gay people may experience some degree of distress and impairment related to behavioral confirmation or internalized stigma, but this symptom picture among homosexuals is more appropriately termed ego-dystonic homosexuality (APA, 1980).

Weinberg (1972) considered the distress experienced by the heterosexual homophobe to be an antagonism directed toward homosexuals. That is, there is no distress per se, but hostile prejudice. Weinberg describes the distress suffered by agoraphobics and claustrophobics in terms of the personal distress the patient suffers and contrasts this distress with that felt by homophobics:

> But here (in homophobia) the phobia appears as antagonism directed toward a particular group of people. This phobia in

operation is a prejudice, which means we can widen our under-
· standing of it by considering the phobia from the point of view of its
being a prejudice and uncovering its chief motives (p. 8).

It will be recalled from Chapter Five that Weinberg attributed the revulsion
toward homosexuals and often the desire to inflict punishment as
retribution to five principal factors.

The distress experienced by the self-labeled heterosexual may never
be felt to be unreasonable; rather, the source of distress or frustration is
reacted to with aggression. Consequently, the distress will not be consciously associated with impairment. Rather, any conscious avoidance will
be defended as normalized preference. For example, if being in a gay bar is
motivationally problematic for the heterosexual, that person may not label
this an impairment in social functioning because of a heterosexual bias that
devalues homosexual contact of any kind.

This same dynamic has led male-dominated science to reject the
study of homophobia, and with it the study of pejorative attitudes toward
the full range of human sexual expression. The need for clarifying sources
of fear in human sexuality is paramount. A discussion of scientific
paradigms and social values is beyond the scope of this chapter and can be
found elsewhere (Sampson, 1978). Also, an excellent discussion of
psychiatry and homosexuality can be found in Silverstein (1976, 1977).

A narrow definition of homophobia for those rare cases warranting
such a diagnosis is possible and necessary (see also MacDonald, 1976).
Moreover, the findings generated by homophobia research can launch
forward the study of prejudice and social perception. The motivational
dynamics related to the focus of the fear, for example, fear of being
homosexual versus fear of mythical homosexuals, provide a compelling
analysis of the distress criterion.

The psychodynamic writers have stressed that phobias are symbols
for other hidden fears. Freud put forward a psychodynamic basis for the
classic case of Hans, a 5-year-old boy with a phobia of horses, namely, that
the manifest phobia was due to the repression of Hans's aggressive
propensities (the hostile ones against his father and the sadistic ones against
his mother). The horse symbolized the feared retaliation from the father.
Thus, a forbidden unconscious wish produced a conflict between ego and
id; this resulted in a conscious fear that became displaced to an apparently
indifferent idea. This is not the place to develop a strict criterion for judging
whether a given phobia is symbolic of other fears or not; but Weinberg
(1972) did not address this issue at all. Freud's development of the idea of
displacement from the case study of little Hans has also been reviewed (see
Wolpe & Rachman, 1960). It should be noted, however, that even where
symbolism can be shown satisfactorily, this does not prove its causative

role—it might simply be a secondary effect of the phobia (see Marks, 1969).

A more cogent theoretical formulation relevant to the personal dynamic view of homophobia was advanced by Freud. It concerns the psychodynamic defenses against homosexual arousal. This formulation is indirectly related to the study of phobia and is relevant to the internal perspective of homophobia because the defenses arise not from a fear of homosexuals per se but from a fear of social condemnation for homosexual behavior. This formulation is accounted for by the advancement of gender role conformity as encompassing at least two second-order associated features: ego-dystonic homosexuality and condemnation of homosexuals.

The strong U.S. sanctions against homosexuality create one of the basic conditions for the development of reaction formation as a defense against whatever love feelings the male may experience toward other males. Freud, believing that we have ascended from the apes, hypothesized that there exists in all of us a homosexual drive. He further hypothesized that some men, upon sensing within themselves an affection for other men, become terrified that their love may manifest itself directly in the form of overt (and societally condemned) homosexual behavior. They defend themselves against the threat by "reversing" their feelings (reaction formation) and vociferously proclaiming the reprehensibility of such feelings.

Freud's (1950/1953) analysis of Daniel Paul Schreber is a pivotal statement of the psychoanalytical theory of psychosis. It is the origin of the view that paranoia arises as a "defense" against homosexual love. The paranoid person feels persecuted by his or her unconscious love, which is experienced as persecution from outside (Scheff, 1975).

Freud thought that the paranoid man replaced "internal perceptions-feelings" by "external perceptions," thus contradicting his love for a man by hating a man.

Freud (1958) saw Schreber as a paranoid. Schreber was also ambivalent about his own father—he loved and hated him. Freud said, in regard to Schreber, "What lies at the core of the conflict in cases of paranoia in males is a wishful phantasy of loving a man . . ." (p. 62).

Thus, according to Freud, if a man loves a man and feels forbidden to, he denies his love and changes it to its opposite by denial and reaction formation. If he feels forbidden to hate a man, he changes his hatred into its inverse: "I hate him" becomes "He hates me" by projection. In the words of Freud, "Consequently the proposition turns into another one: 'he hates (persecutes) me, which will justify me in hating him.' And thus the impelling unconscious feeling makes its external perception: 'I do not love him—I hate him, because he persecutes me' (p. 63).

Direction of Fear

Dividing the fear of others' sexual impulses toward one and the fear of one's own sexual impulses toward others is a relevant differentiation. Weinberg's psychodynamic theory of homophobia does not clarify these differential motivations. According to Weinberg, homophobia is nothing but an irrational social prejudice; homophobia is a catchall concept referable to any nonpositive feeling or attitude toward homosexuals. In this theoretical analysis, no distinction is made regarding the clinical features of distress necessary for the homophobic diagnosis. Weinberg's contribution to society with the study of homophobia is made clear when he describes the function of the study of homophobia:

> The very knowledge that homophobia is being investigated...
> helps people keep in mind that homophobia is a personal problem.
> The mere fact of such study, as it gets publicized, may give great
> numbers of people second thoughts about holding the attitude (p.
> 132).

Morin and Garfinkle (1978) suggest that the fear of others' sexual impulses toward one and the fear of one's own sexual impulses toward others are motivated by different sources. For example, the personal motives that they classify as supporting a fear of others' impulses include: (1) the acceptance of the homosexual stereotype, (2) no knowledge or direct experience with homosexuality, and (3) a basic species-specific reaction to perceived difference. The personal motives that they classify as being the source for a fear of one's own impulses include: (1) the projection of the fear of one's own homosexual impulses onto the expression of the homosexual impulses of others, (2) anxiety or fear surrounding expression of sexual impulses of any sort, and (3) paranoia related to the projection of unconscious and unacceptable impulses.

Marks (1969) finds phobias can be conveniently classified as having external or internal stimuli provoking fear. Marks cites no instances of phobia with both kinds of symptoms. Of course this doesn't mean such syndromes do not exist, but if they do, it is essential to clarify the class of and/or combination of symptoms that must be present for the homophobic diagnosis. The usefulness of the Morin and Garfinkle classification is limited by the fact that they fail to do more than simply differentiate the two sources of fear and suggest they are motivated by different dynamics. We are left with several critical questions in this area. For example, could homophobics seen clinically be classified as internals or externals in terms of the presenting symptomology? Would this classification increase predictions about outcome or mode of therapy? Are the distress and disability experienced by these two types of responders different? It might prove to be helpful to frame the data in a fear-of-others versus a fear-of-self duality. The distress criterion has not to date generated data that would provide support for the validation of the scientific construct homophobia. However, the heterosexual bias toward socially approved defensive aggression against homosexual acts and actors restricts the use of this criterion.

Disability

Lehne (1976) posits that homosexuals are forced to recognize the falsity of the beliefs about homosexual acts and actors that they learn and that they manage to cope rather well. He dismisses the importance of the homophobia concept for homosexuals in the following:

> Homophobia is only incidentally directed against homosexuals, its more common use is against the 49% of the population that is male. This explains why homophobia is closely related to beliefs about sex-role regidity, but not to personal experience with homosexuals or any realistic assessment of homosexuality itself. Homophobia is a threat used in the male role, by homosexist individuals to enforce conformity and maintain social control. The taunt, "what are you, a fag" is used in mary ways to encourage certain types of male behavior and to define the limits of "acceptable" masculinity (p. 78).

Homophobia among heterosexuals is considered by Lehne to be so chronic and pervasive that they do not notice they are in pain or the possible source of their discomfort. However, the impairment for heterosexuals is described as denial of male love, limitation of male interests, activities,and emotional expressions; and competitiveness in work and interpersonal relationships. Clearly the area of impaired functioning is the avoidance of cross-gender behavior.

The gender role source of impairment is incorrectly labeled homophobia as long as we consider *homo* to refer to either homo*sexual* or same-gender contact. Moreover, biases toward normative responsiveness plague this as a criterion for mental illness, particularly when medicine and psychology largely confirm the status quo.

Among most individuals in a culture that prescribes strict gender roles and legally limits individual choice in sexual expression, rigid sextyping will *include* rigid sexuality. The full range of human sexual and social expression is impaired by rigid sex typing whether one examines the literature on socialization (David & Brannon, 1976; Block, 1973; Hantover, 1981; Hartley, 1959), heterosexual relations (Balswick, 1981; Anderson, 1978); homosexual relations (Lewis et al., 1981), or their interaction (Krulewitz & Nash, 1980; Groth & Brugess, 1980). The barriers to male liberation and brotherhood without patriarchy are also more complex than heterosexual prejudice against homosexual relations (Kavaloski, 1981; Sawyer, 1970; Berger, 1979; Pleck, 1981).

Morin and Garfinkle (1978) also emphasize the relationship between homophobia and the male role. In their paper on homophobia and the male role, they see the impairment suffered by "homophobics" as primarily the avoidance of cross-gender behavior such as male-male emotional closeness. Clearly what we are seeing in these formulations of homophobia is gender role conformity, not homophobia per se. Appropriateness of gender behavior is a very salient feature for individuals in most social interactions. The concern for being viewed as a masculine man or feminine woman is quite common. It is also common to associate the word "queer" with "sissy." Both of these can mean either homosexual or womanly man. However, linking homophobia to the male role still does not demonstrate a clinical phobia of homosexuals. Unfortunately, gender role concerns are camouflaged. Care must be taken to partial out the direction and magnitude of the effects of sexual orientation concerns from the effects of gender role concerns. Morin and Garfinkle (1978) begin their section on homophobia and the male role by stating the fact that male homosexuals are commonly seen as feminine. Then they discuss gender role conformity and the fear of being labeled homosexual; they consider the labeling fear motivated by another fear, namely, that of being seen as unmasculine. They conclude that the inappropriate gender role attributions made to people when their sexual orientation label is announced is an evidence of homophobia. This circular logic weakens the theory of homophobia.

Neither the homosexual stereotype of cross-sex mannerisms nor the use of the label queer to encourage gender appropriate behavior demonstrates an impairment sufficient to diagnose a phobia of homosexuals. However, these dynamics of the male role provide some insight into the barriers to intimacy experienced by males. It is not necessary to label these gender-role phenomena homophobia; indeed, it may be inaccurate to do so.

Careful examination of the relationship between gender role and sexual orientation suggests that one's attitudes toward sexuality are assimilated into one's attitudes about gender role. Churchill considered cultural learning regarding gender appropriate behavior to have a powerful influence on attitudes toward homosexuality. Additional support for this observation comes from the work of Bem (1981), who considers the sexuality subschema to be a portion of the gender schema. Bem stresses the strong affect society attaches to this portion of the gender schema: " . . . violation of the prescription to be exclusively heterosexual is sufficient by itself to call into question the individual's adequacy as a man or a woman" (p. 361). Bem's (1981) findings indicate that rigidly masculine or feminine individuals may have a generalized readiness to code members of the opposite sex in terms of sexual attractiveness and that this readiness is a powerful influence on spontaneous social interaction.

Thus, an essential feature of gender role conformity is a pervasive fear and avoidance of cross-gender behavior (see Bem, 1976). Evidence of a readiness to encode and process all interactions in gender relevant terms indicates a cognitive set that guides behavior. This extreme conformity is stress inducing and may be maintained after detrimental outcomes are apparent to the individual; the impairment may be to physical health (Harrison, 1978; Glass, 1977) and/or to interpersonal intimacy (DeGregorio & Carver, 1980; Smith & Brehm, 1981). A confusion of gender role and sexual orientation is invariably present. Two associated features of gender role conformity are observed; they are:

1. Ego-dystonic homosexuality in which the essential features are a desire to acquire or increase heterosexual arousal and a sustained pattern of overt homosexual arousal that the individual explicitly states has been unwanted and a persistent source of distress (APA, 1981), and/or

2. Condemnation of homosexuals to reduce gender role confusion.

THE CULTURAL PERSPECTIVE OF HOMOPHOBIA

The criteria for classifying a culture phobic have been broadly outlined. Churchill (1967) made the first attempt to develop a classification based on the restrictions various cultures placed on homosexual behavior. His classification proved to be a convenient way to order societies. Morin and Garfinkle (1978) outlined general criteria that include language bias as well as legal discrimination; they do not, however, mention fear and avoidance in their criteria. The Morin and Garfinkle criteria have not been tested. Lehne (1976) cites the bases for homophobic social beliefs and views these as support for individual beliefs.

Most of the theories and data generated from the cultural view emphasize the role of religious tradition in maintaining apprehensive expectation toward homosexuals. Cultures that hold a negative view toward all sex practices include various restrictions of homosexual practices. Gender role differentiation appears to be the higher-order variable and the best predicting criterion of these theories. That is, the prescribed social roles for men and women are maintained by a fear of homosexuality, where homosexuality is defined as a deviation from prescribed gender role behavior. "Scientific" theories that generate and publicize a view of homosexuals as deviant and medically aberrant are other cited sources of validation for a cultural view of homophobia. Thus, the cultural perspective has two sources of validation: the classification of cultures as varying in restrictiveness of homosexual practices and, by conjecture, varying in phobia, and the identification of social support for individuals' beliefs and fears.

In 1951 Ford and Beach published a study of different species of animals and of different human groups. Their data suggested an inherent capacity on the part of all mammals to become sexually aroused by stimuli that originate in other individuals of the same gender. Specifically, the cross-cultural and cross-species comparisons suggested that a biological tendency for same-gender sexual behavior is inherent in most if not all mammals, including the human species. Ford and Beach were especially interested in the social definitions and restrictions regarding homosexuality cross culturally. The following passage by Ford and Beach is important because it is the observation that proponents of the homophobia construct have cited to support their theoretical analysis (see, e.g., Churchill, 1967; Morin & Garfinkle, 1978).

> The basic mammalian capacity for sexual inversion tends to be obscured in societies like our own which forbid such behavior and classify it as unnatural. Among these peoples social forces that impinge upon the developing personality from earliest childhood tend to inhibit and discourage homosexual arousal and behavior, and to condition the individual exclusively to heterosexual stimuli. Even in societies which severely restrict homosexual tendencies, however, some individuals do exhibit homosexual behavior. In our own society, for example, homosexual behavior is more common than the cultural ideals and rules seem to indicate. Within the societies which, unlike our own, provide socially acceptable homo-sexual roles, a number of individuals, predominantly men, chose to exhibit some measure of homosexual behavior (p. 151).

Churchill (1967) analyzed the findings of Ford and Beach in his polemic book, *Homosexual Behavior Among Males*. Churchill provided a convenient division of human groups in regard to their acceptance of homosexuality. The first category, referred to as homoerotophobic, represented groups in which homosexual behavior was considered unac-ceptable for all members of the community under any circumstances; the second category, referred to as homoerotophilic, represented those groups in which homosexuality was acceptable for at least some of the members of a community. Churchill's criteria for a culture to be phobic included that the society under question consider any person or any behavior suggesting homosexuality strictly forbidden. Thus, in 1967 Churchill used the word "homoerotophobia" to describe the pervasive cultural fear of erotic or sexual contact with members of the same gender; he stressed, however, the restrictions the cultures placed on homosexual behavior, not individualized phobia. Most importantly, Churchill made specific reference to the observed continuum found in the work of Ford and Beach, and he concluded that attempts to repress homosexuality are a direct result of the socialization practices of cultures that place a negative value on all sex practices. Sex-negative cultures condemned heterosexuality in most forms, as well as homosexuality. Hence, the inclusion of "eroto" in Churchill's scheme.

> ... the history and character of the mystique which surrounds sex in our Judeo-Christian culture ... is obviously a mystique perme- ated by fear, superstition, negativism, and irrationality, and it is precisely these emotions, in an even more exaggerated form, with which we shall meet when we discuss homosexual phenomena between males in our culture (p. 31).

Morin and Garfinkle (1978) cite Churchill's use of the word "homoerotophobia" to describe the continuum observed by Ford and Beach, which characterized the various extant cultures that placed restrictions on various forms of homosexual contact. The word "homo- phobia" is said to have its roots in Churchill's formulation. Three points need to be made clear regarding Churchill's formulation. First, he argued that restrictions on homosexual behavior were greatest among those cultures with negative attitudes toward all sex. Thus, according to Churchill's formulation, negative attitudes toward homosexuality are not isolated but rather a part of a constellation of conservative attitudes regarding gender differentiation and sexuality. Second, Churchill stated that no culture would fit his criteria for homoerotophobic/homoeroto- philic perfectly and that his labels were only for convenience in under- standing restrictions various cultures placed on homosexual behavior (p. 82). In fact, Ford and Beach observed a *variation* of restrictions and a corresponding *variation* in forms and expressions of sexual behavior; other classification systems are plausible. Third, Churchill viewed these cultural restrictions in terms of the processes of cultural learning regarding the appropriate roles for each gender, rather than some individual psycho- pathology.

Morin and Garfinkle (1978) depart significantly from Churchill in defining their criteria for the hypothetical homophobic culture. Specifically, Morin and Garfinkle outline broad criteria, described as follows:

1. Belief systems that hold discrimination on the basis on sexual orientation is justifiable;

2. The use of language or slang, e.g., "queer," that is offensive to gay people; and/or

3. Any belief system that does not value homosexual lifestyles equally with heterosexual lifestyles (p. 30).

Morin and Garfinkle provide equivocal theoretical support for the third point above, namely, that adherence to specific gender appropriate behavior and pejorative views of homosexuals are somehow linked. However, they obscure this link to support the view of homophobia as a superordinate personal pathology. For example, self-report questionnaire data (MacDonald, 1974) that indicated that the need to preserve a double standard between men and women was a more basic component of negative attitudes toward homosexuality than sexual conservatism, was reported as evidence of homophobia.

Lehne (1976) cites three bases for homophobic beliefs on a social level:

1. The religious belief that homosexuality is immoral,

2. The "scientific" theory that considers homosexuality to be a medical sickness or a social deviance, and/or

3. The social belief that homosexuality causes the downfall of a civilization.

These three social beliefs are viewed as support for individual beliefs.

The social function of homophobia, according to Lehne, is primarily to maintain a gender role distinction, in which men support yet oppress women. His theoretical account of the strong association of homophobia with authoritarianism considers the potential for exploitation of homophobia as very real during times of stress and "strong-arm" governments. "This is no accident, but in fact the explanation for the maintenance of homophobia. Homophobia exists as a device of social control, directed specifically against men to maintain male role behavior appropriate to the social situation" (p. 79).

MacDonald et al. (1973) investigated the differential power of explanation offered by two hypothesis about the sources of negative attitudes toward homosexuality:

1. Attitudes are determined by conservative sex morality.

2. Attitudes are determined by a need to preserve a double standard; that is, we may condemn the homosexual ("pansy," "fairy," "butch") in order to reduce sex-role confusion (p. 161).

The subjects of MacDonald et al. were forty-seven male and fifty-seven female students at a large southeastern university (mean age 27–28). The tests administered had reasonably sound reliability and validity; they included: (1) the Intimacy Permissiveness Scale (Christensen & Carpenter, 1962); (2) the Premarital Sexual Permissiveness Scale (Reiss, 1964), male and female forms, (3) a sex-role survey (S-RS), designed to measure support for equality between the sexes, and (4) the Attitude Toward Homosexuality Scale (ATHS).

The findings indicated that more negative attitudes toward homosexuals were associated with stronger support of the double standard. Correlations between sexual permissiveness, attitudes toward homosexuality, and sex role adherence were also significant. Partial correlations were then computed to test the association between attitudes toward homosexuality and support for the double standard, with the permissiveness score and the SRs partialed out and the association between permissiveness score partialed out. The relationship between scores on the Attitude Toward Homosexuality Scale and the sex-role survey remained significant. The relationship between permissiveness and ATHS dropped to zero when the S-RS scores were partialed out. "Thus, it appears that attitudes toward homosexuals are more highly associated with support for a double standard for the sexes than with permissiveness or nonpermissiveness regarding permarital sexual intimacy" (p. 161).

In a subsequent study, MacDonald and Games (1974) addressed certain questions left unanswered by the MacDonald et al. (1973) study. First, the study included separate measures of attitudes toward male homosexuality and attitudes toward lesbianism. Second, the study sought to add information concerning the reliability and validity of the sex-role survey scale and the attitudes toward homosexuality scales. Third, the study intended to extend our knowledge of the characteristics of heterosexuals that are associated with their negative attitudes toward homosexuals.

Data were collected from 94 male (ages 17–35) and 103 female (ages 17–28) undergraduate beginning sociology students at the university. The findings reported satisfactory internal consistency reliabilities for the ATHS[5], with alpha coefficients of .9 or better. The data related to differences between attitudes toward male homosexuality and lesbianism revealed that men are valued and women are devalued when they are seen as potent, especially by males. Higher support for equality between the sexes was associated with more positive attitudes toward male homosexuality and lesbianism. A major determinant of negative attitudes toward homosexuality was the need to keep males masculine and females feminine, that is, to avoid gender role confusion. The highest correlations between sex-role survey scores and attitudes toward homosexuality were almost always on the factor, "sex-appropriate behavior/masculinity-femininity." Furthermore, negative attitudes toward homosexuality correlated significantly with measures of cognitive rigidity, authoritarianism, and low tolerance for ambiguity.

These findings do not support the validity of the construct homophobia as an irrational and isolated phobia of homosexuals. Rather, this research provides validation for the construct of prejudice against homosexuality by demonstrating the lawful relations between homosexual prejudice and gender role conformity.

Homophobia does not appear to be an isolated prejudice or fear of homosexuals. Rather, homophobia is a dynamic feature of gender role conformity. Pejorative attitudes and negative anticipation regarding homosexuals are associated features of a constellation of general social and political attitudes. The individualistic phobia of homosexuals that is based on the irrational or misconceived stereotype of homosexuals has not been shown to be independent of gender role conformity.

A more fruitful analysis would focus on the content of information people have internalized about homosexuals and the salience this information has in their organization of new information about people labeled homosexual. It appears that the "homophobic belief system" is a rationally structured logic, which may be represented syllogistically. Errors in logic may be predicted to support beliefs that reflect social norms, albeit norms based on unfounded, misrepresented, or omitted information. We cannot conclude that the individual's socialized beliefs are "irrational," "abnormal," or indicative of pathology without clearly blaming the victim of social control. The resilience of the unfounded judgment may be accounted for by such concepts as *cognitive gender schema* and *perceptual organization and control*. Pejorative attitudes toward homosexual and homosexuality are central in our system of beliefs regarding external authority. These beliefs may be accounted for by such concepts as *patriarchal procreation*, and *gender differentiation as religious ideology*.

The validity of the homophobia construct from a cultural perspective may be supported somewhat by historical relations between the content of the homosexual stereotype and its distance from gender role ideals. It appears that the content of the male homosexual stereotype as fearful, sexual, womanly, and inferior varies according to some lawful relation between evolutionarily determined gender role demands and material conditions. Creating a social caste homosexual could serve a central function of competitive masculinization. The fear of failure and rejection could motivationally function as a means of social control. *Culturally and historically, the phenomenon labeled homophobia has some validity when viewed as a motivational dynamic in the maintenance of gender roles believed to be syntonic to the functions and material conditions of a society.* "Homophobia" has conceptually developed as a theoretical analysis of the contents and processes of cultural gender role ideals. The term "homophobia," however, is a misleading and unsatisfactory choice of nomenclature. In fact, it distracts us from the truth about patriachal procreation, gender differentiation, and the human potential.

SUMMARY OF CHAPTER SIX

Homophobia was a convenient term designed to interpret cultural restrictions on homosexual behavior, but it became a catchall political concept used to refer to any nonpositive attitude toward gays. However, the descriptions of the concept and the research used to support the theories show neither irrational fear nor a specific reaction toward "homosexuals."

It is important to stress that consideration of fears of homosexuals and anxiety about gender role appropriateness as nonpathological does not imply support for these fears and anxiety. Rather, it permits a reformulation of what has been termed homophobia that focuses on delineation of components of gender role conformity and the associated features concerning issues of sexual preference. In this reformulation the personal characteristics of individuals and their immediate situations, historical processes, and cultural complexes are considered to dynamically correspond. It is recognition of the religious and cultural traditions of homosexual prejudice and hostility that allows one to conclude that the definition of homophobia must be narrowed to meet the criteria for a clinical phobia (see, e.g., Marks, 1969, and APA, 1981). However, total avoidance and irrational fear of homosexuals as an isolated phobia with distress and impairment related to social and occupational functioning has not been demonstrated. Prejudice and hostility toward homosexual acts, actors, and identities have been demonstrated.

The desirability of the construct homophobia as a political strategy for attaining gay rights should be carefully considered. For example, the term might be dropped from the gay lexicon altogether, transforming critical thought with integrity. Otherwise, heterosexual-identified persons with fears of people and behaviors they believe to be homosexual may not resolve these fears out of a rejection of the pathological labeling. Gender role restrictions may be similarly maintained. Moreover, the implications for homosexual-identified persons is that they go public or be considered self-loathing homophobes. This does not serve to unify the social movement against sexual regulation but serves the dominant culture's point of view. The psycholinguistic implications of the diagnostic label must not go unnoticed: The label implies that human nature can be clearly divided into homosexual and heterosexual, that you are either for or against "homosexuals," and that if you are against them, you are mentally sick. The language itself supports victimization. We should be especially aware of false consciousness when combining the ethics of politics and clinical diagnosis.

CHAPTER SEVEN

NEW DIRECTIONS IN METHODOLOGY AND RESEARCH

Progress has been made toward resolving the nature, origin, and impact of pejorative responding to homosexual acts, actors, and identities. Prejudice against homosexuals is expressed by people in various situations and societies through thoughts and attitudes, feelings and emotions, behavior and social roles. Through an enlightened approach to the social psychology of human sexuality, it is possible to proceed toward developing self-help handbooks for self-labeled gays and lesbians, including strategies for social change and methods for clinical intervention. It is my hope that this text will be used to advance a general study that contributes to our understanding of the processes and influences involved in the transformation of belief systems pertaining to the development, function, and stability of the self-concept and specific cognitive schemata.

My primary goals for the research programs outlined below are twofold. First, the data collected from these studies may provide self-help and legal defense for persecuted groups. Second, a critical analysis of the elements central to revolutionary theories may advance us toward a better society. These research programs should be geared toward social action and transformation. An exhaustive discussion of social action research is beyond the scope of this book; the studies described below are intended to supplement ideas in the body of the text and provide further examples of the kinds of studies that would be meaningful.

Future studies using the Nungesser Homosexual Attitudes Inventory (NHAI) should include confirmatory factor analysis in their statistical design. This approach would enable the researcher to test various hypotheses concerning the multidimensionality of the scale and would provide more adequate data to test longitudinal hypotheses about attitudinal changes between various stages of a developmental sequence.

Correlations between the NHAI items and other measures constructed to assess the same factors via different methods, e.g., behavioral observation, associates' reports, physiological responses, and psycholinguistic patterns, will provide the basis for construct validation. For example, pejorative responders may perceive and process information differently than individuals with more positive response sets and more complex impression formation.

It may be possible to show that the pejorative responders look for and recall information consistent with their prejudices when perceiving potentially oppressive situations and when recalling information about homosexual experiences. Furthermore, it has been shown that persons who respond pejoratively on a homosexual attitudes inventory do exhibit speech dysfluency when asked to describe an intimate homoerotic experience (Nungesser, 1979). In addition, it may be shown that *ego-dystonic* persons may have a longer latency in arousal (reaction time) to criterion variables that should be anger-producing stimuli and a high incidence of cardiovascular and gastrointestinal disorders. The psychological and emotional foundations of certain disease states may be clearly shown in cases where social stress is perceived as relentless. Indeed, a disease process of social stigma may place males who negatively identify as homosexual at a high risk for contracting the acquired immune-deficiency syndrome commonly known as AIDS (Coates, Mandel, & Temoshok, 1983). Research studies using the NHAI may focus on the relationship between social oppression and disease. These studies should consider the following the dynamics described below:

> The link between social oppression and psycho-social distress has been explored to some degree in behavioral and social science research. Unfortunately, there has been a paucity of research into the relationship between social oppression and disease. Considering the long-term impact of internalized stigma on the lives of gay people, it seems reasonable to assume such factors directly affect not only psychological but physical health as well.

> Emotions and internal conflict have been associated with both susceptibility to and progression of many diseases. Specifically, suppression of dysphoric or cognitively negatively-judged emotions appear to affect immune competence through neuro-secretory mechanisms which link our affective/cognitive states with regulation of the immune system. Secondly, an inability to ask for help or a perceived lack of need for assistance when faced with a health crisis is a prognostically poor sign in some illnesses (Jeff Mandel, personal correspondance, July 7, 1983).

Researchers should take care that further studies focus on direct experience and record the facts, i.e., affect, personal attitudes, cultural values, physiological arousal, situational influences, and emotional experience, in their qualitative diversity before attempting to reduce them to common form. What the facts mean in the places where they function, and the consequences for these facts when we alter the conditions, should become the guiding questions. In this view, the psychological data collected on pejorative responding to homosexual acts and actors are a part of an intense organization of social facts. Facts of experience provide us with the *what* of our investigation (Asch, 1952). Asch continues, "This requires that we describe with care the content of beliefs, attitudes, and values, and their relation to action" (p. 65). Phenomenal facts are an important source of psychological problems and insight. Indeed, the relations we establish to objects, groups, and individuals depend on information about their properties and processes. It is confusing to make an outright identification between beliefs and emotional processes. Beliefs, however, are often thought to possess a tenacity that does not derive only from their logical consistency. Theories of pejorative responding to homosexual acts and actors must be grounded in an examination of cognitive foundations. These cognitive foundations will reflect personal sentiments, social relations, and the content and quality of knowledge assessable and emphasized.

Sexual preferences may be assessed by verbal self-ratings, behavioral measures of sexual activity, ratings of fantasy content, and psychophysiological measures of pupil dilation or genital enlargement or blood supply (Gonsiorek, 1982). Sexual identities, however, may be assessed by diverse population sampling that would include verbal self-ratings of relevant personal constructs and the meanings these constructs have for individuals in the locality and culture where they function. The relationship between sexual identity and sexual acts/preferences may be seen in the interaction of independent measures. Other important measures may also become meaningful with such an approach. For example, the meaning and impact of life stresses upon personal well-being may indicate why some individuals have problems relating to self-concept, bereavement, and sexual relationships (Parry & Lightbrown, 1981). Moreover, previously unacceptable sampling procedures that tested groups of legally or psychiatrically involved "homosexuals" may be replicated to expose the impact of social labeling. Samples of "homosexuals" who participate in homophile organizations and those who frequent the commercial gay scene may be studied to assess their styles of coping with a hostile culture. This approach essentially studies the complex interaction between homosexual acts and identities within the actor's demographic context.

A possible new direction in research using the NHAI might further our understanding of ego-dystonic homosexuality. The phenomenal facts indicate that the inventory's subscales of disclosure and of attitudes toward one's own homosexuality should be tested as a correlate of, rather than a part of the operational definition of, ego-dystonic homosexuality.

The items on the disclosure subscale measure reactions and oppressive expectations the homosexual had toward others' knowing of his homosexual capacity. As the data indicate, these items correlate highly with whether a person is primarily "in the closet" or "out of the closet." The homosexual actor who is "out of the closet" is better able to estimate the oppressive expectations of coming out and thus responds less negatively to all of the subscale items. This dialectic suggests the delineation of the disclosure subscale from the operational definition of ego-dystonic homosexuality. The subscale measuring attitudes toward the fact of one's own homosexual capacity, or the phenomenon of self-hate among many self-labeled homosexuals, may be shown to be a *result* of internalizing the dominant culture's belief system that stated homosexuals are to be feared, and so on. A more careful analysis of the relationship between self-hate and irrational fears or intolerance of homosexual acts, actors, and identities may resolve questions of causality.

Future research should focus on the *dialectics** of self-disclosure, or coming out. The relationship between self-acceptance, acceptance of other homosexuals, and acceptance of homosexual capacity in general and the issues of coming out and "passing" must be analyzed. The impact of marginal social status and intergroup conflict must be addressed.

These studies should examine the environmental conditions that have an impact on self-esteem and self-concept among homosexual actors. The goal will be to expose the negative impact of hostile social climates on the behaviors, attitudes, and self-preceptions of homosexual actors. This research will demonstrate when it is best to disclose homosexual relations and when it is best to manage one's impressions by conforming to the heterosexual role. This design may test the theory that a person's *positive psychosexual identity* (SI) (defined as genital self-acceptance, low sex guilt for preferred acts, acceptance of similar others, and gender role androgyny) is a function (f) of relevant attitudes in social climate (SC), the person's degree of authoritarianism (A), and the person's self-efficacy (SE) at coping in situations where negative social stereotypes and sexual repression are operating. Thus,

$$SI\,(f) = SC + A + SE.$$

---

*Special thanks to James Dwyer, State University of New York at Stony Brook, and David Funder, Harvey Mudd College, for their helpful comments.

The study proposed for this new direction should contrast groups of subject in a longitudinal design, based on situational criteria, i.e., social climate. Social climate will be determined by:

1. The enforcement of legal sanctions against homosexual behavior and the presence of protective laws for homosexuals.

2. The presence of gay bars, organizations, and social networks.

3. A random survey sample of the heterosexual community regarding its appraisal and acceptance of the homosexual community.

Thus, subjects from three types of social climates would be selected and contrasted. Our climate would be generally very accepting of homosexuals, with social facilities for gays and support from other gays. This social climate would also have protective laws for homosexuals. The second social climate would be somewhat negative in terms of heterosexual appraisal and acceptance of homosexuality. In this situation, there would be gay social networks and access to gay bars. The third social climate would be very negative for homosexuals, i.e., legal sanctions enforced, no heterosexual acceptance, and no gay network or access to gay bars. Population density could be used as another criterion, choosing a city, an urban area, and a rural area that meet the other situational criteria listed above.

The psychological measures for such a study would include items selected from the NHAI, and the Environmental Factors Questionnaire (EFQ). In addition, a social anxiety measure, a self-esteem measure, and a measure of global well-being would be obtained from the subjects. The primary membership and reference groups of the participants should also be studied. Finally, an analysis of the reactions of significant others to the participants' disclosures should be obtained.

There are particular types of measures that may be used to test the broadly defined indicators or correlates stated above. For example, self-report may be used as a measure of the two dimensions of self-esteem, i.e., the NHAI and the MMPI. Reaction to partially structured material relevant to the object is another type of measure. We may ask subjects to complete sentences, for example, or to describe a person or predict one's behavior in ways relevant to several of our theoretical concerns. A direct behavioral measure obtained through observation is yet another type of measure. We may also require the subject to perform an objective task where functioning may be influenced by disposition toward the object. In this measure, subjects may be asked to indicate appropriate conclusions to syllogisms of relevant and neutral content so as to provide measures of the number and direction of errors. Lastly, we may obtain physiological reactions individuals have to themselves as homosexuals, to other individuals labeled homosexuals, and to various social situations or climates.

Another direction this research can take is to assess the personality of situations (Bem & Funder, 1978). In this approach, social climate is characterized by a set of template behavior pairs, which is a set of personality descriptions (Q sorts) of hypothetical "ideal" persons, each one associated with a particular behavior. The Q-sort description of a particular individual is then matched against each template, and that person is predicted to display the behavior associated with the most similar template.

This research would describe situations in terms of personality descriptions of an idealized "type" of person, e.g., the low-homophobic individual, who would be expected to behave in a specified way in that setting. The probability that a particular person will behave in a particular way in a particular situation is then postulated to be a monotonically increasing function of the match or similarity between the person's characteristics and the templates themselves related to the independently assessed properties of the situations. Bem and Funder (1978) studied the functional properties of the forced compliance situation that cause it to evoke attitude change in such individuals. This study demonstrated how the template matching techniques can be employed to test competing theories of a situation; simultaneously, the study illustrates how the templates can be derived from a formal theory.

Since there is a stereotype of homosexuals, and it is in its gestalt negative, it would be possible, it seems, to first map those characteristics (attributes) that are seen as making a person a prototypic homosexual—to then be able to ask the question, "What *type* and *quality* of information are necessary to demonstrate that homosexuals are not prototypical of the homosexual stereotype?" That is, the question would determine what information should be highlighted in order to *disconfirm* the belief systems primed by having access to the one characteristic: homosexuality.*

It also seems that the degree of self-endorsement of prototypical attributes that make up the stereotype could yield measures of how and to what degree the homosexual has internalized the societal stereotype—to what extent the homosexual subscribes to this stigmatized image of self.

An important thesis indicated by the research reported here is that patriarchy, Christianity, and capitalism interact historically and concurrently to reinforce one another. The result of this interaction is not psychological health or social advance but social and individual pathology. A rigorous program of research might find that patriarchy initially

---

*I am grateful to Nancy Cantor at Princeton University for this research question.

reinforced Christianity as a means of economically and spiritually oppressing women. Moreover, Christianity reinforced capitalist profit accumulation by teaching the Protestant work ethic and oppressing males who do not conform. This kind of research program may reveal the contradictions in religious belief systems necessary to induce transformation. It may be shown that the nuclear family is the exploited product of Christianity and patriarchy under capitalist expansion; this is why some gay people jokingly refer to heterosexuals as "breeders for the ruling class." Belief in the traditional family ideology, i.e., authoritarian father, submissive mother, and obedient children, may cause several forms of social psychological pathology, including crime, depression, gender role conformity, and social anxiety.

Social Birth Theory

A meaningful revolutionary theory emerges from the research reported in this book. It involves the "social birth of an individual." Individuals are motivated toward social birth when their personal and private experiences of culture urge them to analyze and confront their culture's rules and regulations. Social birth is the transformation of an individual consciousness resulting from the public and private experience of culture: herein lies the power to create transformed culture in a general sense. The process of coming out homosexually is an example of social birth. In coming out, the person locates him- or herself in relation to significant individuals and reference groups within his or her culture. Social birth is not simply early self-concept formation, or subsequent learning to accept a social stigma. It is an adult experience in consciousness and ideology that results in positive psychosexual identity.

Gay and lesbian identified individuals experience social birth in a profound and intimate way at various times in the life cycle. The individuals may achieve more self-knowledge during times when their private awareness of the self is consciously located within their own culture. Indeed, when gay and lesbian identified people "come out," they bring with them a personal power that comes from first personalizing culture, and later publicizing their so-called "private experience." The process of personalizing culture may be meaningfully developed to include ways in which the individual, in his or her private struggle with his or her culture, can unite with others who share common goals and a common humanity. In this way, information may be transmitted among individuals who experience the truth about human sexual capacities and cultures that would enable them to halt the social stigma process via social birth.

The homosexual prescription in social birth theory is: have absolute confidence in the private experience of culture, and share the experience of your perceptions of culture with others. Furthermore, by personalizing culture, rather than publicizing the so-called "private," a new culture may be created. Social birth is literally the beginning of a new world. Collectively, individuals who shed the labels "homosexual" and "hetero-sexual" in the process of social birth can effectively transmit their message to cultural institutions.

I describe the above as a "prescription," because the outcome of halting the social birth of the individual is often the disease processes of social stigma. It is different than most prescriptions written by gay psychologists, because publicizing the so-called "private" is not the mechanism of this revolutionary theory. The major mechanism of social birth theory is *personalizing culture*. This approach has the dialectic advantage of transforming the cultural categories of public/private, *and* halting the psychosexual processes of social stigma.

Many gay and lesbian individuals have experienced social stigma, via a process of heightened self-awareness that issembles social birth but reflects the regulation of culture. In such cases, "coming-out" as homo-sexual may be a foreclosure of identity based on misinformation about human sexual capacity and culture. Gay and lesbian individuals who identify as such, but believe they are not congenitally so inclined, have experienced the social birth I describe as powerfully healthful for the individual and his or her culture. These people understand that their culture has labeled them in a prejudiced way, but that they have developed particular preferences and are willing to defend them as healthy and legitimate activities and relationships to prefer. The mechanism of social birth is a dialectical power relation between the individual and his or her culture. In social birth, the power relation is strengthened in favor of the individual, because of supporting relationships the individual has with his or her self, and other significant individuals and reference groups. This mechanism may be used to describe personal and cultural changes made by the gay movement, as well as those made by the feminist movement. That people in these movements may believe homosexuality is congenital or immutable attests to the power of culture to regulate information about sexuality. The collective efficacy of revolutionary gender role and sexuality movements may soon alter U.S. culture, with the correct information about sexual acts, actors, and identities. In light of the information contained in this book, it is time for the national character of the U.S. to "come-out" as *human*.

SUMMARY OF CHAPTER SEVEN

The new directions in methodology and research described in this chapter were based on the goals of personal and cultural revolution toward well-being. Future studies using the NHAI may benefit from using confirmatory factor analysis in their research designs. The disease processes of social stigma may be charted in prospective studies correlating the NHAI with measures of immune competence. Sexual preference may be indicated in meaningful ways with certain behavioral measures, ratings of fantasy content, etc. Sexual identities may be assessed by measures of relevant personal and cultural constructs endorsed by the individual. A meaningful focus for research on homosexuality essentially studies the complex interaction between homosexual acts, and identities within the actor's demographic context.

The relationships of the individual with his or her groups, and the relationship of the individual with his or her culture, reveals a dialectical interaction. The dialectics of disclosing homosexual relations and identities were discussed, and studies were presented to explore these dialectics. A functional formula for positive psychosexual identity was proposed:

$$SI(f) = SC + A + SE.$$

The Q-sort method of matching template-behavior pairs was proposed as a method of testing competing theories about positive sexual identity. A study was proposed to explore the type and quality of information necessary to demonstrate that homosexual actors are not necessarily prototypical of the homosexual stereotype. The contradictions in religious belief systems that make transformation imperative may be exposed in a rigorous study of Christianity and patriarchy.

The elements central to a revolutionary theory that may advance us toward a better society were analyzed. Social birth theory was proposed as a meaningful mechanism for creating transformed culture. Social birth is an adult experience in consciousness and ideology that occurs when an individual locates him or herself in dielectical relation to significant individuals and reference groups within his or her culture. *The homosexual prescription in social birth theory is to empower personal experiences of culture and transform the existing categories of sexual meaning.* The message to gay and lesbian identified people, and to heterosexual identified people, is that the sexual preferences they may have developed are not congenital and immutable, but the result of social learning and forced choice. *The prescription for the national character of the U.S. is to "come-out" as human.*

QUESTIONNAIRES

NUNGESSER HOMOSEXUAL ATTITUDES INVENTORY (NHAI)

On the following pages you will find a number of attitude statements that are personal and intimate in nature. These statements pertain to sexual behavior and sexuality. Specifically, the statements fall into three categories: (1) attitudes toward the fact of one's own sexuality, (2) attitudes toward homosexual men and homosexuality in general, and (3) attitudes toward other people's knowing of your own sexual/affectional preference.

No two statements are exactly alike, so consider each statement carefully before responding. We would like you to use these statements in order to describe your own beliefs and attitudes. That is, we would like you to indicate, on a scale from "strongly disagree" to "strongly agree," how much you personally endorse each statement. Please do not leave any statement unmarked.

Example: SD D N A SA   1. Male homosexuals should not be allowed to teach in elementary schools.
Circle SD if you *strongly disagree* with this statement.
Circle D if you *disagree* with this statement.
Circle N if you are *neutral* in regard to this statement.
Circle A if you *agree* with this statement.
Circle SA if you *strongly agree* with this statement.

Some statements may depict situations that you have not experienced; please imagine yourself in those situations when answering those statements.

It is important that you answer as frankly and as honestly as you can. Your answers will be kept in strictest confidence, and, because your responses are anonymous, your privacy will be protected.

SD D N A SA   1. When I am in a conversation with a homosexual man and he touches me, it does not make me uncomfortable.

SD D N A SA   2. I would not mind if my boss found out that I am gay.

SD D N A SA   3. Whenever I think a lot about being a homosexual, I feel depressed.

SD D N A SA   4. Homosexuality is not as good as heterosexuality.

SD D N A SA   5. When I tell my friends about my homosexuality, I do not worry that they will try to remember things about me that would make me appear to fit the stereotype of a homosexual.

SD D N A SA   6. I am glad to be gay.

SD D N A SA   7. Male homosexuality is a natural expression of sexuality in human males.

SD D N A SA   8. When I am sexually attracted to a close male friend, I feel uncomfortable.

SD D N A SA   9. I am proud to be a part of the gay community.

SD D N A SA   10. Male homosexuals do not dislike women any more than heterosexual males dislike women.

SD D N A SA   11. Marriage between two homosexuals should be legalized.

SD D N A SA   12. My homosexuality does not make me unhappy.

SD D N A SA   13. Male homosexuals are overly promiscuous.

SD D N A SA   14. When I am sexually attracted to another gay man, I do not mind if someone else knows how I feel.

SD D N A SA   15. Most problems that homosexuals have come from their status as an oppressed minority, not from their homosexuality per se.

SD D N A SA   16. When women know of my homosexuality, I am afraid they will not relate to me as a man.

SD D N A SA   17. Homosexual lifestyles are not as fulfilling as heterosexual lifestyles.

SD D N A SA   18. I would not mind if my neighbors knew that I am gay.

SD D N A SA   19. It is important for me to conceal the fact that I am gay from most people.

SD D N A SA   20. Whenever I think a lot about being a homosexual, I feel critical about myself.

SD D N A SA   21. Choosing an adult gay lifestyle should be an option for children.

SD D N A SA   22. If my straight friends knew of my homosexuality, I would be uncomfortable.

SD D N A SA   23. If men knew of my homosexuality, I am afraid they would begin to avoid me.

SD D N A SA   24. Homosexuality is a sexual perversion.

SD D N A SA 25. If it were made public that I am a homosexual, I would be extremely unhappy.

SD D N A SA 26. If my peers knew of my homosexuality, I am afraid that many would not want to be my friends.

SD D N A SA 27. Adult homosexual males who have sex with boys under 18 years of age should be punished by law.

SD D N A SA 28. If others knew of my homosexuality, I would not be afraid that they would see me as being effeminate.

SD D N A SA 29. I wish I were a heterosexual.

SD D N A SA 30. When I think about coming out to peers, I am afraid they will pay more attention to my body movements and voice inflection.

SD D N A SA 31. I do not think I will be able to have a long-term love relationship with another man.

SD D N A SA 32. I am confident that my homosexuality does not make me inferior.

SD D N A SA 33. I am afraid that people will harass me if I come out more publicly.

SD D N A SA 34. When I think about coming out to a heterosexual male friend, I do not worry that he might watch me to see if I do things that are stereotypically homosexual.

Environmental Factors Questionnaire (EFQ)

On the following pages you will be presented with a number of questions regarding attitudes toward homosexuality and homosexual men as expressed by those persons who are or have been most significant to you in your current and past environments.

No two questions are exactly alike, so consider each question carefully before answering. Please do not leave any question unmarked.

Section 1

We would like you to use the following statements in order to describe the attitudes of your *closest* gay male friend. On a scale from "strongly disagree" to "strongly agree," please rate each statement with regard to the extent that it describes your friend.

Circle SD if you *strongly disagree* with the statement.
Circle D if you *disagree* with the statement.
Circle N if you are *neutral* in regard to the statement.
Circle A if you *agree* with the statement.
Circle SA if you *strongly agree* with the statement.

SD D N A SA   1. When he is sexually attracted to a close male friend, he feels uncomfortable.

SD D N A SA   2. He wishes he were heterosexual.

SD D N A SA   3. He is glad to be gay.

SD D N A SA   4. Whenever he thinks a lot about being homosexual, he gets depressed.

SD D N A SA   5. He is confident that his homosexuality does not make him inferior to straight men.

SD D N A SA   6. Whenever he thinks a lot about being a homosexual, he becomes critical about himself.

SD D N A SA   7. He would not mind if his neighbors knew he is gay.

SD D N A SA   8. It is important for him to conceal the fact that he is gay from most people.

SD D N A SA   9. When he is sexually attracted to another gay man, he does not mind if someone else knows how he feels.

SD D N A SA   10. He is afraid that if his peers knew of his homosexuality, they would not want to be friends with him.

SD D N A SA   11. He is afraid that people will harass him if he comes out more publicly.

Section 2

The following items concern the attitudes *currently* expressed by your family members, friends, and colleagues. Please use the scale below to rate from one to five how much these people or groups would endorse each of the following statements. If this statement does not apply to you, mark NA. If you do not know, mark DK; otherwise; use the SD–SA scale as in section 1.

1.   2.   3.   4.   5.   6.   7.

___ ___ ___ ___ ___ ___ ___   1. Male homosexuals do not dislike women any more than heterosexual males dislike women.

___ ___ ___ ___ ___ ___ ___   2. Male homosexuals are overly promiscuous.

___ ___ ___ ___ ___ ___ ___   3. Marriage between two homosexuals should be legalized.

___ ___ ___ ___ ___ ___ ___   4. Adult homosexual identity should be an option for children.

___ ___ ___ ___ ___ ___ ___   5. Male homosexuality is a natural expression of sexuality in human males.

___ ___ ___ ___ ___ ___ ___   6. Homosexuality is not as good as heterosexuality.

Section 3

We would like you to use the following statements in order to describe the attitudes expressed at the time you were in high school by your parents, the religious leader in your church with whom you had the most contact, your closest high school friend, and the high school faculty member who had the most impact on you. On a scale from SD–SA, please rate each statement according to how much each individual would have personally endorsed it; keep in mind that these attitudes should have been expressed during the time you were still in high school. If you do not know or cannot remember, mark DK.

1.   2.   3.   4.   5.

___ ___ ___ ___ ___   1. Male homosexuals do not dislike women any more than heterosexual males dislike women.

___ ___ ___ ___ ___   2. Male homosexuals are overly promiscuous.

___ ___ ___ ___ ___   3. Marriage between two homosexuals should be legalized.

___ ___ ___ ___ ___   4. Adult homosexual identity should be an option for children.

___ ___ ___ ___ ___   5. Male homosexuality is a natural expression of sexuality in human males.

___ ___ ___ ___ ___   6. Homosexuality is not as good as heterosexuality.

The following questions concern your own situation while you were in high school.

SD D N A SA 1. My parents are active in the gay rights movement.

SD D N A SA 2. My parents were accepting of my sexual/affectional preference.

SD D N A SA 3. I communicated frequently with my parents.

SD D N A SA 4. I was a part of a social support group that placed a positive value on being gay.

SD D N A SA 5. I was isolated from other gay people.

For questions 6–10, put an asterisk next to those that actually happened. Answer the other questions according to what you think would have happened in the situation described.

SD D N A SA 6. My parents would attend gay meetings.

SD D N A SA 7. My parents would meet and socialize with my gay friends.

SD D N A SA 8. My parents would initiate positive conversations regarding gay issues.

SD D N A SA 9. My parents would read affirmative gay literature that I recommended.

SD D N A SA 10. My parents would permit me to bring home a lover to spend the night.

The following questions concern beliefs expressed by your family *before you graduated from high school.*

SD D N A SA 11. My father believed that young children of different sexes should not be allowed to see each other naked.

SD D N A SA 12. My mother believed that young children of different sexes should not be allowed to see each other naked.

SD D N A SA 13. My father believed that children of the same sex should not be allowed to see each other naked.

SD D N A SA 14. My mother believed that children of the same sex should not be allowed to see each other naked.

SD D N A SA 15. My mother was not embarrassed to be seen naked in front of her children.

SD D N A SA 16. My father was not embarrassed to be seen naked in front of his children.

SD D N A SA 17. My mother dreaded answering questions about sex.

SD D N A SA 18. My father dreaded answering questions about sex.

SD D N A SA 19. My mother did not think children should be given any more sexual information than was absolutely necessary.

SD D N A SA 20. My father did not think children should be given any more sexual information than was absolutely necessary.

SD D N A SA 21. Open discussions about sexuality occurred frequently in our household.

SD D N A SA 22. My family discussions about sex frequently mentioned homosexuality.

SD D N A SA 23. Homosexuality was considered an alternative lifestyle in family discussions.

SD D N A SA 24. My parents were well informed about homosexuality as I was growing up.

SD D N A SA 25. Homosexuality was considered a sexual perversion and/or sinful in family discussions.

SD D N A SA 26. I have a lot of difficulty expressing anger.

SD D N A SA 27. I have a lot of difficulty expressing erotic affection for other men.

SD D N A SA 28. I express my anger as soon as something happens to anger me.

SD D N A SA 29. I have a lot of difficulty expressing affection.

30. At what age were you when you were exposed to material that was positive about being gay? _____

31. At what age were you when you were exposed to a heterosexual person who placed a positive value on being gay? _____

32. How old were you when you found someone you felt comfortable enough with to talk openly about the possibility of your being gay? _____

33. How old were you when you were first aware of erotic feelings for other men? _____

34. How old were you when you first labeled yourself as a homosexual? _____

35. In general, would you describe yourself as feeling good about being gay? _____ If yes, at what age did you first start feeling good about being a gay man? _____

36. Please place a check next to each of the following experiences that you have had as a gay person:
____ Came out to one or both parents
____ Came out to close heterosexual friends
____ Came out to an employer
____ Came out to colleagues
____ Joined a gay organization
____ Marched in a gay pride parade
____ Gave money to a gay cause
____ Read books or articles positive on gay issues
____ Received the support of either or both parents for being gay
____ Received the support of friends for being gay
____ Received the support of a religious leader for being gay
____ Received the support of a teacher for being gay
____ Felt like being a gay male separatist
____ Had a long-term relationship with another gay man
____ Disagreed openly when a fag joke was made
____ Came out to your children and received support
____ Rejected the notion that there are only two kinds of sex roles: those that are masculine and those that are feminine
____ Rejected the notion that there are only two kinds of sexualities: those that are homosexual and those that are heterosexual
____ Felt that the traditional roles for men and women were not necessarily the best way for you to live
____ Created a new mental (cognitive) category for the way you think of your own sexuality and sex role

Section 4

Please use the space provided on this questionnaire to answer the following questions or circle the letter beside the appropriate answer.

1. Would you describe yourself as:
   A. Primarily in the closet
   B. Primarily out of the closet
2. What percentage of your male sexual encounters are with (100% total):
   ____ A. Relatively anonymous partners
   ____ B. Partners who are your friends
   ____ C. Partners with whom you have a long-term relationship
   ____ D. Other (Please specify) _____
3. What percentage of your sexual contacts are with other men? _____

4. How involved are you in the gay rights movement?
    A. Very involved
    B. Somewhat involved
    C. Involved very little
    D. Not at all involved
5. What is your age? _____
6. What is your highest or current level of education?
    A. High school
    B. One year of college attendance
    C. Two years of college attendance
    D. Three years of college attendance
    E. Four years of college attendance
    F. Five or more years of college attendance
7. What is your current occupation? _____
8. On the average, how often do you attempt to "pass" for straight?
    A. Always   D. Somewhat infrequently
    B. Very frequently   E. Very infrequently
    C. Somewhat frequently   F. Never
9. What is the longest that you have ever been in a relationship with one male
    lover? _____
10. Do you have a male lover or "boyfriend"? (   ) Yes   (   ) No
    If so, do you live together? (   ) Yes   (   ) No
11. Do you consider youself:
    A. Homosexual   B. Gay   C. Neither   D. Both, with no difference
    E. Other (please specify) _____
12. On the average, how often do you have sex in each of the following
    places?

            0 Never
            1 Once
            2 Very infrequently
            3 Somewhat infrequently
            4 Somewhat frequently
            5 Very frequently
            6 Always

    (   ) A. Your home
    (   ) B. Your partner's home
    (   ) C. A friend's home
    (   ) D. Gay bath
    (   ) E. Beach
    (   ) F. Park
    (   ) G. Public restroom
    (   ) H. Car
    (   ) I.   Van or camper
    (   ) J. Tent
    (   ) K. Motel or hotel
    (   ) L. Bar

( ) M. Secluded woods or field
( ) N. Barn or farm building
(˙) O. Peep show, pornographic movie house
( ) P. Other (specify) _____

13. Do you consider or have you ever considered yourself "married" to another man? ( ) Yes ( ) No
14. Have you ever had a gay marriage ceremony? ( ) Yes ( ) No
15. How much is your homosexuality or gayness something other than just a sexual preference?
    A. Quite a lot   C. Very little
    B. Somewhat   D. None
16. How important is the concept of a gay community/culture to you?
    A. Very important   C. Somewhat unimportant
    B. Somewhat important   D. Very unimportant

Please use the rating scale on Question 12, above, to answer the next two questions.

17. How often do you socialize with each of the following:
    A. Gay men   D. Bisexual men
    B. Straight men   E. Bisexual women
    C. Lesbian women   F. Straight women
18. How often do you "camp it up" or watch others "camp it up"?
    Camp it up _____
    Watch others camp it up _____
19. Whether or not you camp it up or watch others camp it up, how do you feel about the idea of each of them?

    0 Very negative
    1 Somewhat negative
    2 Neutral
    3 Somewhat positive
    4 Very positive

20. What is your race? (circle one)
    Caucasion   Black   Oriental   Hispanic   Other (specify): _____
20A. What is your annual income? _____
21. What city and county do you currently live in?
    City _____ County _____
22. How many of the following (if applicable) know about your homosexuality?

    0 None
    1 One
    2 Some
    3 Most
    4 All

    ( ) A. Gay male friends   ( ) H. Your employees
    ( ) B. Lesbian friends   ( ) I. Mother

( ) C. Straight friends   ( ) J. Father
( ) D. Neighbors   ( ) K. Sisters and brothers
( ) E. Employer   ( ) L. Your children
( ) F. Teacher   ( ) M. Other children
( ) G. Coworkers   ( ) N. Schoolmates

24. My parents' income falls in the following range (please check appropriate category):

    _____ up to $ 5,000   _____ up to $25,000
    _____ up to $10,000   _____ up to $30,000
    _____ up to $15,000   _____ over $30,000

25. I am dependent upon my parents for the following percentage of my income (please check appropriate category):

    _____ none   _____ up to 75
    _____ up to 25   _____ 100
    _____ up to 50

26. At what age did you consider yourself financially independent from your parents? _____

27. If you are now financially dependent upon your parents for less than 50% of your support, was your independence (check one)

    _____ Your parents' decision   _____ Both
    _____ Your decision   _____ Does not apply

28. Have your parents withheld financial support due to your choice of lifestyle or sexual preference? ( ) Yes ( ) No ( ) Does not apply

29. Have you found it desirable to refuse financial support from your parents?
    ( ) Yes ( ) No ( ) Does not apply

REFERENCES

Abelson, R. Computers, polls and public opinion: Some puzzles and paradoxes. *Transaction*, 1968, *5*, 20–27.

Abelson, R., & Zimbardo, P. *Canvassing for peace: A manual for volunteers.* Ann Arbor, Mich.: Society for the Psychological Study of Social Issues, 1970.

Adorno, T.W., Frenkel-Brunswick, E., Levinson, D.J., & Sanford, R.N. *The authoritarian personality.* New York: Harper, 1950.

Allport, G.W. *The nature of prejudice* (abridged ed.). Garden City, N.Y.: Doubleday/Anchor, 1954/1958.

Altman, D. *Homosexual oppression and liberation.* New York: Avon, 1971.

American Psychiatric Association. *Diagnostic and statistical manual, III.* Washington, D.C.: American Psychiatric Association, 1980.

Anastasi, A. *Psychological testing.* New York: Macmillan, 1976.

Anderson, S. Sex role typing as related to self, acceptance of others, and discrimanatory attitudes toward women. *Journal of Research in Personality*, 1978, *12*, 410–415.

Anderson, S., & Zimbardo, P. Resisting mind control. *USA Today*, Nov. 1980.

Aronson, E. *The social animal.* San Francisco: W.H. Freeman, 1980.

Asch, S. Effects of group pressure upon the modification and distortion of judgment. In M.H. Guetzkow (Ed.), *Groups, leadership and men.* Pittsburgh: Carnegie, 1951, pp. 117–190.

Asch, S. *Social psychology.* Englewood Cliffs, N.J.: Prentice-Hall, 1952.

Asch, S. Studies of independence and conformity: A minority of one against unanimous majority. *Psychological Monographs*, 1956, *70*(9).

Bacon, F. *Novum organum.* (Originally published in 1620.) J. Devey, Ed. New York: P.F. Collier & Son, 1902.

Bailey, D.S. *Homosexuality and the Western Christian tradition*. London: Longmans, 1955.

Bakan, D. *The duality of human existence*. Chicago: Rand McNally, 1966.

Balswick, J. Types of inexpressive male roles. In R. Lewis (Ed.), *Men in difficult times*. Englewood Cliffs, N.J.: Prentice-Hall, 1981.

Bancroft, J. *Deviant sexual behavior: Modification and assessment*. New York: Oxford University Press, 1974.

Bandura, A. The role of modeling processes in personality development. In *The young child: Reviews of research*. Washington, D.C.: National Association for the Education of Young Children, 1967.

Bandura, A. *Social learning theory*. Englewood Cliffs, N.J.: Prentice-Hall, 1977.

Bandura, A., & Huston, A. Identification as a process of incidental learning. *Journal of Abnormal Social Psychology*, 1961, *63*, 311–318.

Bandura, A., Ross, D., & Ross, S. Transmission of aggression through imitation of aggressive models. *Journal of Abnormal Social Psychology*, 1961, *63*, 575–582.

Bartlett, F.C. *Remembering: A study in experimental and social psychology*. London: Cambridge University Press, 1932.

Beck, A.T. *Depression: Clinical, experimental and theoretical aspects*. Philadelphia: University of Philadelphia Press, 1967.

Beck, A.T. Cognitive therapy: Nature and relation to behavior therapy. *Behavior Therapy*, 1970, *1*, 184–200.

Bell, A. Homosexualities: Their range and character. In J.K. Cole & R. Dienstbier (Eds.), *Nebraska symposium on motivation* (Vol. 21). Lincoln; University of Nebraska Press, 1975.

Bell, A., & Weinberg, M. *Homosexualities*. New York: Simon and Schuster, 1978.

Bem, D. *Beliefs, attitudes and human affairs*. Monterey, Calif.: Brooks-Cole, 1974a.

Bem, D., & Funder, D. Predicting more of the people more of the time: Person-situation interaction. *Journal of Personality and Social Psychology*, 1978, 85(b), 485–501.

Bem, S. The measurement of psychological androgyny. *Journal of Consulting and Clinical Psychology*, 1974b, *42*,155–162.

Bem, S. The psychology of sex roles. Lecture presented at Stanford University Department of Psychology, April, 1978.

Bem, S. Gender schema theory: A cognitive account of sex typing. *Psychological Review*, 1981a, *88*(4), 354–364. (a)

Bem, S. Probing the promise of androgyny. In A. Kaplan & J. Bean (Eds.), *Beyond sex role stereotypes: Readings toward a psychology of androgyny*. Boston: Little, Brown and Company, 1976, pp. 47–62.

Bem, S. The BSRI and gender schema theory: A reply to Spence and Helmreich. *Psychological Review*, 1981(b), *88*(4), 369–371.

Bem, S., & Lenney, E. Sex typing and the avoidance of cross-sex behavior. *Journal of Personality and Social Psychology*, 1976, *33*(1), 48–54.

Berger, M. Men's new family roles—Some implications for therapists. *The Family Coordinator*, October, 1979, 638–645.

Berry, D., & Marks, F. Antihomosexual prejudice as a function of attitudes toward own sexuality. In *Proceedings of the 77th annual Convention of the American Psychological Association*, Washington, D.C.: APA, 1969 (Vol. *4*), 573–574. (Summary)

Bieber, I. A discussion of "Homosexuality: The ethical challenge." *Journal of Consulting and Clinical Psychology*, 1976, *44*(2), 163–166.

Bieber, I., Dain, H., Dince, P., Drelich, M., Grand, H., Gundlach, R., Kremer, M., Rifkin, A., Wilber, C., & Bieber, T. *Homosexuality: A psychoanalytic study of male homosexuals.* New York: Basic Books, 1962.

Block, J. *Lives through time.* Berkeley, Calif.: Bancroft Books, 1971.

Block, J.H. Conceptions of sex-role: Some cross-cultural and longitudinal perspectives. *American Psychologist*, 1973, *28*(6), 512–526.

Bogardus, F.S. *Social distance.* New York: Free Press, 1959.

Boswell, J. The Pauline texts. In J. McNeil, *The church and the homosexual.* Kansas City, Mo.: Sheed, Andrews and McMeel, 1976, p. 54.

Boswell, J. *Christianity, social tolerance, and homosexuality: Gay people in Western Europe from the beginning of the Christian era to the fourteenth century.* Chicago: University of Chicago Press, 1980.

Bower, G. Mood and Memory. *American Psychologist*, 1981, *31*, 129–148.

Bramel, D. Some determinants of defensive projection. Doctoral dissertation, Stanford University, 1960.

Bransford, J.D. *Human cognition: Learning, understanding and remembering.* Belmont, Calif.: Wadsworth, 1979.

Brehm, J., & Cohen, A. *Explorations in cognitive dissonance.* New York: Wiley, 1962.

Bronfenbrenner, U. *Two worlds of childhood: U.S. and U.S.S.R.* New York: Russell Sage Foundation, 1970.

Brown, M., & Amoroso, D. Attitudes toward homosexuality among West Indian male and female college students. *Journal of Social Psychology*, 1975, *97*, 163–168.

Bryant, B.S. Lesbian mothers. Master's thesis, California State University, Sacramento, 1975. On file at Lymar Associates, 330 Ellis Street, Room 401, San Francisco.

Buss, A. *A dialectical psychology.* New York: Irvington, 1979.

Cantor, Prototypicality and personality. Unpublished manuscript, Stanford University, 1977.

Cantor, N. & Mischel, W. Information-processing about personality: A pattern-matching process. Paper presented at meeting of the American Psychological Association, San Francisco, August, 1977.

Carlsmith, J.M., Collins, B., & Helmreich, R. Studies in forced compliance: I. The effect of pressure for compliance on attitude change produced by face-to-face role playing and anonymous essay writing. *Journal of Personality and Social Psychology*, 1966, *4*, 1–13.

Carlsmith, J.M., & Gross, A. Some effects of guilt on compliance. In J. Freedman, J.M. Carlsmith, & D. Sears (Eds.), *Readings in social psychology*. Englewood Cliffs, N.J.: Prentice-Hall, 1971.

Cartwright, D., & Zander, A. (Eds.) *Group dynamics*. New York: Harper and Row, 1953.

Cass, V. Homosexual identity formation: A theoretical model. *Journal of Homosexuality*, 1979, *4*(3), 219–235.

Chapman, L.J., & Chapman, J.P. Illusory correlations as an obstacle to the use of valid psychodiagnostic signs. *Journal of Abnormal Psychology*, 1969, *74*, 271–280.

Christensen, H.T., & Carpenter, G.R. Value-behavior discrepancies regarding premarital coitus in three Western cultures. *American Sociological Review*, 1962, *27*, 66–74.

Churchill, W. *Homosexual behavior among males: A cross-cultural and cross-species investigation*. New York: Hawthorn, 1967.

Clark, D. *Loving someone gay*. Milbrae, Calif: Celestial Arts, 1977.

Coates, T., Mandel, J., & Temoshok, L. Behavioral medicine, psychoneuroimmunology and the Acquired Immune Deficiency Syndrome. *American Psychologist*, 1983, in press.

Cofer, C. *Motivation and emotion*. New York: Scott, Foresman, 1972.

Coleman, Eli. Developmental stages of the coming out process. In Gay Left Collective (Eds.), *Homosexuality: Power and politics*. London: Allison and Busby, 1980, pp. 149–158.

Commager, H.S. *Freedom, loyalty, dissent*. New York: Oxford University Press, 1954.

Craik, K.H. The personality research paradigm in environmental psychology. In S. Wapner, S.B. Cohen, & B. Kaplan (Eds.), *Experiencing the environment*. New York: Plenum, 1976.

Cross, W.E. Discovering the black referent: The psychology of black liberation. In V.J. Dixon & B. Foster (Eds.), *Beyond black or white: An alternative America*. Boston: Little, Brown, 1971.

Curran, D., & Partridge, M. *Psychological medicine*. Edinburgh: Livingstone, 1963.

Dank, B. Coming out in the gay world. *Psychiatry*, 1971, *34*, 180–197.

Davenport, W. Sexual patterns and their regulation in a society of the Southwest Pacific. In F. Beach (Ed.) *Sex and Behavior*. 1974,

Huntington, N.Y.: Krieger Publishing Company, pp. 164–207. (Originally published in 1965.)

David, B., & Brannon, R. (Eds.) The male sex role: Our culture's blueprint of manhood and what its done for us lately. In David & Brannon (Eds.), *The forty-nine percent majority*. Reading, Mass.: Addison-Wesley, 1976, pp. 1–48.

Davidson, G. Politics, ethics and therapy for homosexuality. In W. Paul, J. Weinrich, J. Gonsiorek, & M. Hotvedt (Eds.), *Homosexuality: Social, psychological-and biological issues*. Beverly Hills: Sage Publications, 1982, pp. 89–99.

DeCecco, J.P. *The psychology of learning and instruction*. Englewood Cliffs, N.J.: Prentice-Hall, 1968.

DeCecco, J., & Shively, M. Components of sexual identity. *Journal of Homosexuality*, 1978, *4*(1).

DeGregorio, E., & Carver, C. Type A behavior pattern, sex role orientation, and psychological adjustment. *Journal of Personality and Social Psychology*, 1980, *39*(2), 286–293.

DeMonteflores, C., & Schultz, S. Coming out: Similarities and differences for lesbians and gay men. *Journal of Social Issues*, 1978, *34*(3), 59–72.

Deutsch, M., & Gerard, H. A study of normative and informational social influence upon individual judgment. *Journal of Abnormal and Social Psychology*, 1955, *51*, 629–639.

Dollard, J., Doob, L., Miller, N.E. Mowrer, O.H., & Sears, R. *Frustration and aggression*. New Haven, Conn.: Yale University Press, 1939.

Dorner, G., & Hinz, G. Induction and prevention of male homosexuality by androgen. *Journal of Endocrinology*, 1968, *40*, 387–388.

Dunbar, J., Brown, M., & Amoroso, D.M. Some correlates of attitudes toward homosexuality. *Journal of Social Psychology*, 1973, *89*, 271–279.

Dunbar, J., Brown, M., & Vourinen, S. Attitudes toward homosexuality among Brazilian and Canadian college students. *Journal of Social Psychology*, 1973, *90*, 173–183.

Edwards, A.L. *Techniques of attitude scale construction*. New York: Appleton-Century-Crofts, 1957.

Ehrhardt, A. The interactional model of sex hormones and behavior. In H. Katchadourian (Ed.), *Human sexuality*. Berkeley: University of California Press, 1979, pp. 150–160.

Ellis, A. *Reason and emotion in psychotherapy* (2d ed.). Secaucus, N.J.: Lyle Stuart, 1977.

Erikson, E. Identity and life cycle. *Psychological Issues*, 1959, *1*, 18.

Errera, P. Some historical aspects of the concept of phobia. *The Psychiatric Quarterly*, 1962, *36*, 325–336.

Eysenck, H.J. *Behavior therapy and the neuroses*. Oxford: Pergamon Press, 1960.

Farrell, R.A., & Morrione, T.J. Social interaction and stereotypic responses to homosexuals. *Archives of Sexual Behavior*, 1974, *3*, 425–442.

Fasteau, M.F. *The male machine*. New York: Delta, 1976.

Feldman, M., & McCulloch, M. *Homosexual behavior: Therapy and assessment*. Elmsford, N.Y.: Pergamon Press, 1971.

Festinger, L. Behavior support for opinion change. *Public Opinion Quarterly*, 1964, *28*, 404–417.

Festinger, L., & Carlsmith, J.M. Cognitive consequences of forced compliance. *Journal of Abnormal and Social Psychology*, 1959, *58*, 203–211.

Ford, S., & Beach, F.A. *Patterns of sexual behavior*. New York: Harper and Row, 1951.

Foucault, M. *The history of sexuality*. New York: Vintage Books, 1980. (Originally published in 1976.)

Frederiksen, N. Toward a taxonomy of situations. *American Psychologist*, 1973, *27*, 114–123.

Freud, S. Three essays on the theory of sexuality (Originally published in 1905). In J. Strachey (Ed.), *The standard edition of the complete psychological works of Sigmund Freud*. New York: Macmillan, 1953.

Freud, S. Historical notes: A letter from Freud. *American Journal of Psychiatry*, 1955, *CVII*, 786–787. (This letter was written in 1935 and later uncovered by Alfred Kinsey.)

Freud, S. The psychoanalytic notes on an autobiographical account of a case of paranoia. In *The standard edition of the complete psychological works of Sigmund Freud* (Vol. 13). London: Hogarth Press, 1958.

Freund, K. A laboratory method for diagnosing predominance of homo- or hetero-erotic interest in the male. *Behavior Research and Therapy*, 1963, *1*, 85–93.

Freund, K., Langevin, R., Gibiri, S., & Zajac, Y. Heterosexual aversion in homosexual males. *British Journal of Psychiatry*, 1973, *122*, 163–169.

Freund, K., Nagler, E., Langevin, R., Zajac, A., & Steiner, B. Measuring feminine gender identity in homosexual males. *Archives of Sexual Behavior*, 1974, *3*, 249–260.

Gagnon, J. The interaction of gender roles and sexual conduct. In H. Katchadourian (Ed.), *Human sexuality*. Berkeley: University of California Press, 1979, pp. 223–225.

Gagnon, J., & Simon, W. *Sexual conduct*. Chicago: Aldine, 1973.

Gallup, G. Gallup poll on gay rights: Approval with restrictions. *San Francisco Chronicle*, July 18, 1977, p. 1.

Gartrell, N. Hormones and homosexuality. In W. Paul, J. Weinrich, J. Gonsiorek, & M. Hotvedt (Eds.), *Homosexuality; Social, psychological and biological issues*. Beverly Hills, Calif.: Sage Publications, 1982, pp. 169–182.

Gastorf, J., Suls, J., & Sanders, G. Type A coronary-prone behavior pattern and social facilitation. *Journal of Personality and Social Psychology*, 1980, *38*(5), 773–780.

Glass, D.C. *Behavior patterns, stress and coronary disease*. N.J.: Erlbaum, 1977.

Glass, S.J., Denel, H.J., & Wright, C.A. Sex hormone studies in male homosexuality. *Endocrinology*, 1940, *28*, 590–594.

Goffman, I. *Stigma: Notes on the management of a spoiled identity*. Englewood Cliffs, N.J.: Prentice-Hall, 1963.

Green, R. *Sexual identity conflict in children and adults*. New York: Basic Books, 1974.

Green, R. Biological influences on sexual identity. In H. Katchadourian (Ed.), *Human sexuality*. Berkeley. University of California Press, 1979, pp. 115–133.

Green, R., & Money, J. (Eds.). *Transexualism and sex reassignment*. Baltimore: Johns Hopkins Press, 1969.

Groth, N., & Brugess, W. Male rape: offenders and victims. *American Journal of Psychiatry*, 1980, *137*(7), 806–810.

Habermas, J. *Communication and the evolution of society*. Boston: Beacon, 1979.

Hantover, J. The social construction of masculine anxiety. In R. Lewis (Ed.), *Men in difficult times*. Englewood Cliffs, N.J.: Prentice-Hall, 1981, pp. 87–98.

Harrison, J. Warning: The male sex role may be dangerous to your health. *Journal of Social Issues*, 1978, *34*(1).

Hart, J., & Richardson, D. *The theory and practice of homosexuality*. London: Routledge and Kegan Paul, 1981.

Hartley, R.E. Sex role pressures and the socialization of the male child. *Psychological Reports*, 1959, *5*, 457–468.

Hedblom, J.H. Dimensions of lesbian sexual experience. *Archives of Sexual Behavior*, 1973, *2*, 329–341.

Heider, F. An experimental study of apparent behavior. *American Journal of Psychology*, 1944, *57*, 243–259.

Hencken, J. Homosexuality and psychoanalysis: Toward a mutual understanding. In W. Paul, J. Weinrich, J. Gonsiorek, & M. Hotvedt (Eds.), *Homosexuality; Social, psychological-and biological issues*. Beverly Hills, Calif.: Sage Publications, 1982, pp. 121–148.

Hencken, J.D., & O'Dowd, W.T. Coming out as an aspect of identity formation. *Gay Academic Union Journal: Gai Saber*, 1977, *1*(1), 18–26.

Henderson, D., & Batchelor, I. *Henderson and Gillespie's textbook of psychiatry* (9th ed.). London: Oxford University Press, 1962.

Herik, G. Assessing homophobia: A multidimensional approach. Unpublished manuscript, 1978.

Hooker, E. The adjustment of the male overt homosexual. *Journal of Projective Techniques*, 1957, *21*, 18–31.

Hooker, E. Male homosexuals and their "worlds." In J. Marmor (Ed.), *Sexual inversion*. New York: Basic Books, 1965.

Hotvedt, M., & Mandel, J. Children of lesbian mothers. In W. Paul, J. Weinrich, J. Gonsiorek, & M. Hotvedt (Eds.), *Homosexuality: Social, psychological-and biological issues*. Beverly Hills, Calif.: Sage Publications, 1982, pp. 275–286.

Hovland, C., Janis, I., & Kelley, H. *Communication and persuasion*. New Haven, Conn: Yale University Press, 1953.

Hudson, W., & Ricketts, W. A strategy for the measurement of homophobia. *Journal of Homosexuality*, 1980, *5*(4), 357–371.

Humphreys, R.L. *Tearoom trade: Impersonal sex in public places*. Chicago: Aldine, 1970.

Izard, C. *Human emotions*. New York: Plenum Press, 1977, pp. 44–45.

James, W. What is an emotion? *Mind*, 1884, *9*, 188–205.

Jaspers, K. *General psychopathology* (Originally published in 1923; 7th ed.). Manchester University Press, 1963, pp. 136–137.

Jones, E., & Nisbett, R. *The actor and the observer: Divergent perceptions of the causes of behavior*. New York: General Learning Press, 1971.

Joslyn, W.D. Androgen-induced social dominance in infant female rhesus monkies. *Journal of Child Psychology and Psychiatry*, 1973, *14*, 137–145.

Jourard, S.M. *Disclosing man to himself*. New York: Van Nostrand, 1968.

Jourard, S.M. *The transparent self* (2d ed.). New York: Van Nostrand, 1971.

Kagan, J. The concept of identification. *Psychological Review*, 1958, *65*, 296–305.

Kagan, J. Acquisition and significance of sex-typing and sex-role identity. In M.L. Hoffman & L.W. Hoffman (Eds.), *Review of child development research* (Vol. 1). New York: Russell Sage Foundation, 1964. (a)

Kagan, J. The child sex role classification of school objects. *Child Development*, 1964, *35*, 1051–1056. (b)

Kardiner, A. The flight from masculinity. In H.M. Ruitenbeek (Ed.), *The problem of homosexuality in modern society*. New York: E.P. Dutton, 1963.

Karlen, A. *Sexuality and homosexuality: A new view*. New York: W.W. Norton, 1971, pp. 274–275.

Karr, R. *Homosexual labeling: An experimental analysis*. Doctoral dissertation, University of Washington, 1975.

Karr, R. Homosexual labeling and the male role. *Journal of Social Issues*, 1978, *34*, 3.

Katchadourian, H. (Ed.). *Human sexuality*. Berkeley: University of California Press, 1979.

Katz, D., & Braly, K.W. Racial stereotypes of 100 college students. *Journal of Abnormal and Social Psychology*, 1933, *28*, 280–290.

Kavalovski, V. Men and the dream of brotherhood. In R. Lewis (Ed.) *Men in difficult times*. Englewood Cliffs, N.J.: Prentice-Hall, 1981, pp. 199–212.

Kelly, J., & Worell, J. New formulations of sex roles and androgyny: A critical review. *Journal of Consulting and Clinical Psychology*, 1977, *45*, 1101–1115.

Kelly-Gadol, J. The social relation of the sexes: Methodological implications of women's history. *Signs*, 1976, *1*, 809–810.

Kelman, H. Processes of opinion change. *Public Opinion Quarterly*, 1961, *25*, 57–78.

Kinsey, A., Pomeroy, W., & Martin, C. *Sexual behavior in the human male*. Philadelphia: Saunders, 1948.

Kinsey, A., Pomeroy, W., Martin, C., & Gebhard, P. *Sexual behavior in the human female*. Philadelphia: Saunders, 1953.

Knutson, D.C. (Ed.) Homosexuality and the law. *Journal of Homosexuality*, 1980. (Special edition published in New York by Haworth Press.)

Kohlberg, L. A cognitive-developmental analysis of children's sex role concepts and attitudes. In E.E. Maccoby (Ed.), *The development of sex differences*. Stanford, Calif.: Stanford University Press, 1966.

Krafft-Ebbing, R. von. *Psychopathia sexualis* (Originally published in 1906). Wedeck, H.E., Trans. New York: Putnams, 1965.

Krulewitz, J., & Nash, J. Effects of sex role attitudes and similarity on men's rejection of male homosexuals. *Journal of Personality and Social Psychology*, 1980, *38*(1), 67–74.

Landis, C. *Varieties of psychopathological experience*. F.A. Mettler, Ed. New York: Holt, Rinehart and Winston, 1964.

Lang, T. Studies on the genetic determination of homosexuality. *Journal of Nervous and Mental Disease*, 1940, *92*, 55–64.

Larson, P. Gay male relationships. In W. Paul, J. Weinrich, J. Gonsiorek, & M. Hotvedt (Eds.), *Homosexuality: Social, psychological and biological issues*. Beverly Hills, Calif.: Sage Publications, 1982, pp. 219–232.

Laughlin, H.P. *The neurosis in clinical practice*. London: W.B. Saunders, 1956.

Lauritsen, J., & Thorstad, D. *The early homosexual rights movement*. New York: Times Change Press, 1974.

Lee, J.A. Going public: A study in the sociology of homosexual liberation. *Journal of Homosexuality*, 1977, *3*(1), 49–78.

Lehne, G.K. Homophobia in men. In D. David & R. Brannon (Eds.), *The 49% majority: Readings on the male sex role*. New York: Addison-Wesley, 1976, 66–88.

Leventhal, H. Toward a comprehensive theory of emotion. *Advances in Experimental Social Psychology*, 1980, *13*, 139–207.

Leventhal, H. The integration of emotion and cognition: A view from the perceptual-motor theory of emotion. Presented at the 17th Annual Carnegie-Mellon Symposium: Emotion and cognition, May, 1981.

Levitt, E., & Klassen, A. Public attitudes toward homosexuality: Part of the 1970 national survey by the Institute for Sex Research. *Journal of Homosexuality*, 1974, *1*(1), 29–43.

Lewin, E., & Lyons, T. Everything in its place: The coexistence of lesbianism and motherhood. In W. Paul, J. Weinrich, J. Gonsiorek, & M. Hotvedt (Eds.), *Homosexuality; Social, psychological and biological issues*. Beverly Hills, Calif.: Sage Publications, 1982, pp. 249–274.

Lewis, R., Kozac, E., & Grosnick, W. Committment in same-sex love relationships. *Alternative Lifestyles*, 1981, *4*(1).

Lewis, M., & Brooks, J. Self-knowledge and emotional development. In M. Lewis & L. Rosenblum (Eds.), *The development of affect*. New York: Plenum Press, 1978.

Lewis, R. Emotional intimacy among men. *Journal of Social Issues*, 1978, *34*(1), 108–121.

Lichtheim, G. *The concept of ideology and other essays*. New York: Vintage Books, 1967.

Lieberman, S. The effects of changes in roles on the attitudes of role occupants. *Human Relations*, 1956, *9*, 385–402.

Lofland, J. *Deviance and identity*. Englewood Cliffs, N.J.: Prentice-Hall, 1969.

Long, B., & Ziller, R. Dogmatism and predecisional information search. *Journal of Applied Psychology*, 1965, *49*, 376–378.

Lovallo, W., & Pishkin, V. Performance of Type A (coronary prone) men during and after exposure to uncontrollable noise and task failure. *Journal of Personality and Social Psychology*, 1980, *38*(6), 963–971.

Lumby, M.E. Homophobia: The quest for a valid scale. *Journal of Homosexuality*, 1976, *2*(1), 39–47.

Luria, Z. Psychosocial determinants of gender identity, role and orientation.

In H. Katchadourian (Ed.), *Human sexuality*. Berkeley: University of California Press, 1979, pp. 163–193.

Maccoby, E. Gender identity and sex-role adoption. In H. Katchadourian (Ed.), *Human sexuality*. Berkeley: University of California Press, 1979, pp. 194–203.

Maccoby, E., and Jacklin, C. *The psychology of sex differences*. Stanford, Calif.: Stanford University Press, 1974.

MacDonald, A.P., Jr. Identification and measurement of multidimensional attitudes toward equality between the sexes. *Journal of Homosexuality*, 1974, *1*(2), 165–182. (a)

MacDonald, A.P., Jr. The importance of sex-role to gay liberation. *Homosexual Counseling Journal*, 1974, *1*, 169–180. (b)

MacDonald, A.P., Jr., & Games, R. Some characteristics of those who hold positive and negative attitudes toward homosexuals. *Journal of Homosexuality*, 1974, *1*(1), 9–27.

MacDonald, A.P., Jr., Huggins, J., Young, S., & Swanson, R.A. Attitudes toward homosexuality: Preservation of sex morality or the double standard? *Journal of Consulting and Clinical Psychology*, 1973, *40*, 161.

MacDonald, A.P. Homophobia: Its roots and meanings. *Homosexual Counseling Journal*, 1976, *3*(1), 23–33.

Mandler, G. *Mind and emotion*. New York: Wiley, 1975.

Marks, I. *Fears and phobias*. London: Academic Press, 1969.

Markus, H. Self-schemata and processing information about the self. *Journal of Personality and Social Psychology*, 1977, *35*, 63–178.

Masters, W.H., & Johnson, V.E. *Homosexuality in perspective*. Boston: Little, Brown, 1979.

Mayer, R. *Thinking and problem solving*. Chicago, Ill.: Scott, Foresman, 1977

McConaghy, N. Penile volume change to moving pictures of male and female nudes in heterosexual and homosexual males. *Behavior Research and Therapy*, 1967, *5*, 43–48.

McDonald, G.J., & Moore, R.J. Sex role self concepts of homosexual men and their attitudes toward both women and male homosexuality. *Journal of Homosexuality*, 1978, *4*(1), 3–14.

McIntosh, M. The homosexual role. *Social Problems*, 1968, *16*, 182–192.

McNeil, J. *The church and the homosexual*. Kansas City: Sheed, Andrews and McMeel, 1976.

Mead, G.H. *Mind, self and society*. Chicago: University of Chicago Press, 1934.

Mead, M. *Coming of age in Samoa* (Originally published in 1938). New York: Morrow, 1961.

Millham, J., San Miguel, C., & Kellogg, R. A factor-analytic conceptualization of attitudes towards male and females homosexuals. *Journal of Homosexuality*, 1976, *2*(1), 3–10.

Minnigerode, F.A. Attitudes toward homosexuality: Feminist attitudes and social conservatism. *Sex Roles*, 1976, *2*, 347–352.

Minton, H. Homosexual identity formation: A dialectical perspective. Unpublished manuscript, University of Toronto, 1980.

Mischel, W. *Personality and assessment*. New York: Wiley, 1968.

Mischel, W., & Grusec, J. Determinant of the rehearsal and transmission of neutral and aversive behaviors. *Journal of Personality and Social Psychology*, 1966, *3*, 197–205.

Money, J. Prenatal hormones and postnatal socialization in gender identity differentiation. In J.K. Cole & R. Dienstbier (Eds.), *Nebraska symposium on motivation, 1973*. Lincoln: University of Nebraska Press, 1974.

Money, J. Ablatio penis: Normal male infant sex-reassigned as a girl. *Archives of Sexual Behavior*, 1975, *4*, 65–72.

Money, J., & Dalery, J. Iatrogenic homosexuality: Gender identity in seven 46XX chromosomal females with hyperadrenocortical hermaphroditism born with a penis, three reared as boys, four reared as girls. *Journal of Homosexuality*, 1976, *1*, 357–371.

Money, J., & Erhardt, A.A. Prenatal hormone exposure: Possible effects on behavior in man. In R.P. Michael (Ed.), *Endocrinology and human behavior*. Oxford: Oxford Medical Publications, 1968.

Money, J., & Tucker, P. *Sexual signatures: On being a man or a woman*. Boston: Little, Brown, 1975.

Moore, W.E., & Tumin, M.M. Some social functions of ignorance. In B. Rosenberg et al. (Eds.), *Mass society in crisis: Social problems and social pathology*. New York: Macmillan, 1964.

Moos, R.H. Conceptualizations of human environments. *American Psychologist*, 1973, *28*, 652–665.

Morin, S. Educational programs as a means of changing attitudes toward gay people. *Homosexual Counseling Journal*, 1974, *1*, 160–165.

Morin, S. Heterosexual bias in psychological research on lesbianism and male homosexuality. *American Psychologist*, 1977, *32*, 629–637.

Morin, S., & Nungesser, L.G. Can homophobia be cured? In R.A. Lewis (Ed.), *Men in difficult times*. Englewood Cliffs, N.J.: Prentice-Hall, 1980.

Morin, S., & Garfinkle, E. Male homophobia. *Journal of Social Issues*, 1978, *34*, *1*, 29–46.

Morin, S., & Schultz, S. The gay movement and the rights of children. Journal of Social Issues, 1978, *34*(2), 137–148.

Morin, S., Taylor, K., & Kielman, S. Gay is beautiful at a distance. Paper presented at a meeting of the American Psychological Association, Chicago, August, 1975.

Morin, S., & Wallace, S. Traditional values, sex-role stereotyping and attitudes toward homosexuality. Paper presented at the annual meeting of the Western Psychological Association, Los Angeles, April, 1976.

Mort, F. Sexuality: "Regulation and Contestation." In Gay Left Collective (Eds.), *Homosexuality: Power and politics*. London: Allison and Busby, 1980, pp. 38–51.

Myrick, F. Attitudinal differences between homosexually and heterosexually oriented males and between covert and overt homosexuals. *Journal of Abnormal Psychology*, 1974, *83*(1), 81–86.

Newcomb, T.M. *Personality and social change*. New York: Dryden Press, 1943.

Nungesser, L.G. Homophobia and speech disruptions. Unpublished manuscript, Stanford University, 1978.

Nungesser, L.G. *Homophobic prejudice in homosexual males*. Honors thesis, Stanford University, 1979.

Nungesser, L.G. Theoretical bases for research on the acquisition of social sex roles by children of lesbian mothers. *Journal of Homosexuality*, 1980, 5(3), 177–187.

Nutt, R., & Sedlacek, W. Freshman sexual attitudes and behaviors. *Journal of College Student Personnel*, 1974, *15*, 346–351.

Opinion Research Center Poll, 1966. In G. Lehne, Homophobia among men. Unpublished manuscript, 1978.

Ovesey, L. *Homosexuality and pseudohomosexuality*. New York: Science House, 1969.

Padgug, R. Sexual matters: On conceptualizing sexuality in history. *Radical History Review*, 1979, *20*, 3–23.

Parry, G., & Lightbrown, R. Presenting problems of gay people seeking help. In J. Hart & D. Richardson (Eds.), *The theory and practice of homosexuality*. London: Routledge and Kegan Paul, 1981.

Parson, J. Cognitive-developmental theories of sex-role socialization. In Frieze, I., Parson, J., Johnson, P., Ruble, D., and Zellman, G., *Women and sex roles*. New York: W.W. Norton, 1978, pp. 114–134.

Parson, J., & Croke, J. Classic theories of sex-role socialization. In Frieze, I., Parson, J., Johnson, P., Ruble, D., and Zellman, G., *Women and sex roles*. New York: W.W. Norton, 1978, pp. 95–112.

Pattison, E.M. Confusing concepts about the concept of homosexuality. *Psychiatry*, 1974, *37*, 340–349.

Pattison, M., & Pattison, M.L. Ex-gays: Religiously mediated change in homosexuals. *American Journal of Psychiatry*, 1980, *137*(12), 1553–1562.

Paul, W., Weinrich, J., Gonsiorek, J., & Hotvedt, M. (Eds.). *Homosexuality: Social, psychological and biological issues*. Beverly Hills, Calif.: Sage Publications, 1982.

Paul, W. Social issues and homosexual behavior: A taxonomy of categories and themes in anti-gay argument. In W. Paul, J. Weinrich, J. Gonsiorek, & M. Hotvedt (Eds.), *Homosexuality: Social, psychological and biological issues*. Beverly Hills, Calif.: Sage Publications, 1982, pp. 29–56.

Peplan, A. & Amaro, H. Understanding lesbian relationships. In W. Paul, J. Weinrich, J. Gonsiorek, & M. Hotvedt (Eds.), *Homosexuality; Social, psychological and biological issues*. Beverly Hills, Calif.: Sage Publications, 1982, pp. 233–247.

Pettigrew, T.F. Racially separate or together? *Journal of Social Issues*, 1969, *25*, 43–69.

Plant, W., Telford, C., & Thomas, J. Some personality differences between dogmatic and non-dogmatic groups. *Journal of Social Psychology*, 1965, *67*, 67–75.

Pleck, J.H. Man to man: Is brotherhood possible? In N. Glazer-Malbin (Ed.), *Old family/new family: Interpersonal relationships*. New York: Van Nostrand Reinhold, 1975.

Pleck, J. Men's power with women, other men and society: A men's movement analysis. In R. Lewis (Ed.), *Men in difficult times*. Englewood Cliffs, N.J.: Prentice-Hall, 1981, pp. 234–244.

Plummer, K. *Sexual stigma: An interactionist account*. London: Routledge and Kegan Paul, 1975.

Plutchik, R. *The emotions: Facts, theories, and a new model*. New York: Random House, 1962.

Plutchik, R. *Emotion: A psychoevolutionary synthesis*. New York: Harper and Row, 1980.

Rachman, S. *Phobias: Their nature and control*.   Chicago: Ill.: Charles C. Thomas, 1968.

Rachman, S. *The meanings of fear*. Manchester: Philips Park Press, 1974.

Raush, H.L. Interaction sequences. *Journal of Personality and Social Psychology*, 1965, *2*, 487–499.

Reiss, A.J. The social integration of queers and peers. In J. Gagnon & W. Simon (Eds.), *Sexual deviance*. New York: Harper and Row, 1967.

Reiss, I.L. The scaling of premarital sexual permissiveness. *Journal of Marriage and the Family*, 1964, *26*, 188–198.

Rekers, G.A., & Lovaas, O.I. Behavioral treatment of deviant sex-role behaviors in a male child. *Journal of Applied Behavioral Analysis*, 1974, 7, 173–190.

Rekers, G.A., et al. Childhood gender identity change: Operant control over sex-typed play and mannerisms. *Journal of Behavior Therapy and Experimental Psychiatry*, 1976, 7, 51–57.

Richardson, A. The assimilation of British migrants in Australia. *Human Relations*, 1957, *10*, 157–165.

Richardson, D. Theoretical perspectives on homosexuality. In Hart, J., & Richardson, D., *The theory and practice of homosexuality*. London: Routledge & Kegan Paul, 1981, pp. 5–37.

Riddle, D., & Morin, S.F. Removing the stigma: Data from individuals. *APA Monitor*, 1977, 16; 28.

Riegel, K. From traits and equilibrium toward developmental dialectics. In W.J. Arnold and J.K. Cole (Eds.), *Nebraska symposium on motivation*. Lincoln: University of Nebraska Press, 1976.

Riley, M. The avowed lesbian mother and her right to child custody: A constitutional challenge that can no longer be denied. In *San Diego Law Review*, 1975, *12*(4).

Rooney, E., & Gibbons, D. Social reactions to crimes without victims. *Social Problems*, 1966, *13*, 400–410.

Rosenthal, R. *Experimenter effects in behavioral research*. New York: Appleton-Century-Crofts, 1966.

Ross, M.W. Homosexuality, sex roles and societal control. Doctoral dissertation, University of Melbourne, Australia, 1979.

Ross, M.W., Rogers, L., & McCulloch, H. Stigma, sex and society: A new look at gender differentiation and sexual variation. *Journal of Homosexuality*, 1978, *3*, 315–330.

Ross, T.A. *The common neuroses*. London: Edward Arnold, 1937, p. 145.

Rossides, D.W. *The history and nature of sociological theory*. Boston, Mass.: Houghton Mifflin, 1978.

Ruitenbeek, H.M. (Ed.) *The problem of homosexuality in modern society*. New York: E.P. Dutton, 1963.

Sagarin, E. The good guys, the bad guys, and the gay guys. *Contemporary Sociology*, 1973, *2*(1), 3–13.

Sagarin, E. *Deviants and deviance*. New York: Praeger, 1975.

Sampson, E. Scientific paradigms and social values: Wanted—A scientific revolution. *Journal of Personality and Social Psychology*, 1978, *36*, 1332–1343.

San Miguel, C.L., & Millham, J. The role of cognitive and situational variables in aggression toward homosexuals. *Journal of Homosexuality*, 1976, *2*(1).

Sawyer, J. On male liberation. From *Liberation*, 1970, 5, 6–8.

Schachter, S. Deviation, rejection and communication. *Journal of Abnormal and Social Psychology*, 1951, *46*, 190–207.

Schacter, S., & Singer, J. Cognitive, social, and physiological determinants of emotional state. *Psychological Review*, 1962, *69*, 377–399.

Schachter, S. *Emotion, obesity and crime*. New York: Academic Press, 1971, pp. 2–4.

Schatzman, M. *Soul murder: Persecution in the family*. New York: Random House, 1973.

Scheff, Thomas. *Labeling madness*. Englewood Cliffs, N.J.: Prentice-Hall, 1975.

Schultz, R., & Barefood, J. Non-verbal responses and affiliative conflict theory. *British Journal of Social and Clinical Psychology*, 1974, *13*, 237–243.

Scott, R.B. *Price's textbook of medicine* (10th ed.). London: Oxford University Press, 1966.

Sears, R.R. Development of gender role. In F.A. Beach (Ed.), *Sex and behavior*. New York: Wiley, 1965.

Shaver, K.G. *An introduction to attribution processes*. Cambridge, Mass.: Winthrop, 1975.

Shiers, J. Two Steps Forward, One Step Back. In Gay Left Collective (Eds.), *Homosexuality: Power and politics*. London: Allison and Busby, 1980, pp. 140–156.

Shively, M., & DeCecco, J. Components of sexual identity. *Journal of Homosexuality*, 1977, *3*(1), 41–48.

Silverstein, C. Behavior modification and the gay community. Paper presented at the annual convention of the Association for Advancement of Behavior Therapy, New York City, October, 1972.

Silverstein, C. Even psychiatry can profit from its past mistakes. *Journal of Homosexuality*, 1976, *2*(2), 153–158.

Silverstein, C. *A family matter*. New York: McGraw-Hill, 1977.

Silverstein, C. *Man to man: gay couples in America*. New York: Morrow, 1982, pp. 113–195.

Simmons, J.L. Public stereotypes of deviants. *Social Problems*, 1965, *13*, 223–232.

Smith, K. Homophobia: A tentative personality profile. *Psychological Reports*, 1971, *29*, 1091–1094.

Smith, T., & Brehm, S. Person perception and the Type A coronary-prone behavior pattern. *Journal of Personality and Social Psychology*, 1981, *40*(6), 1137–1149.

Snyder, M. Individual differences and the self-control of expressive behavior. Doctoral dissertation, Stanford University, 1972.

Snyder, M., Tanke, E., & Berscheid, E. Social perception and interpersonal behavior: On the self-fulfilling nature of social stereotypes. *Journal of Personality and Social Psychology*, 1977, *35*(9), 656–666.

Snyder, M., & Uranowitz, S. Reconstructing the past: Some cognitive consequences of person perception. *Journal of Personality and Social Psychology*, 1978, *36*(9), 941–950.

Socarides, C. *The overt homosexual*. New York: Grune and Stratton, 1968.

Spence, J.T., & Helmreich, R. *Masculinity and femininity: Their psychological dimensions, correlates and antecedents*. Austin: University of Texas Press, 1978.

Spence, J., & Helmreich, R. Androgyny versus gender schema: A comment on Bem's gender schema theory. *Psychological Review*, 1981, *88*(4), 365–368.

Spence, J., Helmreich, R., & Holahan, C. Negative and positive components of psychological masculinity and femininity and their relationships to self-reports of neurotic and acting behaviors. *Journal of Personality and Social Psychology*, 1979, *37*(10), 1673–1682.

Spence, J., Helmreich, R., & Stapp, J. Ratings of self and peers on sex-role attributes and their relationship to self esteem and conceptions of masculinity and femininity. *Journal of Personality and Social Psychology*, 1975, *32*, 29–39.

Staats, G. Stereotype content and social distance: Changing views of homosexuality. *Journal of Homosexuality*, 1978, *4*(1).

Steffensmeier, D., & Steffensmeier, R. Sex differences in reactions to homosexuals: Research continuities and further developments. *The Journal of Sex Research*, 1974, *10*, 52–67.

Stengel, E. Classification of mental disorders. *Bulletin of the World Health Organization*, 1959, *21*, 601–663.

Storms, M.D. Sexual orientation and self perception. In P. Pliner, K.R. Blaustein, I.M. Spigel, T. Alloway, & L. Krames (Eds.), *Advances in the study of communication and effect* (Vol. 5). *Perception of emotion in self and others*. New York: Plenum, 1978.

Storms, M.D. Sex-role identity and its relationships to sex role attributes and sex role stereotypes. *Journal of Personality and Social Psychology*, 1979, *37*(10), 1779–1789.

Storms, M.D. Theories of sexual orientation. *Journal of Personality and Social Psychology*, 1980, *38*(5), 783–792.

Szasz, T. *The manufacture of madness*. New York: Harper & Row, 1970.

Taft, R. A psychological theory for the study of social assimilation. *Human Relations*, 1957, *10*, 141–156.

Tavris, C. Men and women report their views on masculinity. *Psychology Today*, 1977, *10*(8), 34.

Terhune, W. The phobic syndrome: A study of 86 patients with phobic reactions. Archives of Neurological Psychiatry, 1949, 62, 162–172.

Tomkins, S. The primary site of the affects: the face. In *Affect, imagery, consciousness* (Vol. 1). New York: Springer Publishing, 1962.

Tomkins, S. Affects as amplification: Some modifications in theory. In R. Plutchik & H. Kellerman (Eds.), *Emotion: Theory, research and experience* (Vol. 1). New York: Academic Press, 1980.

Troiden, R. Becoming homosexual: A model of gay identity acquisition. *Psychiatry*, 1979, 42, 362–372.

Warr, P., & Sims, A. A study of cojudgment processes. *Journal of Personality*, 1965, 33, 598–604.

Warren, C. Identity and community in the gay world. Doctoral dissertation, University of Southern California, 1972.

Weeks, J. Movements of affirmation: Sexual meanings and homosexual identities. *Radical History Review*, 1979, 20, 164–179.

Weeks, J. Capitalism and the organization of sex. In Gay Left Collective (Eds.), *Homosexuality: Power and politics*. London: Allison and Busby, 1980, pp. 11–21.

Weinberg, G. *Society and the healthy homosexual*. New York: Saint Martin's Press, 1972.

Weinberg, M., & Williams, C. *Male homosexuals: Their problems and adaptations*. New York: Oxford University Press, 1974.

Weinberger, L. & Millham, J. Attitudinal homophobia and support of traditional sex-roles. *Journal of Homosexuality*, 1979, 4(3), 237–245.

Weinrich, J. Is homosexuality biologically natural? In W. Paul, J. Weinrich, J. Gonsiorek, & M. Hotvedt (Eds.), *Homosexuality: social, psychological, and biological issues*. Beverly Hills, Calif.: Sage Publications, 1982a, pp. 197–208.

Weinrich, J. Discussion of models of sexual orientation. Paper presented at the annual meeting of the American Psychological Association, Washington, D.C., August, 1982b.

Weissbach, T., & Zagon, G. The effect of deviant group membership upon impressions of personality. *Journal of Social Psychology*, 1975, 95, 263–266.

White, B., Alter, R., & Rardin, M. Authoritarianism, dogmatism, and usage of conceptual categories. *Journal of Personality and Social Psychology*, 1965, 2, 104–110.

Wolfgang, A., & Wolfgang, J. Exploration of attitudes via physical interpersonal distance toward the obese, drug users, homosexuals, police and other marginal figures. *Journal of Clinical Psychology*, 1971, 27, 510–512.

Wolpe, J. *Psychotherapy by reciprocal inhibition*. Stanford, Calif.: Stanford University Press, 1958.

Wolpe, J., & Rachman, S. Psychoanalytic "evidence": A critique based on Freud's case of Little Hans. *Journal of Nervous and Mental Disorders*, 1960, *130*, 135–148.

Wright, R., Storms, M., & Duncan, B. Male sexual schemata and responses to male homosexuality. Unpublished manuscript, Department of Psychology, University of Kansas, Lawrence, Kansas, 1976.

Young, W.C., Goy, R.W., & Phoenix, C.H. Hormones and sexual behavior. *Science*, 1964, *143*, 212–218.

INDEX

ABOUT THE AUTHOR

Lonnie Gene Nungesser was born in the Ozark Mountain region of southern Missouri, the second in a farming family of six children. He was licensed as a minister of the Southern Baptist church at age seventeen and served as pastor for the Whetstone Baptist Church in Mountain Grove, Missouri. He moved to San Francisco at the age of nineteen where he served as a patrolman for the United States Coast Guard; he received an honorable discharge and attended the College of Alameda for two years. In 1976, Nungesser was elected the first Caucasian student body president in this East Bay junior college; he successfuly initiated a multiethnic and dual-gender system of self-government for the student body. He appeared in *Who's Who Among Students in American Technical and Vocational Schools* in 1977.

Nungesser entered Stanford University with advanced standing in 1977. He was nominated to the Department of Psychology's Honors Program under the direction of Sandra Bem and Philip Zimbardo. While at Stanford, he was a career adviser and values clarification leader for the Career Planning and Placement Center. It was at Stanford University that many of the ideas expressed in *Homosexual Acts, Actors, and Identities* developed. In the spring of 1979, Nungesser graduated from Stanford's Psychology Honors Program and was awarded one of the first national scholarships presented by the Gay Academic Union.

Nungesser began his doctoral program at the State University of New York at Stony Brook in the fall of 1979. He taught social psychology and introductory psychology courses and developed a course he called "The Psychology of Gender" while at Stony Brook. In the spring of 1980 the *Journal of Homosexuality* published his first article, "Theoretical Bases for Research on the Acquisition of Social Sex Roles in Children of Lesbian Mothers." In 1981, *Men in Difficult Times* was published, which included a controversial article by Nungesser and Steven Morin, "Can Homophobia Be Cured?"

Upon completion of his Master's degree in 1982, Nungesser took temporary leave from academic study. He returned to California to complete *Homosexual Acts, Actors, and Identities*, a project that had captured his passionate devotion for six years. He is currently working as a management consultant in Palo Alto, California.